KT-178-696

STRODE'S COLLEGE

STRODE'S COLLEGE

A CONCISE
ENCYCLOPEDIA OF
THE THEATRE

A scene from the last production of Laurence Olivier's magnificent reign at the National Theatre. The play is Eduardo de Fillipo's Saturday Sunday Monday, *directed by Franco Zeffirelli; the players are Olivier as Antonio and Clive Merrison as Federico. (Photo: Zoe Dominic, Camera Press, London)*

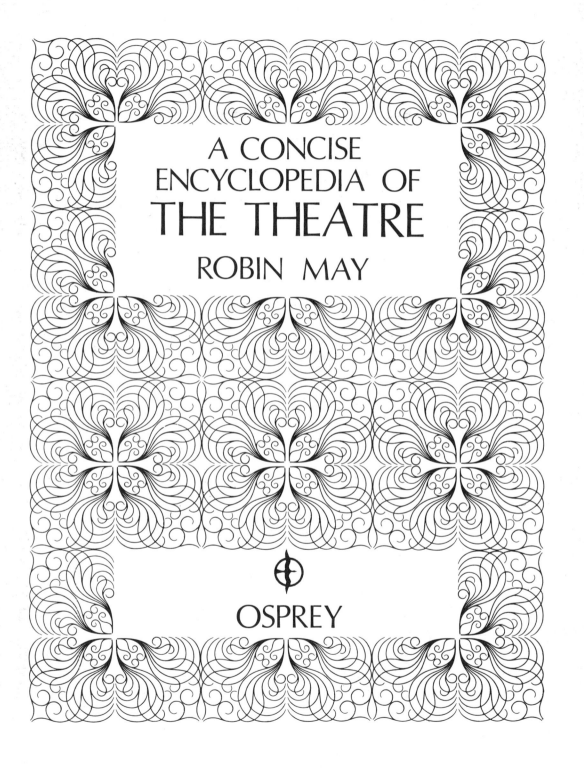

A CONCISE
ENCYCLOPEDIA OF
THE THEATRE

ROBIN MAY

OSPREY

This book was designed and produced by
Alban Book Services Limited
147 London Road, St Albans, Herts, England

OSPREY PUBLISHING LIMITED
Member of the George Philip Group
137 Southampton Street
Reading, Berkshire, RG1 2QZ

First published 1974
© Robin May 1974
Set in French Old Style
Printed in Great Britain on 118 gsm paper by
W. S. COWELL LIMITED
at the Butter Market, Ipswich, England

ISBN 0 540 07005 X

CONTENTS

OTHER BOOKS BY THE SAME AUTHOR:
    OPERAMANIA
    THEATREMANIA
    THE WIT OF THE THEATRE
    WHO'S WHO IN SHAKESPEARE
    A COMPANION TO THE THEATRE

❋ INTRODUCTION AND ACKNOWLEDGEMENTS ❋

This book is for playgoers and students alike and it covers more than 2,000 years of theatrical history. It is too short to give more than a percentage of countries their dramatic due, but the second and longest chapter, a chronological survey of the world's leading playwrights, has representatives from five continents. The book has yet to be written that does full justice to every nation's theatre from Albania to Zaire, and it will be in many volumes.

Cross-referencing has been kept to a minimum, and no individual has more than one biographical entry even though many appear in nearly every chapter. The final chapter, which consists of theatrical terms, is long, but by no means complete, for many of the terms which might have been included are discussed in Chapter 4 part I, the only semi-narrative portion of the book, as befits the subject, the Physical Theatre.

The following individuals have been most helpful: Nanette and Arthur Wise, Frank Seton, Sue Lamb and, as always, my wife. In the selection of pictures I have been greatly helped by members of the staffs of the Italian Institute, the French, German and Japanese Embassies, and Sadie Alford of the Novosti Press Agency.

A bibliography of theatre books would double the length of this one, but it would be churlish not to acknowledge a number of reference and other works which have been especially helpful: *The Reader's Encyclopedia of World Drama*, edited by John Gassner and Edward Quinn, which is a scholarly treasure trove of knowledge about international playwrights; *The Oxford Companion to the Theatre*, whose main strength lies in its historical entries; Elizabeth Locke's brilliantly concise account of the contemporary theatre, brought up to date annually in *Pears Cyclopaedia*; and the *Penguin Dictionary of the Theatre* by John Russell Taylor, a most useful handbook. As always, *The Stage* is a mine of current information, and this year (1973) the staff have banded together to produce *Theatre Review '73*, which historians can only pray will become an annual event. And *Who's Who in the Theatre*, all fifteen editions of it, is essential to all researchers. On the subject of theatre terms two books must be mentioned. One, by Hendrik Baker, who was my tolerant Stage Manager on one occasion when I was a not very good A.S.M., is *Stage Management and Theatrecraft*, and the other is Wilfred Granville's *The Theatre Dictionary*. Not for the first time I am indebted to several books for information on the American scene, especially *The Making of the American Theater* by Howard Taubman and *Broadway* by Brooks Atkinson. Without J. C. Trewin's numerous and detailed theatrical histories a work like this would take twice as long to write, while a number of other writers and critics are acknowledged in the course of the book.

A final word about omissions. Apart from accidental ones, sadly many major figures have been left out on grounds of space, to say nothing of the whole marvellous galaxy of musical hall and vaudeville talent. And the world of the musical is only lightly touched on. If any reader is driven to near-frenzy by the omission of some favourite living or long dead, I will be delighted to hear from him or her for future reference. As an ex-actor but still an avid playgoer myself, it has distressed me having to give the thumbs down to so many of my own favourites. As to the book's objectivity, all I can truthfully say is that when personal feelings intrude, readers will be well aware of the fact.

Robin May
Wimbledon, 1974

TO PAULINE AND CLIVE

CHAPTER 1

DRAMA

A Short Chronological Guide

On this Italian vase of the 4th century B.C. Hermes is taking Zeus (plus ladder) on a nocturnal adventure. The scene is from a south Italian burlesque. (Photo: Mansell Collection)

All theatre springs from the same ultimate source, the religious dances of primitive man. These, which are still performed in some parts of the world, were prayers, dances of thanksgiving, war-dances, dances to exorcize evil spirits, etc. Tribal legends and history could be acted out in dance and song. So it can be reasonably claimed that the history of theatre in its widest sense is as old as the history of mankind.

PRE-GRECIAN DRAMA

3200 B.C.   An Egyptian play about the creation of the world by Betah, god of Memphis, is composed, into which the Isis-Osiris-Horus legend is introduced. Ancient Egyptian plays were religious and essentially ritualistic.

GREEK DRAMA

6th century B.C.   Greek tragedy grows out of the Dithyramb – a hymn to honour Dioynsus (according to Aristotle, though this has been disputed by some, who also dispute that Greek comedy grew out of phallic songs).

534 B.C.   At the first dramatic contest in Athens, Thespis, a poet, wins the prize. He made drama possible by adding an actor, as distinct from the chorus and its leader. The City Dionysia was held every Spring in Athens for four days, the Lenaea every January for three days.

500–300 B.C.   Great age of Greek Drama (Tragedy, Comedy and Satyr, which last was grotesque, obscene farce).

525 B.C.   Birth of Aeschylus, the true founder of European drama and author of the *Oresteia*. Introduces a second actor.

496 B.C.   Birth of Sophocles. He excels in the tragedy of the individual hero and introduces a third actor.

484 B.C.   Birth of Euripedes, a questioning genius, author of *Medea, The Bacchae*, etc.

c. 445 B.C.   Birth of Aristophanes, the great comic

9

	dramatist of Ancient Greece.
384 B.C.	Birth of Aristotle, whose *Poetics* analyse the nature of tragedy.
c. 342 B.C.	Birth of Menander, great master of the 'new comedy' of manners.

ROMAN DRAMA

c. 300 B.C.– A.D. 500	Derived from the Greek, with the chorus mainly discarded and comedy far more popular than tragedy.
c. 251 B.C.	Birth of Plautus, very popular comic dramatist influenced by Menander,. and, in turn, he influences Renaissance writers – Molière, Ben Jonson, etc.
c. 195 B.C.	Birth of Terence, Roman comic dramatist, subtler than Plautus and, like him, influenced by Greeks and influential on later dramatists.
c. 4 B.C.	Birth of Seneca, Roman tragic dramatist, whose plays are written to be read rather than staged.
passim.	CIRCUS: main attraction chariot-racing. MIME: not silent as in modern mime. AMPHITHEATRE (Arena): gladiatorial displays; slaughter of victims by beasts and men; murderous sea-fights in flooded arenas. Cruelty grows during period.
A.D. 326	Condemnation to the beasts stopped.
404	Gladiatorial displays ended.

INDIAN DRAMA

c. 373	Birth of Kálidása, Sanskrit dramatist and the most famous Indian dramatist and poet. (Indian drama has been flourishing for at least two centuries.)
c. 750	Birth of Bhavabhuti, author of the greatest play about Rama. A Sanskrit dramatist.

CHINA

c. 580	Dramatisation of stories, with singing and dancing.
720	The Emperor Ming Huang said to have established a drama school called the Pear Garden in Nanking.

REBIRTH OF EUROPEAN DRAMA

c. 500–1000	A bleak period. In the late Roman Empire Christianity had been hostile to the debased theatre of the time, and the barbarians had no interest in it. For several centuries it virtually disappeared, except for minstrels singing in the halls of chiefs and kings, small troupes of entertainers, tumblers, etc.
c. 900	Beginnings of Church drama.
c. 935	Birth of Hrotsvitha (Roswitha), a German nun, who later writes six short religious plays in Latin.
c. 970	Æthelwold, Bishop of Winchester, writes about how the Easter story shall be performed dramatically in church.

CHURCH DRAMA

c. 1000– 1500	All over western Europe Miracle, Mystery and, later Morality plays flourish, first in the churches, then in the market places. They are first run by priests and monks, then by Trades Guilds. By the late 14th century, the whole Bible has been dramatised.
1210	An edict forbids priests to appear on a public stage. Instead of stopping the performance of plays outside churches, it leads to the secularisation of drama in the vernacular.
fl. 1275	Kuan Han-ch'ing, the most popular Chinese dramatist of the Yaun Dynasty.
1300–1450	Guilds plays at their height.
1363	Birth of Zeami Motokiyo, the most famous of Japanese *noh* playwrights. *Noh* had begun around 1200.
c. 1495	*Everyman*, the most famous Morality, possibly translated from the Dutch.

RENAISSANCE DRAMA

1500–1600	*Commedia dell'Arte*, popular improvised comedies, flourish in Italy and elsewhere (until 18th century). Striking development of theatre buildings in Italy. Skilled use of scenery and perspective. Plays on classical models.

1584	The Teatro Olimpico at Vicenza, built by Palladio, is completed by Scamozzi. Use of changeable painted perspective views, etc.

RISE OF ENGLISH DRAMA

1557	Earl of Surrey devises blank verse for translating Virgil.
c. 1560	*Gammer Gurton's Needle*, first English farce.
c. 1562	*Gorboduc*, first English tragedy. Lope de Vega born.
1564	Births of Shakespeare and Marlowe.
1572	Birth of Ben Jonson.
1576	First permanent English playhouse, The Theatre, erected by Finsbury Fields, London.
1587–1588	Marlowe's *Tamburlaine*, the first great English play, which ushers in the golden age of English drama. The 'age' notably helped by its audiences of all classes, a very rare happening in theatre history. Boy actors play women's parts (as opposed to companies of boy actors who are very popular at this time).
1592	Shakespeare already established as a rising playwright.
1597	Invention of opera by a group of Florentine noblemen, poets and musicians to try to recapture the spirit of Greek drama.
1599	The Globe Theatre built.
c. 1601	*Hamlet*
1604	The Chamberlain's Men (Burbage, Shakespeare, etc.) become the King's Men.
	Masques (entertainments with singing, dancing and acting), having been popular for more than 50 years, now, especially at Court, become very elaborate. Soon professionals (Jonson, Inigo Jones) are staging them, though the performers are amateurs. Women can take part in them.
1608	The King's Men acquire the Blackfriars Theatre (private roofed theatre).
1610	Jonson's *The Alchemist*.
1613	The Globe burnt down during première of *Henry VIII*.

1616	Deaths of Shakespeare and Cervantes.
1618	First theatre with a proscenium arch, Teatro Farnese in Parma, which has a great effect on later theatre architecture.
1623	First Folio of Shakespeare's plays published.
1635	Death of Lope de Vega. Spanish drama in the middle of its golden age. Other great playwrights include Pedro Calderón de la Barca (1600–81).
1637	First public opera house opens in Venice. Spectacular scenery and effects used. Death of Ben Jonson. Corneille's *Le Cid*.
1642	After years of hostility to the English theatre, Puritans finally have the playhouses closed, many being pulled down. Actors are forced into hiding, or the Royal army, or into other occupations.
1640s	Corneille's most productive years launch a great period of French drama.

FRANCE AND ENGLAND

1658	Molière's first success with *Le Docteur Amoureux*.
1660	With the Restoration of Charles II, the English theatre is restored: the Duke's Men under Davenant, the King's Men under Killigrew. First professional actresses in England.
1663	First Theatre Royal, Drury Lane, opened.
1660s–1670s	Lully's opera-ballets at Louis XIV's Court. The King founds The Royal Academy of Dance in 1661.
1660s	Puncinello arrives in London and soon becomes Punch.
1664	Molière's *Tartuffe*.
1667	Racine's first great success, *Andromaque*.
1680	Comédie Française founded.
1695	Congreve's *Love for Love*.
1700	Opera booming in Italy. Venice has ten opera houses.
1707	Death of Farquhar, last great Restoration dramatist.

An 18th century audience as seen by William Hogarth. (Photo: Author's Collection)

1717	Birth of David Garrick, the greatest English actor of the century. First English pantomime.

1720   *Arlequin poli par l'amour*, Marivaux' first big success.

1728   *The Beggar's Opera.*

1747   Garrick manager of Drury Lane.

1755   Birth of Sarah Siddons, née Kemble, greatest of English tragic actresses.

1759   Birth of Schiller, great German dramatist.

1760   Noverre sets down his revolutionary ideas on ballet in his *Letters on Dancing*. The grandfather of today's ballet.

1773   Goldsmith's *She Stoops to Conquer.*

1775   Sheridan's first triumph with *The Rivals.*

THE ROMANTIC AGE

1784   Beaumarchais' *The Marriage of Figaro.*

1787   Schiller's *Don Carlos.* Mozart's *Don Giovanni.*

1788   Goethe's *Egmont.*

1811   Kleist's *The Prince of Hamburg.*

1812   Fourth and largest Theatre Royal, Drury Lane, opened.

1814   Edmund Kean's first great success at Drury Lane as Shylock.

1817   Gas lighting at Drury Lane at the Lyceum.

1820s   The age of melodrama. Drama at a low ebb in Britain. The middle classes desert the theatre. Ballet dancing on toes.

1830   The first night of Victor Hugo's *Hernani*, a turning point in Romantic drama, even greater than Dumas Père's *Henri III et sa cour* (1829).

1835   Büchner's *Danton's Death.*

1838   Rachel first appears at Comédie Française.

1841   Grisi first dances Giselle.

1842	*Nabucco*, Verdi's first great success. Italian opera reaching its period of greatest popularity with all classes.
1843	*The Flying Dutchman*, Wagner's first major opera.
1846	Death of great French mime and Pierrot, Deburau.
1847	Taglioni, supreme dancer of the Romantic era, retires.
1849	*Adrienne Lecouvreur* by Eugene Scribe, the inventor of the 'well-made play'.
1850	Ibsen's first play, *Cataline*.
1860s–1920s	Great age of the Music Hall in Britain and Vaudeville in America.
1867	Tom Robertson's *Caste* and his other plays bring some realism to contemporary British drama.
1871	Henry Irving makes his name as Mathias in *The Bells*. The beginning of a golden age of British theatre, if not of drama. But writers begin to return to the theatre.

RISE OF MODERN DRAMA

1875	*Pillars of Society* by Ibsen, the first of a number of enormously influential plays. *Trial by Jury* by Gilbert and Sullivan.
1876	The first Bayreuth Festival.
1878	Eleonora Duse makes her name in *Les Fourchambault*.
1879–1880	Sarah Bernhardt triumphs in London and New York.
1887	Strindberg's *The Father*. Sardou's *La Tosca*. Buffalo Bill's Wild West Show tours Europe, possibly the most popular show ever to visit Britain.
1892	Shaw's *Widowers Houses* staged.
1893	Verdi's last opera, *Falstaff*.
1896	Chekhov's *The Seagull*. Not until two years later is it understood (see below).
1898	Stanislavsky founds the Moscow Art Theatre and he and Nemirovich-Danchenko revive *The Seagull* triumphantly.
1899	Abbey Theatre, Dublin, founded.
c. 1900–1914	The high noon of the actor-manager system in Britain.

1904–1907	The Granville Barker/John Vedrenne reign at the Royal Court: Shaw, Yeats, Ibsen, Galsworthy, Hauptmann, etc., presented.
1908	Britain's first Repertory Theatre started by Miss Horniman at the Gaiety, Manchester. Feydeau's *Occupe-toi d'Amelie*.
1909	First Diaghilev Russian Ballet season in Paris.
1912	Granville Barker, following pioneer work by William Poel, presents Shakespeare in the simple, swift style of the Elizabethans.
1914	Lilian Baylis presents Shakespeare for the first time at the Old Vic, also opera in English. Georg Kaiser's *The Burghers*.
1919	Theater Guild founded in U.S.A.
1920	*Beyond the Horizon*, Eugene O'Neill's first success.
1921	Pirandello's *Six Characters in Search of an Author*.
1922	John Barrymore's *Hamlet* in New York.
1923	O'Casey's first play, *The Shadow of a Gunman*. *Back to Methuselah* first given at Barry Jackson's Birmingham Rep. Elmer Rice's *The Adding Machine*.
1924	Maxwell Anderson's *What Price Glory?* Noel Coward's *The Vortex*. Death of Puccini.
1925	*A Cuckoo in the Nest*, Ben Travers' first classic farce.
1926	Eva Le Gallienne founds Civic Repertory Theater in New York.
1927	Jerome Kern's *Show Boat*. Robert Sherwood's *The Road to Rome*.
1928	R. C. Sherriff's *Journey's End*. Brecht/Weill's *The Threepenny Opera*.
1929	Mayakovsky's *The Bed Bug*.
1930	John Gielgud's first *Hamlet*.
1931	J. B. Priestley's *The Good Companions*. First performance by the Vic-Wells Theatre Ballet. Group Theater founded in America.
1932	Lilian Baylis re-opens Sadler's Wells. De Fillipo and his family found The Company of the Humorous Theatre.
1933	Lorca's *Blood Wedding*.

1934	Lilian Hellman's *The Children's Hour*.
1935	Clifford Odets' *Waiting for Lefty*.
1937–1938	Gielgud's historic season at the Queen's, notable for casting, repertoire, ensemble and first great Chekhov production in Britain: *The Three Sisters* (Michel St. Denis).
1937	Orson Welles's Mercury Theatre opens.
1939–1945	Tyrone Guthrie in sole charge of the Old Vic and Sadler's Wells.
1942	Anouilh's *Antigone*. Sartre's *The Flies*.
1943	*Oklahoma*.
1944	Golden age of the Old Vic (at the New Theatre) begins under Olivier, Richardson and John Burrell, including Olivier's Richard III. Gielgud's famous season at the Haymarket, *Hamlet*, *Duchess of Malfi*, etc. Wolfit's King Lear.
1945	Tenessee Williams' *The Glass Menagerie*. Richardson's Falstaff. Camus' *The Misunderstanding*.
1946	Royal Opera House, Covent Garden, reopened after the war by Sadler's Wells Ballet. Formation of Covent Garden Opera Co.
1947	Genet's *The Maids*. *A Streetcar Named Desire*.
1948	Ionesco's *The Bald Prima Donna*. Arthur Miller's *Death of a Salesman*. Fry's *The Lady's Not For Burning*. Actor's Studio founded in New York.
1950	Old Vic reopened after wartime closure. Hugh Hunt as Director.
1951	The Wolfit/Guthrie *Tamburlaine*. John Whiting's *Saint's Day*.
1952	Rattigan's *The Deep Blue Sea*.
1953	Beckett's *Waiting for Godot*. Joan Littlewood takes over the Theatre Royal Stratford East for her Theatre Workshop. First Shakespearean Festival at Stratford, Ontario.
1954	Joseph Papp's first New York Shakespeare Festival.
1955	Durrenmatt's *The Visit*. Brook's *Titus Andronicus* at Stratford, with Olivier. American Shakespeare Festival founded at Stratford, Connecticut.
1956	English Stage Co. founded at Royal Court (George Devine). Osborne's *Look Back in Anger*. O'Neill's posthumous *Long Day's Journey into Night* produced in New York. *My Fair Lady*. Berliner Ensemble visits London.
1957	*West Side Story*.
1958	Pinter's *The Birthday Party*. Albee's *The Zoo Story*. Peter Shaffer's *Five Finger Exercise*.
1959	Arden's *Sergeant Musgrave's Dance*.
1960	Peter Hall becomes Director of the Royal Shakespeare Co. with a London base at the Aldwych. Mermaid Theatre, Puddle Dock, opened. Henry Livings's *Stop It, Whoever You Are*.
1961	*Beyond the Fringe* (Peter Cook, Jonathan Miller, Dudley Moore, Alan Bennett).
1962	First Chichester Festival. *Who's Afraid of Virginia Woolf?*
1963	National Theatre opens under Olivier with *Hamlet*. *The Wars of the Roses* at Stratford. Theatre Workshop's *Oh What A Lovely War*.
1964	Weiss's *Marat-Sade*. Olivier's Othello. Lincoln Center Repertory Theater founded.
1965	Edward Bond's *Saved*. Osborne's *A Patriot for Me*. Pinter's *The Homecoming*.
1966	Joe Orton's *Loot*. Brook's *US*.
1967	Peter Nicols' *A Day in the Death of Joe Egg*. Tom Stoppard's *Rosencrantz and Guildenstern are Dead*. David Storey's *The Restoration of Arnold Middleton*.
1968	Hochhuth's *Soldiers* in London. End of theatre censorship in Britain. Trevor Nunn succeeds Peter Hall as Director of Royal Shakespeare Co.
1969	Leonard Rossiter in *Arturo Ui*. Ian McKellen as Richard II and Edward II.
1970	Peter Brook's *Dream*. David Storey's *Home*. Opening of the Young Vic. Paul Zindel's *The Effect of Gamma Rays on Man-in-the-Moon Marigolds* in New York.
1971	Simon Gray's *Butley*. John Mortimer's *A Voyage Round My Father*. Peggy Ashcroft in *The Lovers of Viorne*. Ariane Mnouchkine's *1789* in Paris and London. Death of Tyrone

Guthrie.

1972 *The Romans* at Stratford. National Theatre's *Long Day's Journey Into Night*. *Cowardy Custard* at the Mermaid. Opening of Sam Wanamaker's Globe Theatre on Bankside.

1973 Christopher Hampton's *Savages*. Peter Hall succeeds Olivier as Director of the National Theatre. Death of Noel Coward. Joseph Papp, producer and director of the New York Shakespeare Festival, becomes Director of both the Vivian Beaumont Theatre and the Forum Theater at the Lincoln Center.

Laurence Olivier as Hotspur, and Margaret Leighton as Lady Percy in John Burrell's production of Henry IV Part I in 1945. The Company was the Old Vic, the theatre, the New, and the production, which had Ralph Richardson as Falstaff, is now a theatre legend. (Photo: John Vickers)

A relief from Pompeii showing a scene from a Graeco-Roman comedy. (Photo: Mansell Collection)

CHAPTER 2
DRAMATISTS
A Chronological Survey

AESCHYLUS (525–456 B.C.). Greek dramatist, author of some 90 plays, both satyrs and tragedies, seven of the latter surviving complete. They are *The Suppliant Women*, *The Persians* (against whom he had fought at Marathon, Salamis and Plataea), *Seven Against Thebes*, *Prometheus Bound* and his trilogy, *The Oresteia*. These plays and his innovations can be claimed to make him the founder of European drama.

He found tragedy given by an actor and a chorus, and, by adding a second actor, created true theatrical dialogue and therefore true drama. Except in

16

The Suppliants, he cut the chorus from 50 to 12, and he encouraged fine costumes and introduced the *cothurnus* (high boot) to give his actors extra stature. He also liked colourful spectacle and, after Sophocles had introduced one, included a third actor in his plays.

As a dramatic poet he is Shakespeare's only rival, though his verse is rougher than that of Sophocles. His language is monumental, not colloquial, as befits his themes, and his surviving plays are astonishingly wide-ranging. The most famous is the triology, about the family of Agamemnon, the doomed house of Atreus and their crimes against the gods. A series of vengeful events show sin begetting sin, resulting in suffering and counter-sin and, finally, divine justice. The Olympian characters are descended from gods and men.

For more information on the nature of Greek drama, see page 103, but it should be stressed that such were the powers of characterisation possessed by Aeschylus, that modern audiences, who know nothing of its traditions, are enthralled by his plays if they are well done.

SOPHOCLES (496–406 B.C.). Greek dramatist of whose 120-odd plays only seven tragedies and part of one satyr and a few fragments survive: *The Women of Trachis, Ajax, Antigone, Oedipus Rex, Oedipus at Colonus, Electra* and *Philoctetes*. The satyr play is *Ichneutae* ('Trackers'). He introduced a third actor into his plays, which are more complex, intimate and full of human interest than those of Aeschylus. He excels in the tragedy of the individual hero, in relationships between a person or persons and fate and the gods. His idea of sin is non-Christian in that the hero suffers for the sin regardless of his innocence or his intention. His plots are less simple than those of Aeschylus, and he increased his chorus from 12 to 15 and made it a lyrical commentator rather than an intervener in the action. In *Oedipus at Colonus*, produced after his death, he included a fourth actor, and yet another introduction (or use) was *periaktoi*, a form of painted scenery. No Greek dramatist appeals more to modern taste, and no Greek play is better known than *Oedipus Rex*, with its six speaking parts, two of which, Oedipus and his mother Jocasta, are as famous as any in drama except that of Shakespeare. It is also called *Oedipus Tyrannus*. As well as his fame as a playwright – he won the first prize in the dramatic competitions 18 times – Sophocles was a leading civil servant and a general.

EURIPIDES (484–406 B.C.). Greek dramatist, 18 of whose 92 or so plays survive. His realism startled his contemporaries and, indeed, the Victorians who felt it reduced heroic tragedy to everyday life. He is a questioning, intellectual humanist, who is prepared to criticise the unreasoning gods, and he usually presents stories of personal emotions, not universal dramas of principle. He exposes the wickedness of vendettas and he assumes that there can be no guilt unless there is intention of sin. War and politics are among his themes, and some of his plays are tragi-comedies. Many of his later plays have women as their leading characters; he introduced prologues to drama and, not very satisfactorily, included a *deus ex machina* at the end to sort things out.

His first extant tragedy is *Alcestis* (438), though the drunken, comic Heracles perhaps turns it into tragi-comedy. The sensational nature of some of his plays is indicated by their themes: *Medea*, a mixed marriage and infanticide, *Hippolytus*, the unfair treatment of illegitimate children and infanticide, *Electra*, matricide. In *Iphigenia in Tauris* he mixes comedy with tragedy and allows a happy ending, as he does in *Helen*. Other plays include *Orestes, Hecuba, The Suppliant Women* and two posthumous pieces, *Iphigenia in Aulis* and *The Bacchae*, one of the most elemental, explosive plays ever written, and one which speaks directly to our own age. Though it is the tragedy of the puritanical King Pentheus, the main character is the god Dionysus (Bacchus), the personification of joyous passions and desires which, if forbidden, can destroy a man and in themselves become evil. The play is an ecstatic, electrifying masterpiece. Euripedes greatly influenced later Greek dramatists and the Roman dramatist, Seneca.

ARISTOPHANES (448–380 B.C.). Greek dramatist, of whose 40 comedies 11 survive complete. Nine are 'old comedy', in which the chorus plays a major part in the action, which is linked to the original ritual action, and in which both people and state are ridiculed. The plots are usually fantastic and, with no censorship, anyone and any institution could be attacked with impunity. So these comedies were essentially topical and local. The chorus was 24 strong, and to the masks were added padding, exaggerating both stomach and rump, and, often, a phallus.

His early surviving plays are *The Acharnians* (425), *The Knights, The Clouds, The Wasps, Peace,*

The Birds, Lysistrata and *Thesmophoriazusae*. In all of them the convention of the *parabasis* was observed, in which the chorus became the dramatist putting across his own views directly at the audience. The best known of this group is *Lysistrata*, in which the women of Greece refuse to sleep with their husbands until the war between Athens and Sparta is ended.

The later plays tend towards 'middle comedy' in which the rôle of the chorus is lessened and the plots are more involved: *The Frogs, The Parliament of Women, Ecclesiazusae* and *Plutus*. The dramatist's bawdy outspokenness has assured his plays of revivals in modern times, despite the difficulty of translating his comedies and the loss of topical allusions. His masterpiece is generally considered to be *The Birds*, though no one is sure what it is about. It is set in the kingdom of Cloudcuckooland, a land of birds and men, and seems to be a satire on Athens, written in matchless comic poetry.

ARISTOTLE. See ARISTOTELIAN PLAY, page 158.

MENANDER (*c.* 342–*c.* 292 B.C.). Greek dramatist, none of whose work was known until four incomplete plays were found in 1905. He was the supreme master (by reputation) of the 'new comedy', comedy of manners with stock characters and with the chorus confined to occasional musical relief. The four plays were *Hero, Samia*, the *Epitrepontes* and *Perciromene*, which last was complete enough to allow Gilbert Murray to turn it into *The Rape of the Locks* (1957). That year the *Dyskolos* was found, and half *The Man from Sicyon* was discovered in 1963. In contrast to Aristophanes's topical plays Menander's sophisticated social comedies, with the chorus kept to a minimum, can be considered the ancestors of modern comedy. They were to influence greatly the Romans, Terence and Plautus.

PLAUTUS (*c.* 251–184 B.C.). Roman comic dramatist about whose life very little is known. He was an actor, possibly a clown, which helps to account for his mastery of farce, comedy and stagecraft. Twenty-one of his plays survive, a number of which may be translations from Greek originals. He was a comic genius, influenced by the 'New Comedy' of Menander (see above) and possibly by earlier forms of Italian drama, and was very popular in his own day.

His plots are full of mistaken identities, trickery,

disguises, etc., and his characters are family figures, courtesans, cunning slaves and boastful warriors, the settings sometimes being brothels. His style is broader than Terence's (see below) and modern audiences find him funny. The musical *A Funny Thing Happened on the Way to the Forum* was based on several of his plays. More important, Plautus greatly influenced Renaissance writers of comedy, including Molière, Ben Jonson and Shakespeare (in *The Comedy of Errors*, based on the *Menaechmi*).

CAECILIUS (*c.* 219–168 B.C.). Roman comic dramatist who only survives in some 300 lines quoted by other writers and in 40 titles. He was considered by some to be finer than Plautus or Terence.

TERENCE (*c.* 195–159 B.C.). Roman comic playwright who came to Rome from Carthage as a slave, but was educated and freed by his master. His six known plays are adaptations of Greek originals, better constructed and subtler than Plautus's, and peopled by fewer stock characters. He cut plot summaries from his prologues and, in *Andria* had a young gentleman fall in love with a girl of his own class, something which never happened in Greek comedy. (Young ladies were kept in seclusion in Athens). Terence's servants were bunglers rather than rogues. He was criticised for daring to adapt Greek originals to suit his own tastes and was less popular than Plautus, but this was partly because the public was beginning to prefer gladiators and circuses to plays. His finest play is possibly *Hecyra*, a serious comedy of marriage, though some have found it lacking in laughs and action. Its première was not helped by the fact that the audience could see a rope-dancer in action in a side show.

Terence's plays continued to be read and were to be very influential in Renaissance times onwards, notably on Molière.

SENECA, Lucius Annaeus (*c.* 4 B.C.–A.D. 65). Roman tragic dramatist, philosopher and statesman, whose nine tragedies comprise the only surviving drama of the Roman Empire. They were written to be read, not staged, which is just as well for they contain unstageable scenes. In one, the sorrowing father of Hippolytus puts together his son's dismembered body. The construction of the plays, too, is essentially non-dramatic: we cannot tell whether certain characters are on stage or not. Yet the horrors and sensational events, inspired by Greek legends and also, perhaps, by the grim reality of Nero's court, are paraded for the reader, even if characterisation is fairly crude. Some believe that the plays were staged, with the horrors being done in a stylised manner. How else?

Seneca's plays, which include *Hercules Furens* and *Oetaeus*, *Medea*, *Phaedra* and *Agamemnon*, were very influential during the Renaissance, sparking off the Elizabethan school of revenge tragedy, inspiring Marlowe and Shakespeare, first in *Titus Andronicus*, then in the masterpiece of the genre, *Richard III*. Seneca's own life ended tragically but stoically and nobly, when he was forced to commit suicide on Nero's orders.

KÁLIDÁSA (*c.* 373–*c.* 415). Indian (Sanskrit) dramatist and the most famous of Indian dramatists and poets. His life and his dates are mysteries. Three of his plays survive, *Malavikagnimitra*, a romantic comedy, *Vikramorvvasiya*, in which a human marries a nymph and fights in Heaven, and

Sakuntala, about a king who marries a hermit's foster daughter. Western readers have compared the plays to Shakespeare's late Romances, like *Cymbeline*. The delightful *Sakuntala* had some influence on European taste when it was first translated in the late 18th century, as it helped the swing to romanticism.

HARSHRA, Sri (*c.* 590–647). King of northern India and a notable dramatist. *Priyadarsika* is a court comedy, as is the finer *Ratnavali*, which has a clown keeping the intrigue going. After this charming piece came *Nagananda*, a play with a Buddhist theme.

BHAVABHUTI (*c.* 750). Indian (Sanskrit) dramatist, the finest and most famous of his plays being *Rama's Later History*, an epic about Rama, who is a manifestation of the god Vishnu. It followed an earlier work, *The History of Rama*, about his triumphs in war and his coronation and is superb

The great French comic dramatist, Molière, acting in Corneille's La Mort de Pompée *in 1659. (Photo: The Cultural Attache, French Embassy)*

drama – poetically, psychologically and theatrically. The part children play in a marriage is a key theme. It is considered the greatest of all the enormous number of works of art about Rama.

HROTSVITHA, or **Roswitha** (*c.* 935–*c.* 1001). German dramatist, poet and historian, and a nun at Gandersheim. Her six short religious plays in Latin link classical with medieval drama and have been staged in modern times. Though chastity as opposed to passion is a regular theme, the plays are not too narrow, and range from comedy to tragedy. She had read Terence and was influenced by his form and style, though the stories of *Paphnutius, Dulcitius, Sapientia, Gallicanus, Calimachus* and *Abraham* (not the Old Testament figure) are all drawn from Christian history, tradition and legends.

KUAN HAN-CH'ING (*fl.* 1275–1300). Chinese dramatist, the most popular of the Yuan dynasty (1280–1368) and still widely performed today. Eighteen of his plays survive, the most remarkable and loved being *Snow in Midsummer*, whose leading character is a much-persecuted heroine, wrongly executed for murder.

MOTOKIYO, Zeami (1363–1443). Japanese dramatist and the most famous of *noh* playwrights. He was known as Zeami and, like his father, ran his own company. Nearly 100 plays survive, which make up almost half the *noh* repertoire. They include the 'revengeful ghost piece', *Aoi-no-ue*, the moving *Atsumori*, and *Takasago*, a 'god-dance' drama which celebrates in religious and solemn form many glories of Japan from its rulers to its landscape and art.

VICENTE, Gil (*c.* 1465–*c.* 1536). Portuguese dramatist and actor who became a court dramatist, writing suitable plays for his office. He also wrote moralities and comedies and found himself in trouble with the Inquisition for daring to ridicule the clergy (along with judges and the nobility). His titles include *Monologue of the Cowboy* and *The Farce of the Muleteers*.

MACHIAVELLI, Niccolo (1469–1527). Italian dramatist and master political theorist, who wrote the first comic masterpiece in Italian. This was *La Mandragola* (1520), a witty prose portrayal of a corrupt society and, in particular, how the heroine Lucrezia is betrayed by a well-drawn gallery of rogues. The play was inspired by Boccaccio, though other plays by the author of *The Prince* were based on classical models.

ARIOSTO, Lodovico (1474–1533). Italian dramatist and poet, a courtier's son who lived in the then-theatrical capital of Italy, Ferrara. In a theatre designed by himself for the ducal palace, he gave his own comedies, also acting in them on occasion. He based his work on the Latin dramatists, the finest play being *La Lena* (1528). Lena is a bawd who helps two young lovers, and the play is rich in social history as well as being fun.

LINDSAY, Sir David (1490–1555). Scottish dramatist and poet, author of the enjoyable and famous political Morality, *The Three Estates* (1540).

ARETINO, Pietro (1492–1556). Italian dramatist and painter, who wrote one tragedy, *Orazio*, and a number of amusing comedies, stocked with realistically drawn courtiers, criminals and other characters including one in *Lo Ipocrito* who is a forerunner of Tartuffe. The plays are not based on classical models, but splendidly and satirically Italian.

SACHS, Hans (1494–1576). German dramatist, mastersinger and cobbler, best known as the hero of Wagner's *Die Meistersinger*. The original wrote over 100 forgotten tragedies and comedies, but is remembered for his contribution to the *Fastnachtsspiele* (carnival plays), pleasing folk-comedies in simple verse. He wrote some 200 of them.

HEYWOOD, John (*c.* 1497–1580). English dramatist and poet whose interludes bridge medieval drama and the Elizabethans. He was also a musician and married Sir Thomas More's niece. His playlets avoid moralising, the best being *The Playe called the foure P.P.; a newe and a very mery enterlude of a palmer, a pardoner, a potycary, a pedler* – who all try to out-lie each other.

BEOLCO, Angelo (1502–1542). Italian dramatist and actor, and a rich doctor's son who wrote his plays in the Paduan dialect. He peopled them with peasants and ordinary folk, playing Ruzzante in them, a cheerful, simple frisky peasant who earned his creator the nickname, *Il Ruzzante* (the playful one). His finest play is *La Moschetta* (The Coquette) of 1528. Though he was popular with his aristocratic audiences, perhaps because of his elegant writing, his ordinary folk were splendidly drawn.

UDALL, Nicholas (1505–1556). English dramatist and headmaster (of Eton and Westminster), and author of *Ralph Roister Doister*, the first true English comedy (*c.* 1553). Influenced by Terence and Plautus, it was given by boys and is a bustling

The great Spanish poet and dramatist, Lope de Vega, who is credited with 2,000 plays. Some 470 of them survive. (Photo: Mansell Collection)

verse comedy about a vainglorious warrior trying to win a wealthy widow.

STEVENSON, William (1521–1575). English fellow of Christ's College, Cambridge, who may have written *Gammer Gurton's Needle* (*c.* 1560), a racy, earthy, play in rhymed verse, which ranks as the first English farce, and is both effective and folksy. Though influenced by classical models, its characters, plot and scenes are English and original. The character Hodge has given his name to the typical English village labourer.

GASCOIGNE, George (*c.* 1542–1577). English dramatist and poet, who wrote the first English prose comedy, *Supposes* (1566), based on Ariosto's *I Suppositi*. This clever farce is the source of the Bianca-Lucentio sub-plot in Shakespeare's *The Taming of the Shrew*. In *The Glass of Government* (*c.* 1575) he pioneered English tragicomedy. He also produced pageants and wrote the first English novel, *The Adventures passed by Master F.J.*, and his *Jocasta* is the first English play based on Greek drama.

TASSO, Torquato (1544–1595). Italian dramatist and poet, who plays include the pastoral drama, *Aminta*, and the romantic tragedy, *Torrismondo*, which has elements of horror that anticipate later tragic pieces. *Aminta* (1573) was the most successful play of its type, which was to spread over Europe.

GARNIER, Robert (*c.* 1545–1590). French dramatist and the finest native writer of tragedies of his century. He was far ahead of his rivals in dramatic skill and lyricism, also in doom-laden emotion and, though he drew on classical and Biblical themes, he related them to current events. Perhaps his finest achievement was *Les Juifves* ('The Jewish Women') of 1583.

CERVANTES, Miguel de (1547–1616). Spanish novelist, dramatist and poet and the author of *Don Quixote*. A great theatre-lover, he wrote a number of plays and comic interludes, some of which have vanished. The interludes are his finest works for the stage, being truthful, realistic and satiric comments on his times. The Senecan tragedy, *El cerco de Numancia*, in which a Spanish city is besieged by the Romans, has inspired Spaniards at critical moments in their history, and Frenchmen during the German occupation. Other fine plays are *El rufian dichoso* about a blackguard who becomes a saintly friar and *El trato de Argel* about men captured, as was Cervantes, by pirates; but none of these match the best of the *entremeses*, as the comic interludes are called.

LYLY, John (*c.* 1554–1606). English dramatist, the grandson of William Lyly, whose Latin Grammar was in use for 300 years. A courtier, his plays were written for small educated audiences, and he helped inaugurate the golden age of Elizabethan drama, influencing Shakespeare, amongst others. Best known for his novel, *Euphues*, whose style gave us the word 'euphuism', the best of his artificial and elegant plays is probably *Endimion, the Man in the Moon*. He used classical themes and Terence as a model for his comedies, *Midas and Mother Bombie*. Though a key figure, because he was the first to write sophisticated English comedy, and for his introduction of prose into his dramas, his plays lost their popularity even in his own day.

PEELE, George (*c.* 1557–1596). English dramatist and friend of Marlowe, Greene and Nashe and other 'University Wits'. His plays include the historical drama, *Edward I*, and his two best-known works, the pastoral *The Arraignment of Paris* and, sometime in the early 1590s, *The Old Wives Tale*, part romance, part folklore, and more subtle than earlier English comedies. He was a fine lyric poet.

GREENE, Robert (1558–1592). English dramatist, pamphleteer and poet, whose famous attack on Shakespeare in *A Groatsworth of Wit Bought with a Million of Repentance* is crucially important because it is the first reference to his theatrical status (1592). Though he may have had a hand in other plays of his time, the best of those undoubtedly by him are *Friar Bacon and Friar Bungay* (*c.* 1590) and *James IV of Scotland* (*c.* 1591). Both have heroines who are 'not unworthy prototypes of the heroines in Shakespeare's romantic comedies' (Edward Quinn) and both are charming and inventive and have double plots. Scottish readers should be warned that *James IV* is pure fiction.

LODGE, Thomas (*c.* 1558–1625). English dramatist whose *Rosalynd* (1590) gave Shakespeare the plot of *As You Like It*. His best play is *Wounds of the Civil War* (1587).

KYD, Thomas (1558–1594). English dramatist, whose popular *The Spanish Tragedy* (*c.* 1588) triggered off a line of revenge tragedies. In the Senecan tradition, its strength lies not in its language but in its exciting plot which thrilled audiences. *Cornelia* (*c.* 1593) is also known to be his and he is thought to have written two early versions of Shakespearean plays, *The Taming of the Shrew* and *Hamlet*, both lost. Shakespeare may have been influenced by him in *Titus Andronicus*. Kyd was arrested with Marlowe for atheism in 1593 and died a year later in disgrace and poverty.

CHAPMAN, George (*c.* 1559–1634). English dramatist and poet, famous for his translation of Homer which so thrilled Keats. His finest tragedy is *Bussy d'Ambois* (*c.* 1604), a Senecan melodrama showing a Herculean hero at odds with a corrupt society. Perhaps his most delightful comedy is *All Fools* (*c.* 1604), based on two plays of Terence, and greatly admired by Swinburne. With Jonson and Marston, he wrote *Eastward Ho!* (1605) and was imprisoned with them because it offended James I: there was a flippant allusion in it to the Scots. He offended the French Ambassador with *Charles, Duke of Byron*, and two of his patrons, Raleigh and Somerset suffered respectively imprisonment and death, and a trial for murder. He died in poverty.

CHETTLE, Henry (*c.* 1560–*c.* 1607). English playwright and printer, who apologised to Shakespeare after Greene (see above) had attacked him. Few of his plays have survived, only one of them being solely by him: *The Tragedy of Hoffman* (*c.* 1602). This is a revenge tragedy crammed with horrors, with a hero-villain as an avenger.

VEGA, Lope de (1562–1635). Spanish dramatist, poet and novelist, who is thought to have written over 2,000 plays, though less than 500 survive. He simultaneously followed an astonishingly adventurous and romantic life, including service with the Armada as well. He ranged from dramatised lives of the saints to farce, inventing cloak-and-dagger drama, though the majority of his plays are tragicomedies. His verse is very fine, as is his theatrical flair. Modern in outlook, as it seems today, he influenced among others, Molière, but has never had his due in English-speaking countries. His plays include *Fuenteovejuna* ('The Sheep Women', *c.* 1612) about rebellious villagers, which has been hailed as the first proletarian drama; *El mejor alcalde el rey* ('The King's the Best Magistrate', 1620), in which a peasant bride is violated on her wedding eve, but is later saved by the King; and (much admired today) *El Caballero de Olmedo* ('The Knight from Olmedo', *c.* 1620), a magnificent poetic tragedy. A delightful comedy is *El perro del hortelano* ('The Dog in the Manger', *c.* 1613), in which a Neapolitan countess falls in love with her secretary, but, not being able to demean herself by marrying him, will not allow her maid to do so either. If his plays about the wrongs of the Spanish peasantry and their efforts to right them seem his finest achievements today, his career as a whole is one of the greatest in dramatic history, and not because he was so prolific, staggering as his output is.

MARLOWE, Christopher (1564–1593). English dramatist and poet whose *Tamburlaine* (1587–8) was the first great English play and ushered in the golden age of Elizabethan drama. In this and later plays Marlowe transformed blank verse into an instrument of power and passion, as well as extreme lyrical splendour. His short career paved the way for Shakespeare.

A Cambridge-educated, Canterbury shoemaker's son, his stormy and mysterious private life ended with a tavern brawl in which he was stabbed. His first play was probably *Dido, Queen of Carthage*, very closely based on Virgil. *Tamburlaine* is an epic about a superman, a hero flawed by lust for power and not, as in earlier English tragedies, merely a great man who 'falls'. Marlowe's 'mighty line' (Ben Jonson) in this and later plays is splendidly powerful and often extremely beautiful, though as a playwright he lacked both humour and the ability to create characters in Shakespearean depth. His plays are even harder to date than Shakespeare's. *The Jew of Malta* is a study in villainy which contrasts sharply with *The Merchant of Venice*, Shylock being a greater and more human creation than Marlowe's Jew. It has been success-

fully staged as a horror comic in modern times. *The Massacre at Paris* survives in very corrupt form and is about the Massacre of St. Bartholomew. Finally came Marlowe's greatest achievements, *Edward II*, both a chronicle play and a tragedy (which influenced Shakespeare's *Richard II*) and also a bleak comment on humanity and power, and *Doctor Faustus*, a tragedy shot through with extreme lyricism. *Edward* especially showed a great advance in stagecraft, while *Faustus* marked the true dawn of English tragedy. Its comic scenes are considered to be additions by other hands.

Greater as a poet than a playwright (though one should remember his early death), he inspired Shakespeare, who yet teased him on occasion: Pistol in *Henry IV* and *V* is regarded by some as a walking parody of the plays, *Tamburlaine* included, performed by the Admiral's Men. And the confrontation between Hotspur and Glendower in *Henry IV* Part I parodies Faustus's efforts at magic. Yet Shakespeare's final tribute was a beautiful one; in *As You Like It* he wrote: 'Dead shepherd, now I find thy saw of might, "Who ever lov'd that lov'd not at first sight?"'

SHAKESPEARE, William (1564–1616). English dramatist and poet, very successful in his own day and, over the last 200 years or so, reaching a pinnacle of fame as the greatest, most admired, and most widely popular of all playwrights.

Born into a fairly prosperous middle class family in Stratford-upon-Avon, where the education was good (idiot Baconians and others of that ilk who do not believe he wrote his own plays, please note), he reached London around 1587. His life is better documented than any other playwright's of his day except Jonson's, but is still maddeningly wrapped in many mysteries. By 1592, he was successful enough as a playwright and actor to be abused by the jealous, dying Greene and defended (including favourable comments on his character) by Henry Chettle. Hailed by many of his contemporaries, he was however one star amongst many. Jonson, who nevertheless could criticise him, hailed him as being 'for all time', and Leonard Digges (in the preface to the 1640 edition of the poems) gave clinching evidence of his tremendous drawing power in the theatre.

Dramatically, he excelled in storytelling (many of the stories being from earlier sources), themes, characterisation, poetry, prose, and imagery – all being part of his whole, unique talent. His amazing

23

neutrality enabled him to create more *different* characters than any other writer, while his boundless humanity embraced nearly every type of man and woman. In *Henry IV Part I*, Falstaff and Hotspur, whose conceptions of honour are totally different, are both heroes.

The dating of the plays which follow is approximate: lack of space forbids discussion. *The Comedy of Errors* (*c.* 1590–4) is a skilful and farcical early comedy, its source being Plautus. *Titus Andronicus* (*c.* 1589–94) is wholly or partly Shakespeare's and, though a chapter of horrors, 'works' in the theatre. Its hero is truly tragic, its villains are splendid and there are signs of future glory. The three parts of *Henry VI* (*c.* 1589–92) show Shakespeare in his first chronicle plays developing swiftly from the crude effectiveness of Part I to Part III which prepared the way for his first masterpiece, *Richard III* (*c.* 1592–3) with its superb, sardonic, Satanic super-villain hero. Holinshed and Halle were the main sources for the plays.

The Taming of the Shrew (*c.* 1593) is lively and effective, especially in performance, while *The Two Gentlemen of Verona* (*c.* 1590–5), from a Spanish source, is an early attempt at a romantic comedy, not very interesting by Shakespearean standards, but with flashes of inspiration, not least Launce and his sour-natured dog, Crab. There followed the poems and possibly the sonnets, with the theatres closed because of plague.

Love's Labour's Lost (*c.* 1594), whose plot was mainly invented despite topical allusions, is a near masterpiece with plenty of action and wit and vivid characterisation, including Berowne – an early sketch for Benedick. *King John* (*c.* 1595–7) is fascinating, though flawed by too many themes, not all of them dramatic. The Bastard is a major creation, there is some superb verse, and several characters make their mark, including the King and the distraught Constance. An earlier play about John was the main source, while *Richard II* (*c.* 1595–6) drew on Holinshed and Daniel's *Civil Wars*. In this play Shakespeare achieved total mastery, especially in his handling of Richard, brought down by weaknesses in his nature, but ennobled by suffering. He and others are obsessed by the very earth of England. There are fewer vivid characters than in the later chronicles, but the play is a notable work of art.

The very popular *Romeo and Juliet* (*c.* 1595–6), based on an old Italian story, is another triumph,

of dramatic skill and matchless early lyricism – sometimes lyricism for its own sake – but its decorative nature adds to the intense feeling generated by the play. The lovers are star-crossed, but Romeo's impetuosity intensifies a tragedy engendered by events. Proof of Shakespeare's new maturity is in the wealth of good parts, while Juliet develops from an inexperienced girl into his first great tragic heroine.

A Midsummer Night's Dream (*c.* 1595–6), its plot Shakespeare's own, is a masterly romantic comedy, with the dramatist miraculously creating several worlds – the fairies, the lovers, the mechanicals, the Court – with different languages to match. Modern efforts to strip away some of the romanticism and find a sinister note in the forest have only made the play more interesting. It remains adored. So does *The Merchant of Venice* (*c.* 1596–8), from Italian sources and with topical allusions in it (as nearly always with Shakespeare). Criticised now for the characters of some of the Gentiles, and with Shylock far more a tragic figure than he was in Elizabethan times, the play works marvellously, despite a wide variety of elements, from a fairy-tale way to choose a husband to the reality of a pound of flesh. Shylock is a great creation. His implacability is due to his daughter's defection and continued insults to his race – not inherent evil.

The two parts of *Henry IV* (*c.* 1597–8) are summits of Shakespeare's early achievement. They are epics which range England from the Court to the Boar's Head Tavern, a Tudor view of the 14th century, with a huge procession of vivid characters of all classes, and with themes ranging from honour to kingship, friendship and joy. Falstaff is the greatest comic creation in English Literature, witty in himself and the cause of wit in others. Prince Hal's rejection of him was understood by Elizabethans who adored Henry V, though today it seems very unattractive. The two plays are national glories. *Henry V* (1599) is less remarkable, but fascinating because so many points of view are expressed, while the rhetoric thrills all but the most cynical and pacific. Holinshed was the main source of *Henry IV*, while an earlier play was an additional source for *Henry V*. The plot of *The Merry Wives of Windsor* written, it is said, by Royal Command to show Falstaff in love, was Shakespeare's own. Falstaff is a butt, a shadow of himself, but the play works well in the theatre.

Julius Caesar (1599), drawn from Plutarch, is a

A scene from Hamlet *at the Old Vic in 1937. From left to right are Robert Newton as Horatio, Laurence Olivier as Hamlet and Alec Guinness as Osric. (Photo: British Theatre Museum)*

masterly political play with three great creations, Brutus, Cassius and Mark Antony, and tauter in construction than the English histories. Shakespeare was by now the complete professional and his understanding of human nature had reached new heights. The character of Caesar causes argument, but Caesarism and the spirit of Caesar dominate the play. Beatrice and Benedick dominate *Much Ado About Nothing* (1598–9); they are Shakespeare's creations, though the plot is mainly from Italian sources. This is a great romantic comedy and, the matchless, witty pair apart, is full of good things and interesting parts. More unified is *As You Like It* (1599–1600), with its enchanting heroine, Rosalind, found in an earlier novel, and many original creations including Touchstone (very hard to play today) and the melancholy Jaques. Finest of the three great romantic comedies is *Twelfth Night* (*c.* 1600), with its marvellous sub-plot (and its characters) Shakespeare's own – the main plot coming from Italian and English sources. The play was often called *Malvolio* after its most remarkable creation; but the other main characters are superbly drawn, and the play is a masterpiece and an enchantment.

There followed three Dark Comedies, *All's Well that Ends Well* (*c.* 1602, unless it is an earlier play called *Love's Labour's Won*, mentioned by Francis

Meres in 1598), *Troilus and Cressida* (1601–2) and *Measure for Measure* (*c.* 1604). The second of these plays, cynical, political, anti-military and anti-disturbers of the peace, is the most popular today, sour and bitter as it is. It is full of good parts, which *All's Well*, cursed with a boorish hero, Bertram, and a controversial heroine, Helena, is not. *Measure for Measure*, however, is a fascinating yet grim comedy, with a major creation in Angelo (icy exterior covering lust), splendid bawdy, and a heroine, Isabella, who divides opinion after refusing to save her brother by surrendering to Angelo.

Hamlet (*c.* 1601), the most famous of all plays, dates from this period. A revenge play, drawn from ancient Norse tradition, its hero has attracted more attention than anyone else in fiction, the ultimate Renaissance Man, about whose every action or every failure to act arguments rage endlessly. None of the millions of words written about him ultimately explain his theatrical magic. His language and thought affects every generation, while the play as a whole and its other characters show Shakespeare's now-total mastery. *Othello* (1604) is less complex and subtle, partly because the Moor is less given to philosophising than Hamlet, but its power is as lethal as its language is magnificent, powerful and, on occasions, shattering. Othello himself, proud, noble and trusting, is brought down to savagery by his catastrophic jealousy yet is raised to volcanic force by the malignant Iago. This villain has been seen as purely evil, the personification of Vice, and as a monstrous practical joker (W. H. Auden), while Othello has been hailed as a flawless hero until tragedy overwhelms him. But recently he has been dubbed proud to the point of arrogance and a self-dramatiser by some, including F. R. Leavis and T. S. Eliot. Desdemona, innocent, dignified and strong in character, is one of Shakespeare's noblest heroines, and the play (from an Italian source) is universally popular, notably in Russia and India.

Shakespeare next unleashed an even greater thunderbolt, *King Lear* (*c.* 1605–6), partly based on an earlier play, though he invented Lear's madness and took the Gloucester sub-plot from Sydney's *Arcadia*. Lear's pride and abdication are personally and politically disastrous, and rage, foolishness and impulsiveness bring about both his downfall and madness. Yet he comes through his ordeal and finds nobility in misfortune, where he is supported by those he has rejected. Shakespeare uses the trappings of melodrama and Grand Guignol (the blinding of Gloucester etc.), yet studies mankind even more deeply, if pessimistically, than before, placing his play in a pagan world of epic grandeur. *Macbeth* (1606) is less complex, but Shakespeare uses all his dramatic and imaginative powers to chart the progress of a man from ambition, though murder and tyranny, to ruin and death. Miraculously he creates a villain who is a tragic hero, for his verse grows more impressive (and pessimistic) as his crimes multiply. The soldier-poet is one of Shakespeare's greatest though most difficult parts (few actors are right for both aspects), and Lady Macbeth, a cold villainness, devoted to her husband's cause, but remorseful under her surface of steel, is a supreme rôle for a great actress.

Antony and Cleopatra (1607–8), based mainly on Plutarch, divides opinion. Some find the verse rich to the point of cloying, others golden and incomparable. For them the play is the equal of the other supreme tragedies and they are stirred by the theme of love or duty, and revel in the play as a gigantic love duet and love duel, born from a chronicle play. It is hard to believe that Shakespeare was detached from his lovers (as some claim). He knew their faults, but the verse proclaims he gave his heart to them. And there are many other fine rôles in the play. Antony's greatness has to be taken partly on trust, but not Cleopatra's. She is frank, funny, fascinating, clever, sensual, passionate, hot-tempered and capricious to a degree, and is Shakespeare's supreme female rôle.

There followed *Timon of Athens* (*c.* 1605–9) and *Coriolanus* (*c.* 1608). Timon only makes sense as a tragic satire, for the hero is transformed from the most magnanimous of men into the complete misanthrope, with scalding language to match. *Coriolanus* is much finer, its anti-hero proud to the point of folly, snobbish (inherited from his alarming mother, Volumnia) and graceless. Yet there is nobility in him and his demagogic enemies are despicable, and the people of Rome an unlikeable lot. One of the strengths of the play is that it is always uncomfortably topical. Next came the Romances, *Pericles* (*c.* 1607), *Cymbeline* (*c.* 1609–10), *The Winter's Tale* (1611) and *The Tempest* (1611), all of them presumably written for the indoors Blackfriars Theatre. *Pericles* is sensational and unsubtle – an odd, enjoyable piece with good low scenes. John Gower acts as Chorus, whose 14th-century reworking of a Latin story provides the plot. *Cymbeline*, based mainly on legendary history, is an attractive piece, Masque-like in places, and with two great parts, the enchanting Imogen and the villainous Iachimo. The several plots are linked less well than usual, but much of the play delights. So, to a greater degree, does *The Winter's Tale*, again full of sensations and surprises, but with Shakespeare making everything credible in terms of a Romance. There is a wealth of good characterisation, including the insanely jealous Leontes and the Elizabethan super-spiv in the pastoral Act IV, Autolycus. This act is part-dream, part-Warwickshire and pure enchantment. *The Tempest* divides opinion: like its main figure Prospero, who (for all his fine verse) is too omniscient for some, yet for others is Shakespeare himself and utterly human. It is not so action-packed as the other romances and obeys the unities of place, time and action (unique therefore in Shakespeare) and has much in common with a Masque. Arguments continue as to whether the play is an allegory on Shakespeare's life or simply the culmination of his art, but it survives extremes of interpretation, like all his greatest works; the deformed and brutish Caliban is a final example of Shakespeare's humanising powers, for the monster is allowed the incomparable speech beginning, 'Be not afeard: the isle

David Warner as Hamlet in Peter Hall's 1965 production at Stratford, designed by John Bury. (Photo: British Tourist Authority)

is full of noises.'

Shakespeare seems to have collaborated with John Fletcher on several occasions, most notably in *Henry VIII* (1613), the finest parts of which, it is generally agreed, are his. By no means the equal of the earlier chronicle plays, it is full of interest, and Wolsey, Queen Katharine and, perhaps, Henry live. It is a pageant play and a historical masque for the Globe's public and is based on Holinshed and Halle. Some believe that Shakespeare had a hand in *The Two Noble Kinsmen* and *Cardenio*.

By 1594 Shakespeare had become a leading member of the Chamberlain's Men – later the King's Men – and in 1599 he was a shareholder (with responsibilities for choosing plays, directing them, etc.) in the new Globe Theatre. Even after he retired sometime around 1610 to live the life of a gentleman at Stratford, he remained associated with his company, apart from writing plays for them. The line of parts he is alleged to have played were old men, the Ghost in *Hamlet*, etc., but this may have been due to his writing duties his colleagues wishing to keep his parts small. He would have been responsible for directing his own plays whenever possible. He was immortalised in 1623 when his friends, John Heminge and Henry Condell, collected his published and unpublished plays together – there were eighteen of the latter – and produced the First Folio.

MIDDLETON, Thomas (*c.* 1570–1627). English dramatist and poet, and author of several outstanding plays: *A Chaste Maid in Cheapside* (with Dekker) (1611), which is a fine contemporary comedy; *Women Beware Women* (*c.* 1623) about incest, adultery and murder; and *The Changeling* (*c.* 1623), his finest tragedy and a strong study in corruption and murder, with a heroine who seems to be virtuous but gradually disintegrates into a villainess. William Rowley (see below) collaborated with him in this last. He had a genius for portraying depravity, a strong satiric gift, and a remarkable ability to make his finest characters psychologically real. This notable pessimist also produced pageants and masques.

BARNES, Barnabe (1571–1609). English dramatist and poet, only one of whose plays, *The Devil's Charter* (1607), survives. It is a tragedy based on Pope Alexander VI and modelled on *Dr. Faustus*. Some believe that he was the 'rival poet' mentioned by Shakespeare in his Sonnets.

DEKKER, Thomas (*c.* 1572–*c.* 1632). English playwright and pamphleteer, who between 1598–1602 was turning out plays fast for the shrewd and tight-fisted manager, Henslowe. He wrote more than 40 plays, many with others, between the 1590s and the 1620s, spending some time in a debtors' prison. About 15 survive, by far the most famous being *The Shoemaker's Holiday* (1599), a vigorous comedy full of London characters, which he never again equalled. Two more comedies, both with John Webster, were *Westward Ho!* (1604) and *Northward Ho!* (1605) both set in London. He is thought to have collaborated with John Ford in *The Witch of Edmonton* (1621). The most important of his pamphlets, theatrically speaking, is *The Gull's Hornbook* (1609), an invaluable picture in parts about the Jacobean Theatre, satirical as it is: 'By sitting on the stage, if you be a Knight, you may happily get yourself a Mistresse: if a mere Fleet Street Gentleman, a wife.' He seems to have been a delightful man.

JONSON, Ben (1572–1637). English dramatist, poet and friend and critic of the less academic and far more popular and successful Shakespeare. Unlike his 'gentle' rival, he was quarrelsome to the point of duelling and often arrogant, dismissing most of his fellow-playwrights (except Shakespeare) as hacks. His comments on Shakespeare in prose and verse are invaluable.

This apprentice bricklayer (turned soldier, turned playwright) was imprisoned for being part author of the slanderous, *Isle of Dogs* (1597). His first comedy (with Shakespeare in the cast) was *Every Man in his Humour* (1598), in which he first made every character embody a 'humour'. It was then supposed that the human body was controlled by four liquids – blood, black bile, yellow bile and phlegm – and these 'humours' needed to be balanced harmoniously for good health in body and mind. Many of Jonson's characters were dominated by a single 'humour' with comic results so that many of them were caricatures; indeed, his greatest admirers put him in the class of Dickens as a delineator of character by broad methods. Others find Dickens' creations far more believable. Nevertheless, from 1606, he wrote a series of major comedies which are classics. *Volpone* (1606) is the story of a cunning old miser and a brilliant study of gullibility. *Epicoene, or the Silent Woman* (1609) is a lively, clever comedy, while *The Alchemist* (1610) returns to gullibility. *Bartholomew Fair*

(1614) is a bustling, noisy portrait of Jacobean London on the spree.

In these 'humours' plays lie Jonson's real genius. Tragedies like *Sejanus* (1603) and *Cataline* (1611) were not even widely popular in his own day. These too are satirical-tragic satires. Much more successful were the Court masques, spectacles which he produced with the great architect, Inigo Jones. Jonson raised masques from pleasant entertainments to works of literary merit. Performed by amateurs, they were, with Jonson and Jones in charge, very professionally staged and were given between 1605–12. His final plays are little known. One of them, *The Staple of News* (1625) is about the rise of the news industry. On his tombstone is written 'O rare Ben Jonson'; indeed, though even his best plays have long absences from the repertory, he ranks second only to Shakespeare in Elizabethan–Jacobean drama.

DAY, John (1574–*c.* 1640). English dramatist who wrote several plays for the Children of the Revels, including the *Isle of Gulls* (1606), which disgraced the children and others concerned with it because of apparently satirical references to a number of courtiers. His finest work, *The Parliament of Bees* (1608, part play and part masque), consists of delightful sketches adapted from Dekker, who may have collaborated on them with Day.

HEYWOOD, Thomas (*c.* 1574–1641). English dramatist who claimed to have had a hand in almost 200 plays, though only a score survive. By far his most famous and best play known to us is his *A Woman Killed with Kindness* (1603), a domestic drama which combines warm humanity with feeling and strong characterisation. His portraits of English social life are invaluable, even if his plays vary widely in quality.

ROWLEY, Samuel (*c.* 1575–1624). English playwright and actor, with Shakespeare's rivals, the Lord Admiral's Men. The probable co-author of a number of plays, he is thought to have helped to add a comic sub-plot to *Doctor Faustus*. He wrote *When You See Me, You Know Me* (1605) one of the sources of *Henry VIII*.

TOURNEUR, Cyril (1575–1626). English dramatist, usually regarded as the author of *The Revenger's Tragedy* (published 1607) and *The Atheist's Tragedy* (*c.* 1611), the first of which is sometimes revived and is darkly chilling and very impressive.

A scene from Goldini's The Servant with Two masters *in a production at the Piccolo Theatre, Milan. (Photo: Italian Institute, London)*

MARSTON, John (1576–1634). English dramatist and satirist, eight of whose plays survive. The most important is the tragicomic satire, *The Malcontent* (1603), about a deposed duke who returns to his court in the disguise of a discontented jester to observe and manipulate his former subjects. Marston escaped imprisonment over *Eastward Ho!* for which he was more responsible (rude references to Scots at Court) than its co-authors, Jonson and Chapman, who were imprisoned. Jonson and Marston continually quarrelled, and Jonson satirised him as Crispinus in *The Poetaster* (1601). However, the quarrel was patched up and *The Malcontent* was dedicated to Jonson. Marston was imprisoned for an unknown reason in 1608, and then became a priest. Honesty and great intensity were his chief characteristics as a playwright. As well as his comedy masterpiece, *The Dutch Courtesan* (1605) is occasionally revived.

FLETCHER, John (1579–1625). English dramatist, best known for his long collaboration with Francis Beaumont (see below) from 1608–16. Their plays have been claimed as the finest English examples of the romantic tragicomedy. They include *Philaster* (1610), *A Maid's Tragedy* (1611, their finest tragedy proper), *A King and No King* (1611) and *The Scornful Lady* (1613). Both well-born, their plays were geared to the private audiences of the Blackfriars Theatre, Fletcher being the finer poet of the two. Fletcher probably collaborated with Shakespeare in *Henry VIII* (1613), and certainly in *The Two Noble Kinsmen*, and in *Cardenio*, which is lost. His other collaborators included Massinger and Rowley, while some of his own plays are *The Faithful Shepherdess* (1608), *The Woman's Prize, or The Tamer Tamed* (*c.* 1611, a sequel to Shakespeare's *Shrew*) and *The Humorous Lieutenant* (1619).

Beaumont and Fletcher knew what their audiences wanted and provided it. Fletcher was more popular in Restoration times than Shakespeare.

WEBSTER, John (*c.* 1580–*c.* 1634). English dramatist whose life is obscure even by Elizabethan standards. Almost forgotten until Lamb re-discovered him, he now ranks second only to Shakespeare in English dramatic poetry because of his two dark, deeply pessimistic masterpieces, *The White Devil* (published 1612) and *The Duchess of Malfi*, acted by the King's Men in 1613–14. He also wrote *The Devil's Law Case* and collaborated with others, notably with Dekker in *Westward Ho!* and *Northward Ho!*; also with Dekker, Ford and Rowley in the sensational melodrama, *Keep the Widow Waking* (1624). Bernard Shaw hopelessly underrated him, calling him 'Tussaud laureate', but the 20th century knows better than to mock at his gloomy vision. However, as Rupert Brooke noted, 'A play of Webster's is full of the feverish and ghastly turmoil of a nest of maggots. . . . Human beings are writhing grubs in an immense night.' What makes his two great plays bearable is their language and the chances they give for fine acting. Both are passionate dramas set in Renaissance Italy, indeed *The White Devil* is based on fact, and both have lines and speeches which are Shakespeare's only rivals, though starker: 'I have caught An everlasting cold. I have lost my voice Most

irrecoverably.' Yet his most famous line, which has never been bettered by anyone, is anything but stark, for all its matchless concision. In *The Duchess of Malfi*, Ferdinand looks down at his dead sister and says: 'Cover her face: mine eyes dazzle: she died young.'

ALARCON, Juan Ruiz (*c.* 1581–1639). Spanish dramatist, born in Mexico, and author of comedies of manners which influenced Corneille. The most famous is *La Verdad sospechosa* ('Truth under suspicion').

MASSINGER, Philip (1583–1640). English dramatist, many of whose plays were in collaboration with Fletcher and sometimes, it is thought, Beaumont and Fletcher. When Fletcher died, he became the King's Men's chief playwright. Two of his own plays are the comedy, *The City Madam* (1623) and *A New Way to Pay Old Debts* (*c.* 1625), with its famous part, Sir Giles Overreach, in which Edmund Kean sent Lord Byron into a convulsion. It contains this passage: 'Ha! I am feeble: Some undone widow sits upon mine arm, And takes away the use of it; and my sword, Glued to my scabbard with wronged orphans' tears, Will not be drawn.' Only great actors need attempt . . .

BEAUMONT, Francis (*c.* 1584–1616). English dramatist, whose plays with John Fletcher have been referred to above. His earliest piece, *The Woman Hater* (*c.* 1606) was a Jonsonian 'humours' play for the Children of St. Paul's. Only one other play still exists that was his alone, and it is sometimes given: *The Knight of the Burning Pestle* (1607). Inspired by *Don Quixote*, it burlesques historical romances and, in particular, the audiences who adored them, satirising London playgoers by using a play-within-a-play technique.

MOLINA, Tirso de (1584–1648). Spanish dramatist and priest, and the first to use the legendary Don Juan on the stage in his *The Deceiver of Seville and the Stone Guest*. Of his huge output, many of them comedies, some 80 survive, the best known being *Don Gil de las Calzas Verdes*.

BREDERO, Gerbrand (1585–1618). Dutch dramatist, influenced by Lope de Vega in his romantic comedies, but writing brilliant farces and comedies in his own idiom, which have never been surpassed in Dutch. His finest farces include *Klucht van de Koe* ('Farce of the Cow', 1612), while in *De Spaansche Brabander* ('The Spanish Brabanter', 1618) he put his native city of Amsterdam on the stage. His characterisation in his farces and comedies is sharp and his mastery of ordinary people's language is notable.

ROWLEY, William (*c.* 1585–*c.* 1642). English dramatist and actor who some believe was the brother of Samuel Rowley, referred to earlier. He collaborated, as noted, with Middleton in *The Changeling*. Of his own four plays the best known is *The Birth of Merlin* (*c.* 1608), partly because when published in 1662, Shakespeare was alleged to have been the co-author. Some have claimed that he wrote the non-Shakespearean parts of *Pericles*.

FORD, John (1586–*c.* 1639). English dramatist who collaborated with Dekker, Webster and Rowley, while himself writing one magnificent play, *'Tis Pity She's a Whore* (*c.* 1630), with incest as its theme. Apart from this passionate tragedy, his best known play is *The Broken Heart* (1633). He also wrote a good chronicle play, *Perkin Warbeck* (1634). The last of the great Elizabethan dramatists, his work is full of compassion and understanding of human nature. He was influenced by Robert Burton's *Anatomy of Melancholy* (1621).

FIELD, Nathan (1587–1620). English dramatist and actor, despite a Puritan preacher for a father. Apart from collaborating with Fletcher and Massinger, he wrote two Jonsonian comedies, *A Woman is a Weathercock* (*c.* 1609) and *Amends for Ladies* (1611). A better actor than a playwright, he rose from child star to sharing leads with Burbage.

VONDEL, Joost van den (1587–1679). Dutch dramatist and poet. A Humanist who was inspired by Terence and Plautus as well as the Bible, his masterpiece is *Lucifer* (published 1654), which dramatically relates the revolt and fall of the Angels. In *Adam in Ballingschap* ('Adam in Exile', published 1664) he portrayed the ideal man. Vondel's poetry matches his superb imaginative gifts.

BROME, Richard (*c.* 1590–1652). English dramatist, who began in the service of Ben Jonson. Apart from collaborating with others, he wrote at least 15 plays, including *The Antipodes* (1638) about an attempt to mend a marriage, and his finest piece, *A Jovial Crew* (1641) about two daughters who join a gypsy band led by their father's steward. Social comment was his forte.

DESMARETS de SAINT-SORLIN, Jean (1595–1676). French dramatist, poet and novelist, and a founder member of the French Academy. His finest play is the comedy, *Les Visionnaires* (1637),

written at the request of Cardinal Richelieu; an amusing comment on high society, it portrays a number of harmless eccentrics in an original and high literary way.

SHIRLEY, James (1596–1666). English dramatist, 31 of whose plays survive. His best comedy is *The Lady of Pleasure* (1635), a witty satire on Charles I's London, while his tragedies include *The Traitor* (1630) about Lorenzo de Medici, *Love's Cruelty* (1631) and, his finest piece, *The Cardinal* (1641), a powerful play not unlike *The Duchess of Malfi*. This play was the last major work written before the Puritans closed the theatres, the last of a line of plays spanning more than half a century which are unequalled in the history of drama.

OPITZ, Martin (1597–1639). German poet from Silesia who diverted his native drama to classical models and to Italy and France, not for the better. He translated a number of classical and Italian plays, wrote some plays of his own, and purified and improved the German language; but he made it seem that drama was for clever people, and his influence was therefore not very happy.

CALDERÓN de la BARCA, Pedro (1600–1681). Spanish dramatist and poet who wrote over 200 plays, more than half of which survive, and who ranks with de Vega as a supreme Spanish playwright. Possessor of a strong dramatic sense, fine imagination and a keen intellect, his plays range widely, his religious pieces never descending to conventional clichés. Some of these are one-act *autos sacramentales*, the best known being *El Gran teatro del mundo* (1649) and *La cena de Baltasar* ('Baltassar's Feast', *c.* 1634). He also wrote full length religious plays, including *La devocion de la cruz* (*c.* 1633), while *El alcalde de Zalamea* ('The Mayor of Zalamea', 1640) is a fine historical play. *La vida es sueno* ('Life is a dream', *c.* 1635) is a famous metaphysical play about a prisoner who finds that a spell outside prison is only a dream. He also wrote *pundonor*, or point of honour plays, including *El medico de su honra* (*c.* 1629), also comedies, romances, cloak-and-dagger plays and folklore and legendary pieces. He was a superb poet and his influence stretched out far beyond Spain, including adaptations in Restoration England. He became Philip IV's Court Playwright and Master of the Revels, having written his first play at 14. Ordained a priest in 1651, he only wrote *autos sacramentales* from that time onwards, apart from plays commanded of him at Court.

MAIRET, Jean (1604–1686). French dramatist, even more highly thought of in his own day than Corneille. His first play was a tragicomedy, *Chryséide et Arimand* (1625), thereafter achieving many successes, becoming the leading French dramatist. *Sophonisbe* (1634) is the first French tragedy to obey the Unities. He quarrelled with Corneille over *Le Cid*, which did his reputation with later generations no good. His *Les Galanteries du Duc d'Ossone* (1632) is one of the best comedies of his times. In 1640, he gave up playwriting for the diplomatic service.

CORNEILLE, Pierre (1606–1684). French dramatist and poet, and France's first great tragic playwright, though his first play, *Mélite* (1629) is a farcical comedy. His first tragedy is *Médée* (1635). His most famous – and successful – play, written after a quarrel had ended his employment by Richelieu as an official dramatist, is *Le Cid* (1637), a tragicomedy. It created a storm because though it seemed to observe the Unities, it was more truly a romantic drama in classical guise. But it made his name and, after Mairet's retirement he had no rival until the appearance of Racine. The 1640s were his most productive years, his plays including *Horace* (1640), *Cinna* (1641), *Polyeucte* (1642), *La Mort de Pompée* (1643) and the comedy, *Le Menteur* (1643). After the failure of *Pertharite* (1652) his career was less successful, though he had lesser triumphs to come, including the spectacular *La Toison d'or* (1660) and *Tite et Bérénice* (1670) on the same subject as Racine's *Bérénice*, which had the gossips clucking.
Corneille was a magnificent creator of tragic, heroic men and women, boldly, sometimes superhumanly drawn. Duty and reason conflict with hatred and love in them. He shaped French tragedy by focusing on the soul, not, as had earlier dramatists, simply on actions. Racine surpassed him, but he remained in his lifetime *le grand Corneille*. A difficult man, he enjoyed a happy home life. His brother, Thomas Corneille (1625–1709), was a successful playwright in his own day, though without Pierre's genius. His most famous works were the romantic tragedy *Timocrate* (1656) and the heroic tragedy *Ariane*, one of Rachel's great rôles.

DAVENANT, Sir William (1606–1668). English dramatist, theatre manager, soldier, and Poet Laureate, and abuser of Shakespeare's plays. He may have been Shakespeare's godson and enjoyed the rumour that he was his illegitimate son. He collaborated with Inigo Jones in three Court masques before the Civil War, produced the first English opera, *The Siege of Rhodes* in 1656, and at the Restoration took over the running of one of the two new licensed companies of players, The Duke of York's. In his theatre at Lincoln's Inn, he produced doctored (usually butchered) versions of Shakespeare's plays, one of his most famous 'improvements' being on *Macbeth*, 'being dressed in all its finery, as new clothes, new scenes, machines, as flyings for the witches, with all the singing and dancing in it', etc. He judged the taste of the day perfectly and his (profitable) sins cannot disguise the fact that he had a marvellous career and did much for the theatre he so loved. *The Siege of Rhodes* saw the first appearance of a woman on the public stage (not an actress but a singer) and was an early heroic play, apart from its operatic importance.

MILTON, John (1606–1674). English poet, author of the masques *Arcades* (1633) and *Comus* (1634), also the great dramatic poem, *Samson Agonistes* (1671). Though not meant for the stage, it has been performed in modern times, as has *Comus*. The greatest of English non-dramatic poets, his work can only be the passing concern of this book.

ROTROU, Jean (1609–1650). French dramatist, who was almost the equal of Corneille. Thirty of his plays have survived. His first great success was *La Bague de l'oubli* ('The Ring of Oblivion', 1629), inspired by a play of de Vega's. It ranks as the first French non-farcical comedy. Perhaps his best play is *Les Sosies* (1637) based on the story of Amphitryon. A later triumph was *La Soeur* (1645), a five-act high comedy in verse full of disguises, kidnappings and false identities in the manner of Italian Renaissance plays. He sold his *Venceslas* (1647) to pay off a gambling dept, having created a part in it, Ladislas, which was to give great opportunities to many leading actors. Like several of his last plays, it is a tragicomedy, based on a Spanish play. A much-liked man, he died at Dreux during a plague, refusing to escape as he was civil lieutenant there.

SUCKLING, Sir John (1609–1642). English dramatist, far more famous as a lyric poet. His best known play is *Aglaura* (1637), a tragedy with a happy ending (at King Charles I's request), set at the Persian Court. *The Goblins* is freely drawn from *The Tempest* (c. 1638), while *Brennoralt* (c. 1639), a tragicomedy with a Byronic hero, is probably his best play.

SCARRON, Paul (1610–1660). French dramatist, poet and novelist. A witty man, crippled by rheumatism at 30, he wrote many comedies and farces, his masterpiece being *Don Japhet d'Armenie* (1647), a burlesque which mocks both noble and heroic pretentions. Many of his plays are high comedies styled on Spanish models. A remarkable man who could even mock his own infirmities, he married the future Mme. de Maintenon, who married Louis XIV.

KILLIGREW, Thomas (1612–1683). English dramatist and theatre manager, a page to Charles I and Groom of the Bedchamber to Charles II, who gave him a patent to form The King's Company. They played in Vere Street, then at the new Theatre Royal, Drury Lane, less successfully than Davenant's rival company, but at least not butchering the Bard so disgracefully. Killigrew's plays were written before the Civil War. They include two tragicomedies, *The Prisoners* (1635) and *Claracilla* (1636) and *The Parson's Wedding* (1641) which even seemed over-bawdy to Restoration audiences. It is also very witty. In 1682, the King's Company was forced to merge with its rivals. Pepys called Killigrew 'a merry droll'.

GRYPHIUS, Andreas (1616–1664). German (Silesian) dramatist and poet, rarely performed today, but the author of a number of important tragedies and comedies. The tragedies were mostly about kings and the upper nobility, including *Charles Stuart* (1649), a static piece about 'Majesty Murdered' – its sub-title. It dates from 1649, the year Charles I lost his head, so was topical, if more 'book drama' than stage play. His comedies concentrate on the lower classes, *Die geliebte Dornrose* ('The Beloved Dornrose', 1660), written in Silesian dialect, being realistic in a way then unusual in German drama. Perhaps the best of his comedies, which are prose works, is *Horribilicribrifax* (published 1663) which exposes every sort of contemporary folly.

MOLIÈRE (Jean Baptiste Poquelin's pen-name, 1622–1673). French dramatist, actor and director, and the greatest of all French writers of comedy. Deserting a possible legal career, he became an actor in 1642, joining the Béjarts, an acting family, then, with Madeleine Béjart, founding the Illustre-Théâtre. It ran into debt and Molière had a spell in prison, after which he joined another company,

writing short *commedia dell'arte*-like farces for them and acting in them. It was a good training.

The turning point came in 1658 when the company played before the 20-year-old Louis XIV at the Louvre. After giving a Corneille tragedy, Molière came on and announced his own farce, *Le Docteur amoureux*, which was a success and revealed his own gifts for comic acting. The King granted the troupe the right to stay in Paris and they took over the Théâtre du Petit-Bourbon, sharing it with Italian players, who influenced Molière greatly. Later, he took over the Théâtre du Palais-Royal. Tragedies were not proving the company's forte, but Molière saved the day by writing *L'Etourdi* ('The Blunderer', 1655) and *Le Dépit amoureux* ('The Amorous Quarrel', 1656), then in 1659 had a huge success with *Les Precieuses Ridicules*, which offended the fashionable young but delighted everyone else. This one-acter was his first triumph.

Scandal (because of Molière's choice of subjects) was to haunt the company, but the King and the unbiased public adored Molière's plays, Louis act-

Friedrich von Schiller, German dramatist and poet, and a supreme figure in the European Romantic Movement. (Photo: The Cultural Attaché, French Embassy)

ing as a firm and vital patron for several years. It was needed, though it meant that Molière had to provide court entertainments. His private life was attacked, while *L'Ecole des Femmes* (1662) had the prudish combining with the learned to attack him. And his great *Tartuffe* (1664), a superb exposé of religious hypocricy, shocked the righteous. Louis gave way to them a little, ordering the play only to be given privately. In 1665, Molière's troupe became the King's Company, the same year that *Dom Juan, ou le festin de pierre* ('Don Juan, or the Stone Guest') was alleged to be atheistical. Some demanded that Molière be burnt, but he went on writing comedies. In 1666 he was at the height of his powers with *Le Misanthrope* and *Le Médicin malgré lui* ('The physician in spite of himself'). *Amphitryon* and *L'Avare* ('The Miser') appeared in 1668. Perhaps his best-known Court play is *Le Bourgeois gentilhomme* (1671), then followed, amongst others, yet another great satire, *Les Femmes savantes* ('The Learned Ladies', 1672) and his last play, *Le Malade Imaginaire* (1672), written when the King was withdrawing his support for religious and political reasons. It was in this play that Molière died on stage. Though, contrary to legend, his friends just managed to secure him a Christian burial, it was done at night to avoid a scandal. Even in death it seemed he could cause trouble.

Molière's supreme achievement was to raise French comedy to the heights and prestige of French tragedy. Under his guidance it became part satire, part social comment, part character comedy, and his plays admonished as well as entertained their audiences. Sadly, though his plays are universal in that they can be applied to all of us, they are very difficult to translate and still retain their wit. His dramatic construction is as fine as his verse and superb sense of comedy, even if some of his endings are arbitrary; while if he tends to create types rather than individuals, his range is enormous. He rises to his greatest heights when attacking hypocrisy and vice, and remains unrivalled in drama as a delineator of character through comedy.

DRYDEN, John (1631–1700). English dramatist, poet, satirist and critic, regarded by some as the greatest of the Restoration dramatists, though the works of others are more frequently performed. His supreme poetic achievements are non-dramatic satires, including the political *Absolom and Achitophel*. He wrote nearly 30 plays, some in collabora-

tion, ranging widely: comedy, tragi-comedy, blank verse tragedy, adaptations of Shakespeare, an English style of opera (part play, part musical spectacle, as in *King Arthur*, with Henry Purcell) and heroic tragedy in rhyming couplets, a form he did more than any other English writer to develop.

For all his importance, few of his works are now given. However, *Marriage à la Mode* (1672) is occasionally revived because the comedy of the second plot is brilliant and very funny. His best play is *All for Love* (1678), a blank verse tragedy about Antony and Cleopatra, which held the stage until the 19th century when Shakespeare's play was at last recognised. *The Conquest of Granada* (part I, 1669; part 2, 1670) should be read for its bad as well as its good sections. It is an epic in rhyming couplets, packed with incidents; Buckingham's *The Rehearsal* (1671) guyed it so successfully that the genre was doomed, but not before Dryden had written another such play, *Aureng-Zebe* (1675). His Prologues and Epilogues, for the plays of others as well as his own, are not only good verse but marvellous sources of theatrical information.

ETHEREGE, Sir George (*c*. 1634–*c*. 1691). English dramatist, the first to develop the English comedy of manners. Influenced presumably by Molière after living in France in Cromwell's time, he wrote *The Comical Revenge, or Love in a Tub* (1664), mixing drama and comedy, the plot being given in serious verse, the sub-plot in lively comic prose. The latter proved to be his strongest point in *She Would if She Could* (1668) and *The Man of Mode* (1676), a masterpiece which is still seen, and which contains a superb creation, Sir Fopling Flutter, a Restoration dandy.

QUINAULT, Phillipe (1635–1688). French dramatist and poet, very popular in his own day, not least for his libretti for Lully's operas. His assets are stage sense and ability to portray passion; his faults, lack of originality, insipidity and, according to Boileau, the excessive tenderness of his characters. His finest comedy is *La Mère coquette* (1665) while his most popular tragedy was *Astrate, Roi de Tyr* (1664).

RACINE, Jean (1639–1699). French dramatist and poet whose tragedies, with those of Corneille, tower above the drama of their age. La Bruyère said that Corneille showed men as they ought to be and Racine as they are, meaning it as a criticism (which few would now accept) of Racine. He was one of the supreme tragic poets and the greatest of all writers of classical tragedy in alexandrines.

Orphaned at the age of four he was educated by the Jansenists at Port-Royal, where his aunt became the Abbess. The excellent teachers there preferred French to dead languages, Greek to Latin, and encouraged logical thought and influenced their pupil for life. After three tragedies had been turned down, Racine's fourth, *La Thébaïde, ou les frères ennemis* (1664) was given by Molière, who had outlined it for the young man. Molière also presented *Alexandre*, about Alexander the Great (1665), but Racine secretly gave it to the rival Hôtel de Bourgogne, so falling out with his patron, as well as quarrelling with the Jansenists, who were hostile to the stage.

His first great success was *Andromaque* (1667), with his mistress who had also been with Molière, in the lead. This resulted in fame, theatrical rivalry with Corneille, and in Molière never speaking to him again – with reason. It should be noted that Racine preferred women in the leading rôles of his plays. His only comedy, *Les Plaideurs* (1668) followed, based partly on *The Wasps* of Aristophanes; then came the great but not very successful *Britannicus* (1670), set in Nero's time. *Bérénice* (1670) came out by accident or design just before a similar play by Corneille; then followed plays which consolidated his position as the leading tragic dramatist of the day: *Bajazet* (1672), *Mithradate* (1673) – both eastern subjects treated in an up-to-date French style – and *Iphigénie* (1674), based on Greek legend. His career in the theatre ended with *Phèdre* (1677), which was less successful than a play on the subject by one Pradon, who was persuaded to write his piece by Racine's enemies, of whom there were plenty. In *Phèdre*, Racine combined fate in the Greek sense with a modern person wracked with guilt, yet condemned to evil ways.

An additional reason for retirement was his appointment as the King's histographer, and he only returned to drama to write two biblical plays at the request of Mme de Maintenon, *Esther* (1689) and *Athalie* (1691), for performances at her girls' school. After his death, they entered the repertoire of the Comédie Française, the latter becoming one of Racine's most acclaimed plays. He was reconciled to the Jansenists before his death and ended his life, which had been so full of intrigue, passion and quarrels, as a good father and good Christian.

By his passionate intensity he humanised French classical drama, obeying the rules, yet transforming them and giving an unequalled line of fierce yet tender heroines to the theatre. Bruntetière said that Racine was the first to write 'the literature of the passions of the heart' which, applied to France, was certainly so.

WYCHERLEY, William (1640–1716). English dramatist, author of four Restoration comedies, robustly coarse, funny and full of well-observed contemporary types. They are *Love in a Wood* (1671), *The Gentleman Dancing Master* (1672), his masterpiece, *The Country Wife* (1675) and *The Plain Dealer* (1676). He gave up playwriting when the stage was 'purified' having earlier suffered imprisonment for debt. In *The Country Wife*, which is quite frequently revived, the libertine Horner pretends to be impotent to avert the suspicions of husbands. The 'wife', Margery Pinchwife, who thoroughly enjoys the pleasures of the town, is a famous comedy rôle.

SHADWELL, Thomas (*c.* 1641–1692). English dramatist who deliberately modelled himself on Ben Jonson in comedies like *Epsom Wells* (1672), *The Squire of Alsatia* (1688), *Bury Fair* (1689) and other efficient, quite lively comedies. He also played the Restoration game of 'improving' Shakespeare in *The Enchanted Island* (1674), a version of *The Tempest*. He followed Dryden as Poet Laureate.

WEISE, Christian (1642–1702). German dramatist and teacher, author of many long serious plays. He was one of the first Germans to portray the middle classes realistically on stage.

CRUZ, Sor Juana Inés de la (*c.* 1648–1695). Mexican dramatist, poetess and nun and South America's finest 17th-century lyric poet. She wrote some excellent interludes and comedies.

LEE, Nathaniel (*c.* 1648–1692) English dramatist, author of a number of grim tragedies, featuring corpses, lunatics, etc. He ended his life in Bedlam. His best play is *The Rival Queens* (1677), about Alexander the Great's jealous wives, which held the stage for a century or more.

OTWAY, Thomas (1652–1685). English dramatist, author of *The Orphan* (1680) and *Venice Preserved*, the best post-Jacobean tragedy which has often been revived. Very popular in his own day, one of his successes was a translation of Molière's *Les Fourberies de Scapin*.

CAMPISTRON, Jean Galbert de (1656–1723). French dramatist who wrote plays and libretti in the style of Racine. His most famous and best is *Andronic* (1685), contemporary history in a Roman setting.

CHIKAMATSU MONZAEMON (1653–1725). Japanese dramatist especially well-known for his puppet plays, though between 1695–1705 he concentrated on Kabuki and afterwards Joruri; these forms are explained in Chapter 4. He was the leading dramatist of the period of the *noh* plays from which he inherited various conventions and, though more read than performed today, is regarded as one of the great playwrights. His range and width of outlook was as wide as Shakespeare's, his domestic tragedies being particularly notable. His first known play is *The Soga Successors* (1683) for puppets, like the ones that followed, including the heroic drama, *Kagekiyo Victorious* (1686). His return to puppets later was due to the retirement of the Kabuki actor, Sakata Tojuro, and the success of the puppet play *The Love Suicides at Sonezaki* (1703). A famous historical drama is *The Battles of Coxinga* (1715). The sophistication of his art is in striking contrast to its sensational, often primitive aspects, and he has been compared to Marlowe and Dekker as well as Shakespeare. Despite Japanese ideals and attitudes that make parts of his plays difficult for Westerners, there is no reason for their merits not to be appreciated.

REGNARD, Jean-François (1655–1709). French dramatist and (for two years) a slave after being captured by pirates. He wrote many farces for Italian actors and fairground theatres (1688–96), then, almost until his death, had his comedies given by the Comédie Française. The most famous are *Le Joueur* ('The Gamester', 1696) and *Le Legataire universel* ('The Residuary Legatee', 1708). His plays are fast, funny, cynical and highly theatrical, though critics have tended to claim him as a Molière without the genius. Certainly character development was not his strong point though he created plenty of lively types, and he also developed the valet as a leading character, thus anticipating Figaro.

DANCOURT, Florent Carton (1661–1725). French dramatist and actor, author of some 60 plays, the best of them witty, lively and cynical. Many are set in the country. Well-known examples include *Le Chevalier à la Mode* (1687), *Les Bourgeoises à la Mode* (1692) and *La Fête de village* (1700), and he

also wrote a number of one-act comedies.

VANBRUGH, Sir John (1664–1726). English dramatist and major architect (Blenheim Palace, etc.), and author of two classic comedies, *The Relapse, or Virtue in Danger* (1696), and *The Provoked Wife* (1697). These witty plays were coarse enough (at a time when public taste was changing) to provoke the wrath of Jeremy Collier in his famous attack on the immorality of stage (1697); indeed, until modern times Sheridan's watered-down version of *The Relapse, A Trip to Scarborough*, was given. Now we are allowed to enjoy Lord Foppington and other superb creations in all their naughty glory.

LESAGE, Alain René (1668–1747). French dramatist and novelist who fell out with the Comédie Française and was forced to write for fair theatres. Before that he had written one major play, the 5-act prose comedy, *Turcaret* (1709), satirising a financier and, indeed, a whole society obsessed with money.

CONGREVE, William (1670–1729). English dramatist, the greatest of the Restoration writers of comedy of manners. His first success was *The Old Bachelor* (1693), followed by *The Double-Dealer* (1694). He wrote three more plays, the tragedy, *The Mourning Bride* (1697), a piece beloved by tragediennes for many years because of the rôle of Almeria; and two masterpieces of comedy, both of them glories of the English language, *Love for Love* (1695) and *The Way of the World* (1700). The former is perhaps more loved, as the latter's plot is a trifle complicated; but the witty dialogue of *The Way of the World* is of an unsurpassed perfection, its supreme parts being Mirabell and Millamant, the captivating heroine.

The play was less well received than *Love for Love* and that, plus a controversy with Jeremy Collier (see Vanbrugh above) which had occurred two years earlier and may have influenced the public against him, led him to retire from the theatre. He enjoyed the life of a gentleman, which annoyed Voltaire when he visited him. It is still frustrating to think of the masterpieces that might have been written in the last 29 years of his life.

CIBBER, Colley (1671–1757). English dramatist, manager, actor and play doctor: his adaptation of *Richard III* held the stage for many years and had one famous addition: 'Off with his head! So much for Buckingham.' His *Love's Last Shift, or the Fool of Fashion* (1696) began the swing to sentimental comedy compared with the racier Restoration plays. Other successes were *The Careless Husband* (1705) and *The Non-Juror* (1717), from *Tartuffe*. For many years one of the managers of Drury Lane, this confident, influential snob became Poet Laureate, and more importantly, wrote a key book, *An Apology for the Life of Mr. Colley Cibber, Comedian*, an invaluable guide to Restoration actors and acting.

STEELE, Richard (1672–1729). Irish-born English dramatist, essayist, soldier and pamphleteer, who softened the sharpness of Restoration comedy by sentiment and the introduction of moral themes. His first three plays were *The Funeral* (1701), satirising fashionable displays of grief, *The Lying Lover* (1703) and *The Tender Husband* (1705). There followed his famous association with the *Spectator* and the *Tatler*. His last and finest play, *The Conscious Lovers*, is highly moral and was a great success.

CRÉBILLON, Prosper Jolyot de (1674–1762). French dramatist whose nine tragedies were hugely successful in his own day. On the horrific side, his work was strictly more melodramatic than tragic, and Boileau called him a 'Visigoth in an age of good taste', Perhaps his best play is *Rhadamiste et Zénobie* (1711). He was regarded as a French Aeschylus by his admirers.

ROWE, Nicholas (1674–1718). English dramatist whose tragedies showed some power in an age whose standards were low. The finest are *The Fair Penitent* (1703) and *The Tragedy of Jane Shore* (1714), which were very successful for a century or so. He had theatrical flair but his work lacks vitality.

FARQUHAR, George (1677–1707). Irish-born English dramatist whose short career produced one excellent comedy, *The Constant Couple, or a Trip to the Jubilee* (1699) and two great ones, *The Recruiting Officer* (1706), based on his own Army experiences, and *The Beaux' Strategem* (1707), which is a transition between the Restoration and Sheridan and, more importantly, one of the most delightful and best comedies in the language.

DESTOUCHES, (Phillipe Nericault, 1680–1754). French dramatist, author of a number of moral, sentimental comedies, including *Le Philosophie marié* ('The Married Philosopher', 1727) and *Le Glorieux* ('The Conceited Count', 1732).

HOLBERG, Ludvig (1684–1754). Danish–Nor-wegian dramatist, satirist and historian, and the virtual creator of Scandinavian drama. Inspired by Plautus, the *commedia dell'arte*, Molière and English prose writers, he yet created native comedies in his short theatrical career, most of them being written while Director of the Danish Theatre in Copenhagen (1721–8). When the theatre reopened after a long closure he wrote more plays. His first original play was *Den Politiske Kandestober* ('The Political Tinker', 1722), and one of his finest is *Den stundeslose* ('The Fussy Man', 1726), about a man obsessed with his life's trivialities.

GAY, John (1685–1732). English dramatist and poet whose *The Beggar's Opera* (1728) was a sensational success and has frequently been revived. Usually alleged to be part political satire (rather obscure today, except for experts on Sir Robert Walpole) and part satire on the Italian opera of the day, it has been pointed out by Dennis Arundell in *The Critic at the Opera* that the latter theory makes no sense as it is not remotely like the opera of the day, being a ballad piece. Arundell claims that it satirises the abysmal translations of the Italian libretti of the day. Now it is simply enjoyed. Brecht transformed it into *The Threepenny Opera* (1929). Gay also wrote *Polly*, a sequel, and twelve plays.

MARIVAUX, Pierre (1688–1763). French dramatist, essayist and novelist, author of short, delicate plays more highly regarded now than in his lifetime. *Arlequin poli par l'amour* ('Harlequin refined by Love', 1720) was his first big success staged, like many of his plays, at the Comédie-Italienne. Of his other 34 plays, most of them are love comedies; some of the finest are *La Surprise de l'amour* (1722), *La Double Inconstance* (1723) and *Le Jeu de l'amour et du hasard* ('The Game of Love and Chance', 1730), full, like all his plays, of changes of mood and psychological nuances, rather than much in the way of plot.

IZUMO, Takeda (1691–1756). Japanese dramatist, successor to Chikamatsu, best known for his *kabuki* plays, though he also wrote for the puppet theatre. One of his most popular plays is *Sugawara Denju Tenarai Kogami* ('The House of Sugawara', 1746), originally written for puppets, but later given by actors. It is about a faithful retainer who sacrifices his child to save his lord's heir.

VOLTAIRE, (François Marie Arouet, 1694–1778). French dramatist, novelist, poet, historian, and the great philosopher who embodied 18th-century 'enlightenment'. Though his plays are not now performed, he was devoted to the theatre, writing over 50 plays, half of them tragedies, and ranging from farce and satires to bourgeois dramas. His tragedies, classical and cold, include *Oedipe* (1718) and his two finest, *Zaire* (1732) and *Mérope* (1743). *Nanine* (1749) is a bourgeois drama based on Richardson's *Pamela*.

METASTASIO, Pietro (1698–1782). Italian dramatist and poet, many of whose plays have been used by operatic composers. He wrote 27 dramas for music including *Didone Abbandonata* (1724) which was later used by over 50 composers, *L'Adriano* (1731), *La Clemenza di Tito* (1734) used by Mozart, etc., and *Attilio Regolo* (1740) considered his masterpiece. Though very successful his characters lack passion and feeling.

GOTTSCHED, Johann Christoph (1700–1766). German critic who wrote a few dramas, but whose importance lay in steering the German stage towards the French drama of Racine and Corneille. He advocated 'comedy according to the rules' and had Harlequin banished from the German stage. Though mocked now, he paved the way for Lessing and others. In *Agis* he treated a social problem for the first time in German drama.

SILVA, Antônio José da (1705–1739). Portuguese dramatist, whose seven plays include the witty comedy, *Guerras do alecrim e mangerona* (1737), not about war as the title suggests but about love and disputes among young people. Born in Brazil, he and his family were taken to Portugal by the Inquisition when he was eight. He was tortured and burnt at the stake for being a practising Jew, and Brazil's first national play, *Antônio José* (1838), was written about him by Domingo de Magalhaes (1811–82).

FIELDING, Henry (1707–1754). English dramatist, journalist and major novelist (*Tom Jones*, etc.), whose most famous play is *The Tragedy of Tragedies; or, The Life and Death of Tom Thumb the Great* (1731), a more elaborate version of his *Tom Thumb* of the previous year; it is an uproarious burlesque of tragedies by John Dryden, etc. His satires on politics and politicians, including *The Historical Register for the Year 1736* (1737) were so excellent that Walpole introduced censorship via the Lord Chamberlain which lasted until the 1960s. Fielding switched to novels.

GOLDINI, Carlo (1707–1793). Italian dramatist who wrote over 200 plays, some in French and some in the dialect of his native Venice. A major reformer, his aim was to substitute the now decadent *commedia dell'arte* improvised plays with written drama, in his case all comedies. He also rejected the current mannered verse plays of the time. Aiming at a middle class audience, he was critical in his plays of the aristocracy. His women are better drawn than his men, being less conventional and full of charm. He was the founder of the bourgeois theatre. His most famous plays include *La Locandiera* ('The Mistress of the Inn', 1753), which gave Duse a favourite rôle more than a century later; *I Rusteghi* ('The Boors', 1760), turned into a delightful opera by Wolf-Ferrari (1906); and *Le Baruffe Chiozzotte* (1762), set among Venetian fishermen.

DIDEROT, Denis (1713–1784). French dramatist, philosopher and novelist, whose plays, including *Le Fils naturel* (1757), *Le Pére de famille* (1758), etc., helped establish bourgeois drama and were widely translated in his own day. Far more important now are his writings on the theatre; these include *On Dramatic Poetry* (1758) and essays on actors of his day, including Garrick. He was concerned with the relationship between the actor and his part, and stressed the need for a true company ensemble.

SEDAINE, Michel Jean (1719–1797). French dramatist and poet, influenced by Diderot's ideals, who wrote many good libretti for light operas and a number of plays, the best known being *Le Philosophe sans le savoir* (1765), which was a finer bourgeois drama than any of his master's.

GOZZI, Carlo (1720–1806). Italian dramatist who, unlike Goldini, tried to improve the decadent *commedia dell'arte* of his day by turning it into written theatre. His finest works are possibly *Turandot* (1764), later used by Puccini in his last opera, and *L'Augellino belverde* ('The Beautiful Green Bird', 1764). He was considered extravagant even in his own time and, despite his wit, he lacked insight into his characters.

LESSING, Gotthold (1729–1781). German dramatist, critic, thinker and scholar whose first important play was *Miss Sara Sampson* (1755), a bourgeois tragedy influenced by Richardson and other English novelists. In this and other plays he observed the unities of Aristotle. A particular success was *Minna von Barnhelm* (1767), which firmly established middle class drama in Germany. His *Nathan der Weise* (produced 1783) is a fine poetic plea for religious toleration. Unlike many of his contemporaries, he was a true man of the theatre.

GOLDSMITH, Oliver (*c.* 1730–1774). Irish dramatist, novelist, poet and essayist, both of whose two comedies are still played today: *The Good-natured Man* (1768) and *She Stoops to Conquer* (1773), which has always been very popular. In a dismal period of genteel comedy he, like Sheridan, stands out as a good dramatic deed in a feeble world, his plays being lively and robust without the vulgarity of the Restoration period and the insipidity of his contemporaries.

BEAUMARCHAIS, Pierre Augustin Caron de (1732–1799). French dramatist, best known for inspiring Mozart's *The Marriage of Figaro* and Rossini's *The Barber of Seville*, but a major figure in his own day, whose criticisms of the aristocracy and exposures of incompetence and fraud in high places got him into trouble, which he survived. He even survived the Revolution, despite spells in prison, his riches putting him under suspicion. *The Barber* was first given in 1775, *Figaro* in 1784 and caused an even bigger storm than its predecessor. None of his other plays matched these two masterpieces which, along with the writings of Voltaire, Diderot, Rousseau and others, proved so subversive and so influential in encouraging the middle classes to take action, or at least support it.

EWALD, Johannes (1743–1781). Danish dramatist and poet whose florid plays paved the way for Scandinavian bourgeois tragedy. His greatest success was the musical play *Fiskerne* ('The Fishermen', 1778). A major lyric poet, he was influenced by French classical form, by Germans and by Milton, but developed into a truly national voice.

FONVIZIN, Denis (1745–1792). Russian dramatist, strongly influenced by the leading French thinkers, but writing plays which were recognisably Russian. *The Minor* (1762, rewritten, 1781) was the first genuinely Russian play and had great influence on later writers. It satirises provincial landowners and their politics, and they later helped force him to retire from public life. *The Brigadier-general* (1769) portrays the gentry as either being snobbishly devoted to all things French, or denouncing such things as being effete.

ALFIERI, Vittorio (1749–1803). Italian dramatist, best known for his classical verse tragedies, often peopled with superhuman figures drawn from historical, biblical and mythical sources. His first language was French, but he switched to Italian and wrote concise, unsentimental, romantic pieces, using his new language musically and very finely. His comedies were soon forgotten, while the finest of his tragedies include *Antigone* (1777), *Oreste* (1778), *Virginia* (1778) and *Saul* (1782). *Oreste* was revived in 1962 by Vittorio Gassman. With *Mirra* (1786) it is possibly his finest work.

GOETHE, Johann Wolfgang von (1749–1832). German dramatist, poet, novelist and Germany's supreme man of letters. His *Götz von Berlichingen* (1773), a romantic, full-blooded play about a robber baron, introduced *Sturm und Drang* ('storm and stress', a German off-shoot of the Romantic movement, its disciples worshipping Shakespeare, wild emotions and individual battling against misunderstanding and hostility, the plays and poems being free, even rambling in form). Goethe's next major play was *Egmont* (1788), based on the historical hero of the Netherlands revolt against Spain. It followed closely on his very influential novel, *The Sorrows of Werther*. Two dramatic poems, *Iphigenie auf Tauris* and *Torquato Tasso* followed a trip to Italy (1786), but they are more for reading than acting. His masterpiece, *Faust* (Part I pub. 1808: Part 2, 1832) is too vast a conception to be judged as a conventional play. Part I is practical enough, being the Faust story that most know in one form or another. Part 2 is a huge philosophical, satirical and symbolic fantasy on a cosmic scale, whose influence has been collosal on literature — less so, somewhat naturally, on drama.

SHERIDAN, Richard Brinsley (1751–1816). Anglo-Irish dramatist, theatre manager (Drury Lane) and politician. Apart from *Pizarro* (1799), a verse melodrama adored in its day and absurd now, his whole theatrical career as a playwright was packed into the years 1775–9, which produced three masterpieces, *The Rivals* (1775), *The School for Scandal* (1777) and *The Critic* (1779); also *St. Patrick's Day, or The Scheming Lieutenant* (1775); the comic opera, *The Duenna* (1775), and a watered-down version of Vanbrugh's *The Relapse, A Trip to Scarborough* (1775). He managed Drury Lane (1776–1809), building a new theatre in 1794, and only giving up when it was burnt down in 1809. His greatest plays have been called High Georgian comedies, laughing comedies, comedies of manners,

Restoration comedies without the licentiousness of the earlier plays, but with all the wit. Written in prose that is a national glory, they are sometimes sentimental but never too much so, constructed brilliantly, peopled with immortals (Mrs. Malaprop, Lady Teazle, etc.) and in an uncynical way mock and satirise human folly. Like Goldsmith, Sheridan – the greater artist – promoted a sense of good will for all his sharp observation, and he is very funny. *The Critic*, which partly burlesques Buckingham's *The Rehearsal*, is also a hilarious farce. *The Rivals* and, especially, *The School for Scandal* are, except for those who compare their sentimental comedy unfavourably with the finest Restoration plays, twin triumphs, always adored and never out of fashion.

TYLER, Royall (1757–1826). American dramatist, author of the first American comedy to be professionally performed: *The Contrast* (1787). In it he portrayed New York society, native honesty and the hypocrisy of mere foreigners, also Jonathan, the first of many stage Yankees. His other plays, some of which are lost, were less good.

IFFLAND, August Wilhelm (1759–1814). German dramatist and actor whose sentimental plays were very popular in his day, though he indulged in over-sentimentality and too much moralising. His most successful play was *Die Jäger* ('The Hunters', 1785). He ran the Gotha, Mannheim and finally, the National theatre in Berlin, training young actors well, but being criticised for his cautious repertoire.

SCHILLER, Friedrich von (1759–1805). German dramatist, poet, historian and critic, whose famous costume dramas are typical of *Sturm und Drang* (see Goethe above), and who gradually developed a classicism which, combined with his Romanticism (in subject matter), produced plays which still grip audiences today outside, as well as in, Germany. His first play, *Die Räuber* ('The Robbers', 1781) concerned hostile brothers; then came *Kabale und Liebe* ('Cabal and Love, 1784). His first grand historical tragedy was *Don Carlos* (1787), set in Philip II's Spain; the character of Carlos' friend Posa, who strives for freedom of thought, saw Schiller working towards the play of ideas. His historical trilogy, *Wallenstein* (1799) set in the Thirty Years War, shows a growing realism and deeper characterisation.

His final historical dramas appeared rapidly: *Mary Stuart* (1800), *Die Jungfrau von Orleans* (1801) about Joan of Arc, *Die Braut von Messina* ('The Bride of Messina', 1803) and *Wilhelm Tell* (1804). *Mary Stuart*, about Mary, Queen of Scots, has a famous confrontation between her and Elizabeth I, unhistorical but highly effective. His Joan of Arc falls in love with an (invented) British Lord. In *Die Braut von Messina*, Nemisis attacks a princely house, while *Wilhelm Tell*, perhaps his masterpiece, is not a tragedy, but a dramatic idyll both classical and romantic. Schiller died young at the very height of his powers. Rossini's *William Tell* and Verdi's *Don Carlos* are the two finest operas inspired by him.

KOTZEBUE, August von (1761–1819). German dramatist who wrote over 200 plays, many of which were very popular, sometimes equally so abroad through translations. He wrote every kind of play, though sentimental comedy was his chief genre and strong emotion his forte. Perhaps his best comedy is *Die deutschen Kleinstädter* ('The German Provincial', 1803), while *Menschenhauss und Reue* ('Misanthropy and Repentance', 1789) was among his most successful. His *Die Spanier in Peru* (1796) was turned by Sheridan into *Pizarro*. He is rarely given today.

DUNLAP, William (1766–1839). American dramatist and manager, the author or part-author of 29 plays, which range from comedies to historical tragedies and ballad operas. His first success was *The Father, or American Shandyism* (1789), while perhaps his most interesting play is *André* (1798) about a tragic incident in the Revolutionary War, Major André being a British officer hanged as a spy.

His importance lies in his preparing the ground for American playwrights and encouraging others to follow him, as he followed Royall Tyler (see above).

WERNER, Zacharias (1768–1823). German dramatist and preacher, who established German Fate-Drama with his one-acter, *Die vierundzwanzigste Februar* ('The 24th of February', 1810): a peasant family fights against a curse that has them killing each other on the fatal date. Religious mysticism is strongly present in some of his plays, though in *Die Mutter der Makkabaer* ('The Mother of the Maccabeans', 1820), the mysticism turn into ravings and even horrors. His power is seen best when he mixes realism with strange fantasies.

PIXÉRÉCOURT, Guilbert de (1773–1834). French dramatist who has been dubbed 'the Corneille of melodrama'. A hugely popular second-rate playwright he wrote, or collaborated on, about 120 plays and influenced Dumas, de Vigny and Victor Hugo. His best known melodrama is *Coelina, ou l'enfant du mystère* (1798), and his influence spread to Britain.

TIECK, Ludwig (1773–1853). German dramatist, novelist and poet, famous for his fairy tales whose themes he borrowed for some of his plays: *Ritter Blaubart* ('Bluebeard the Knight', 1796), etc. His finest play is *Der gestiefelte Kater* ('Puss in Boots', 1797) which shows him a master of romantic irony. Not only does he tell the traditional story, but he mocks the conventions of the day by having the author interrupt the play and discuss it with both audience and stagehands.

KLEIST, Heinrich von (1777–1811). German dramatist whose reputation has soared in the 20th century. Lack of recognition increased his own morbid pessimism which finally drove him to suicide. His complex, subtle plays show remarkable psychological insight. Part of his attraction for today's audiences is that his characters are often vacillating, insecure and nervous. *Der zerbrochene Krug* ('The Broken Jug', 1808), a clever comedy about a corrupt magistrate with a genius for lying, used to be regarded as his greatest work. Now the classical tragedy, *Penthesilea* (1808) and, especially, *Der Prinz von Homburg* ('The Prince of Homburg', 1811) are much acclaimed. The latter is both a romantic, patriotic drama and a psychological study; it examines Kleist's eternal problem – whether self-mastery is also self-denial. Other plays include a family tragedy, *Die Familie Schroffenstein* (1793), *Käthchen von Heilbronn* (1810) about a woman's obsessive devotion, and the historical drama, *Die Hermannschlacht* ('The Battle of Arminius', 1808).

BYRON, George Gordon, Lord (1788–1824). English poet who wrote eight plays, though only *Marino Faliero* (1821) was given in his lifetime. His influence on other dramatists and composers was colossal. *The Two Foscari*, set like the former in Venice, was a success in 1838. His most objective play, *Werner, or The Inheritance*, was much admired in the 19th century and, generally, his plays are less literary and more stageworthy than those of most of his contemporaries. Though it has been staged, his *Manfred* is a dramatic poem.

RAIMUND, Ferdinand (1790–1836). Austrian dramatist, actor and manager who brought humanity and artistry to Viennese folk and fairy tales. A delightful example of his plays is *Das Mädchen aus der Feenwelt, oder der Bauer als Millionär* ('The Girl from the World of Fairies, or the Millionaire Farmer', 1826). These very Viennese plays have not been translated into English.

GRILLPARZER, Franz (1791–1872). Austrian dramatist and poet, whose sensitive and unhappy nature is reflected in his plays. Two of his most famous works are *Die Jüdin von Toledo* ('The Jewess of Toledo', completed in 1855) and *Ein Bruderzwist im Habsburg* ('Family strife in Hapsburg', completed in 1850). He wanted both destroyed, but they were saved, revealing harsh self-appraisals.

SCRIBE, Eugène (1791–1861). French dramatist much abused for inventing the 'well-made play', mechanically clever, but lacking true characterisation and psychology. He wrote nearly 400 vaudevilles (featherweight pieces with musical interludes), over 100 libretti and 35 full-length plays, including one famous tragedy, *Adrienne Lecouvreur* (1849), with Ernest Legouvé; he had a number of collaborators, but the stagecraft was his. However he lives for his French and Italian opera libretti, not entirely thanks to the composers: *La Sonnambula* and *L'Elisir d'Amore* are among a number of good ones and *Le Comte Ory* is even better, though the first two are adaptations of his plays by Romani.

KLICPERA, Vaclav (1792–1859). Czech dramatist and novelist who helped awaken the spirit of Czech nationalism in his dramas and comedies. Though his final poetic dramas, commissioned by intelligensia, were more influential later, more typical is his *Hadrián of Rímsy* (1822) with a stupid knight who is a parody of plays of chivalry. In this and other comedies his satiric, comic talent is shown, the later ones often being concerned with provincial officials.

SHELLEY, Percy Bysshe (1792–1822). English poet whose dramatic poems are not suitable for the stage, but whose *The Cenci* (1819) is sometimes performed, and with success. Following Elizabethan models, it is based on a true Italian Renaissance story about a tyrant and his daughter, whom he rapes. She has him murdered.

FREDRO, Count Aleksander (1793–1876). Polish dramatist whose finest works are perhaps *Damy i huzary* ('Ladies and Hussars', 1825), a good farce, and *Sluby panienskie* ('Maidens' Vows', 1833), a pleasant comedy. Assailed by Romantics and revolutionaries for alleged conservatism, he has since come into his own again.

GRIBOYEDOV, Alexander (1795–1829). Russian dramatist who often collaborated with friends, but not on his masterpiece, *Woe from Wit* (1823), a brilliant comedy about an idealistic young man up against a corrupt society. Banned in his own lifetime, it was the first dramatic attack on Tsarist society, and is still played today – for its wit as well as its sentiments.

VIGNY, Alfred de (1797–1863). French dramatist and poet whose love of Shakespeare led him to adapt *Romeo*, *The Merchant* and *Othello* in the late 1820s partly as a broadside against Racineian classical methods. He wrote one major work, *Chatterton* (1835), which inspired Romantics; it concerns a tragic love between a poet and a sensitive wife of a gross businessman. Two costume plays were less successful.

GARRETT, Almeida (1799–1854). Portuguese dramatist, poet and novelist who brought Romanticism to Portugal and renewed her drama. His most significant play is *Frei Luis de Sousa* ('Friar Luiz of Sousa', 1843), an historical prose drama.

PUSHKIN, Alexander (1799–1837). Russian poet of great influence on Russian literature and music, etc., whose finest play, *Boris Godunov* (1819, performed 1870) is truly Shakespearean, as is its more famous operatic version by Moussorgsky. He wrote a few short plays including *Mozart and Salieri* (1832). Russian opera is more indebted to him than is the Russian theatre.

GRABBE, Christian Dietrich (1801–1836). German dramatist and poet, whose heroes are overwhelmed by the forces and furies of history, as in *Napoleon, oder die hundert Tage* ('Napoleon and the Hundred Days', 1831). Though no great dramatist himself, he paved the way for modern epic drama.

NESTROY, Johann (1801–1862). Austrian dramatist and actor and the original Sarastro in *The Magic Flute*. He wrote a number of folk-plays full of satire, wit and vitality, using Viennese dialect. They include *Der böse Geist Lumpazivagabundus* ('The Evil Spirit Lumpazivagabundus', 1833) and *Das Mädel aus der Vorstadt* ('The Girl from the Suburbs', 1841).

DUMAS, Alexandre, père (1803–1870). French dramatist and novelist whose romantic melodramas were hugely successful. Alone and in collaboration he wrote more than 90, which ranged from Roman stories to those of his own day. He also adapted his novels, sometimes in collaboration with Auguste Maquet. With Victor Hugo (see below) he fathered French Romantic drama, though his plays were more viable than Hugo's. His first major success, and the first Romantic drama to be performed, was *Henri III et sa cour* (1829) which began the Romantic revolution. Later big successes included *La Tour de Nesle* (1832) and *Kean* (1836), re-written in 1952 by Jean-Paul Sartre and widely performed. *The Three Musketeers* and *The Count of Monte-Cristo* are among his novels that he turned into plays. *Antony* (1831), a modern, middle-class romantic tragedy, which caused a scandal because it was about one of his mistresses and had two more acting in it, looks forward to a genre which was to become very popular. Also see **Dumas fils** (1824–1895).

HUGO, Victor (1802–1885). French dramatist, poet, novelist and politician. A champion like Dumas (above) of the Romantic drama, his Preface to his unstageable *Cromwell* (1827) was a rallying-cry for free and outspoken plays, to be Shakespearean in their mixture of tragedy and comedy, and written in dramatic poetry. His *Hernani* (1830) provoked riots and changed the course of the European theatre, for all that it now seems no more than an extravagant melodrama, splendidly rhetorical but, like his other plays, peopled with near-puppets – unless played by fine actors in the grand manner. Yet the revolution the young Hugo brought about was a life-giving one – in *Hernani*, *Le Roi s'amuse* (1832, banned after one performance, but the inspiration of Verdi's *Rigoletto*), *Lucrèce Borgia* (1833), *Marie Tudor* (1833) and his superbly theatrical *Ruy Blas* (1838); that only this last play has real merit in its own right does not detract from his achievement.

BIRD, Robert Montgomery (1806–1854). American dramatist and novelist, author of a number of romantic tragedies in blank verse: *Pelopidas* (1830), *The Gladiator* (1831) made famous by Edwin Forrest, *Oralloosa* and *The Broker of Bogota* (1834), also a revision of John Stone's *Metamora*. His popularity, especially with *The Gladiator*, about Spartacus, made him little money because of the current state of the copyright laws, so he abandoned the theatre and a possible major dramatic talent was lost.

TYL, Josef (1808–1856). Czech dramatist whose plays formed the basis of his country's national drama, though only some of them are still given. They form a link between Romanticism and realism. His farce *Fidlovacka* (1834) about the patriotic lower middle classes and the Germanised bourgeoise has a song in it which became part of the Czech national anthem. He wrote social dramas, dramatic fairy tales and historical plays including *Kutnohorsti haviri* ('The Miners of Kutna Hora', 1848), significant because it portrayed the working class on stage. His most popular play abroad has been the fairy tale, *Strakonicky dudak* ('The Bagpiper of Strakonice', 1847).

GOGOL, Nikolai (1809–1852). Russian dramatist and novelist whose theatrical fame rests on one masterpiece, the satiric comedy *The Government Inspector* (1836). Though the Tsar liked this attack on municipal corruption – triggered off by a clerk appearing and claiming to be the inspector general – it was bitterly attacked. The farce *The Marriage* (1842) is vividly and grotesquely characterised and has been revived; with other dramatic sketches it influenced the early one-acters of Chekhov.

SLOWACKI, Juliusz (1809–1849). Polish dramatist and poet who wrote a number of historical dramas, including *Kordian*, most of them not performed in his lifetime. His finest comedy is *Fantazy* (c. 1841) which satires the Romantics of his day.

TENNYSON, Alfred, Lord (1809–1892). English dramatist and major poet whose plays, for all their fine poetry, fatally lack drama and dramatic skill. The best, *Becket* (1893), gave Henry Irving one of his greatest successes.

MUSSET, Alfred de (1810–1857). French dramatist, poet and novelist, the most gifted of the Romantics of his day, and the only one whose works are still regularly staged. With a gift for dialogue, and using humour, irony, delicate fantasy and melancholy, he has been seen as classical as much as Romantic. Much of his work was written for reading, but proved stageable and successful. His plays include *Fantasio* (1833), *Lorenzaccio* (1834) and *Les Caprices* (1851), the first two being acted years after writing them. All are amusing and fantastic, and tinged with bitterness and romantic extravagance. He also wrote one-act 'proverbs' which are not extravagant, including *Il faut qu'une porte soit ouverte ou fermée* ('A Door must be kept Open or Shut', 1848).

Victor Hugo in his old age. When he was a young man his Hernani *caused riots and revolutionised the French theatre.* (Photo: The Cultural Attaché, French Embassy)

BROWNING, Robert (1812–1889). English poet whose verse plays belong to literature rather than drama: the true drama is in his poems. However *Strafford* (1837) was given by Macready, for whom it was written, and *Pippa Passes* (1841) has been staged occasionally. The British theatre of his day was at a sadly low ebb, which hardly encouraged major poets.

KRASINSKI, Zygmunt (1812–1859). Polish dramatist and playwright whose two major works are *Irydion* (staged in 1908) and *Nieboska* (staged in 1902); the latter is a masterpiece of Polish Romanticism.

BÜCHNER, Georg (1813–1837). German dramatist and poet whose two main plays, *Danton's Death* (1835) and *Woyzeck* (1837, left unfinished) have been frequently and widely performed in modern times. Büchner reacted against the extreme romanticism of Schiller and Goethe, and anticipated the more natural drama that came in half a century after his death, and also the later Expressionists, his plays being full of violence and morbid psychological insight. Widely regarded today as a great playwright, his early death was a disaster. Berg's famous opera *Wozzeck* is closely based on his depressing portrait of an illiterate soldier, while his play about the great French revolutionary Danton reflects his passionate love of freedom and his deep pessimism.

HEBBEL, Friedrich (1813–1863). German dramatist and poet who wrote a number of plays about victimised women, including *Judith* (1840) and *Maria Magdalena* (1844); also historical dramas, including *Genoveva* (1843) and *Herodes und Marianne* (1850), his characters being given a modern treatment. He had a tragic view of life.

LUDWIG, Otto (1813–1865). German dramatist and novelist whose finest play, *Der Erbförster* ('The Hereditary Forester', 1850) is a painfully realistic study of bourgeois life. *Die Makkabäer* ('The Maccabees', 1854) a historical – mythical drama, is more romantic.

GOMEZ DE AVELLANEDA, Gertrudis (1814–1873). Cuban dramatist and poetess whose finest play is *La hija de las flores* ('The Child of the Flowers', 1852), a delightful Romantic comedy, but full of believable people.

LABICHE, Eugene (1815–1888). French dramatist who alone or in collaboration, wrote 150 or more farces and comedies. He became the scourge of the middle classes who repaid him by adoring him. Many of his plays are brilliantly constructed and, however farcical, reflect the social climate of his time. His older men are his most successful creations. Popular from the start, his most famous plays include *Le Chapeau de paille d'Italie* ('The Italian Straw Hat', 1851), written with Marc Marcel and well-known outside France, *Le Voyage de Monsieur Perrichon* (1860) with Edouard Martin, *La Poudre aux yeux* ('Dust in Your Eyes', 1861) also with Martin. Living in the country from the 1850s, he gave many of his plays a rustic setting. He also wrote vaudevilles (comedies with songs). Before he died he was generally recognised as France's leading comic dramatist, if not the world's.

PENA, Martins (1815–1848). Brazilian dramatist best known for his comedies, notably *O novico* ('The Novice, 1845), his most famous play – which is an amusing, graceful, portrait of his period. His *O Juiz de Paz na Roca* ('The Justice of the Peace in the Country', 1838), ranks as Brazil's first national comedy.

MOKUAMI, Kawatake (1816–1893). Japanese dramatist regarded as the last major *kabuki* playwright. Outlaws and thieves often feature in his plays, notably in *Aoto Zoshi Hana no Nishikie* ('Benten the Thief', 1862).

SUKHOVO-KOBYLIN, Alexander (1817–1903). Russian dramatist, author of an impressive trilogy: *Krechinsky's Wedding*, *The Case* and *Tarelkin's Death*, written in the 1850s but which, the first apart, took long to get staged. The themes are Russian patriarchal and country house life in decay, the corruption of the bureaucracy and the decadent nobility, and the plays offended the Censor. The playwright finally gave the theatre up in despair, especially as his life had been soured by the false accusation of murdering his mistress. He settled in France.

TURGENEV, Ivan (1818–1883). Russian dramatist and major novelist, author of *A Month in The Country* (1850), the first Russian psychological drama; a subtle, hauntingly atmospheric work, it is by far his most famous and influential play, though he wrote a number of comedies full of well-observed characters, including *The Bachelor* (1849).

AUGIER, Emile (1820–1889). French dramatist, a notable author of comedies of manners. He was one of those to rebel against the excesses of the Romantics, concentrating on social and domestic dramas, the best-known being *Le Gendre de Monsieur Poirier* ('Mr. Poirier's son-in-law', 1854). His *Le Mariage d'Olympe* (1855) is a portrait of a courtesan in striking contrast to Dumas' idealised Lady of the Camelias, and was meant to be. Augier believed in bourgeois ideals and was prepared to comment on social and moral evils.

BOUCICAULT, Dion (1822–1890). Irish dramatist and actor, most of whose 150 or so plays were adaptations, often from the French. Very popular in his own day in Britain and America, his most successful plays were *The Corsican Brothers* (1852) and *The Coleen Bawn* (1860). His theatrical flair was considerable, as a London revival in the 1970s of *London Assurance* by the Royal Shakespeare Co. has proved. He was one of the only authors to write a serious play about the American negro and the subject of slavery: *The Octoroon* (1859).

NORWID, Cyprian (1821–1888). Polish dramatist whose historical and contemporary plays are better known now than in his own lifetime. They include a historical tragedy, *Caesar and Cleopatra* (1878).

BOKER, George Henry (1823–1890). American dramatist, poet and diplomat, author of a number of verse dramas, his best being *Francesca da Rimini* (1853).

OSTROVSKY, Alexander (1823–1886). Russian dramatist and author of more than 80 plays, the first of which, *The Bankrupt* (1848), made his name by being banned; it attacked unscrupulous merchants. He wrote historical plays and fantasies, including *The Snow Maiden* (1873), better known as an opera, also successful comedies and social dramas. They include his best-known play, *The Storm* (1860), another attack on the merchant class and its way of life, and on religious intolerance. Its unfortunate heroine is Katya Kabanova, the title of Janacek's opera based on the play. Most of his plays were given at Moscow's Maly Theatre.

DUMAS, Alexandre, fils (1824–1895). French dramatist and novelist, son of Dumas père, see above (1802–1870). His first and most famous play *La Dame aux Camelias* (1852), a semi-autobiographical story dramatised from his novel about a repentant courtesan, is still staged, though less than the opera it inspired, Verdi's *La Traviata*. But his later plays, as if in rebellion against his upbringing, are concerned with the importance of marriage and home, including *Le Demi-monde* (1855), *Le Fils naturel* (1858), *Le Père Prodigue* (1859) and *Francillon* (1887).

IBSEN, Henrik (1828–1906). Norwegian dramatist, often cited as 'the father of the modern theatre' and undeniably the father of the modern problem play and one of the very few supreme dramatists. He moved from historical and verse dramas to apparently naturalistic social plays constructed with great mastery. His final plays were even more richly symbolic than anything he had written since his earliest works: symbolism is never absent from his plays, even his most realistic ones, adding to their stature and giving even the most prosaic and less successful a poetic quality that ensures revivals. Ibsen's triumph was all the greater because he was one of the only great dramatists whose plays tend to be humourless.

After his father's bankruptcy he became (at 15) a druggist's apprentice. His first play, *Cataline* (1850), was modelled on Schiller and Scribe. Other historical dramas followed, including *The Vikings at Helgeland* (1858) and *The Pretenders* (1864); meanwhile in 1851 he had become literary editor of the national theatre at Bergen, then (1857–62) director of the Norske Theatre at Christiana. A

state pension (1862) gave him financial security; it was prompted mainly by the publication of *Brand* (1865, produced 1885), his first major play – a bleak, huge, symbolic drama about a fanatical pastor, his mission and his behaviour to man and God: he sacrifices his family for his ministry.

The poetic fantasy, *Peer Gynt* (1867), followed; its reckless, irresponsible hero, richly human in his compound of good and bad, lives in reality and fantasy. In this play at least there is some humour; Peer has been called 'a romantic folk precursor of existential man' (Richard Vowles). After the light-hearted *League of Youth* (1869) and the vast *Emperor and Galilean* (1869–73), Ibsen wrote four enormously influential plays set in small Norwegian towns. They are *Pillars of Society* (1875–7), *A Doll's House* (1878–9), *Ghosts* (1881) his most notorious play, and *An Enemy of the People* (1882); the subject matters are (in order): public life based on a lie, the truth and falsehood of a marriage, venereal disease (a past lie) poisoning a family, and municipal corruption and the downfall of Doctor Stockman, who dares to tell the truth (that a spa is polluted).

Symbolism flows more strongly in *The Wild Duck* (1884), a masterpiece in which a real, but unseen duck symbolises the plight of the heroine. Another exceptionally memorable character is the well-meaning, but terrible Gregers Werle whose determination to unravel the truth at all costs leads to tragedy. *Rosmersholm* (1886), with its 'new woman' heroine, Rebecca West, followed; then came *Hedda Gabler* (1890), with Ibsen at the height of his powers; Hedda's bored destructiveness is memorably shown, but the other characters – the virtuous ones included (Tesman and Mrs. Elvsted) – are also brilliant creations. In *The Lady from the Sea* (1888), *The Master Builder* (1892) and *Little Eyolf* (1894) the symbolism is almost too strong; respectively, the 'lady's' dreams about the sea, the Master Builder Solness' buildings which have sexual symbolism, and the rôle of the Rat Wife in *Eyolf*.

Finally came a study of a man whose lust for power led him to sacrifice love, *John Gabriel Borkman* (1896), and *When we Dead Awaken* (1899), in which artistry replaces power as the reason for sacrifice.

In his own day it was Ibsen's realistic plays and their plots that were so influential. Now it is the poetic nature of his work and the enriching quali-

A scene from Ibsen's Hedda Gabler, *with Jill Bennett as Hedda and Ronald Hines as George Tesman, produced at the Royal Court Theatre in 1972 and directed by Anthony Page. (Photo: Peggy Leder)*

ties of his symbolism, also his incomparable build-up towards his climaxes, which are subtly and gradually prepared for, that enthral audiences. He has taught even those playwrights who reject him.

TOLSTOY, Lev Nikolayevich (1828–1910). Russian dramatist and great novelist who admitted that his main concern as a playwright was to preach. His first play, the comedy *The Contaminated Fami-*

ly (1862–4), is a comment on Russian nihilism after the freeing of the serfs, and is not liked by Soviet critics. *The First Distiller* (1887) is about peasant drunkenness; *The Power of Darkness* (1889) is a very forceful peasant drama based on an actual crime; while *The Fruits of Enlightenment* (1891) is another hostile comment on Russian attitudes, plus an attack on spiritualism. *The Living Corpse*, also known as *Redemption* (1900, produced 1911) is an attack on official justice (the marriage laws in this case, based on fact); while *Light Shining in Darkness* (which was unfinished) is autobiographical and deals with the problems of disinterested unworldliness in an alien world. His last play was *Everything Stems from it*, a harking back to *The First Distiller*.

ROBERTSON, Thomas William (1829–1871). English dramatist and actor, whose plays, especially *Caste* (1867), are historically of great importance, for they started a school of realistic drama in a period of melodramatic and romantic excess and sheer badness. He was concerned with 'real' settings and props, credible dialogue and sensible plots (even if they seem artificial now). His plays were dubbed 'cup-and-saucer drama', but it was meant as a compliment, and he directed them himself. Even his first and untypical *Garrick* (1864) from the French has a great number of stage directions and demands for realistic scenery, and from *Society* (1865) onwards the new pattern was established – including simple titles: *Ours* (1866), *Caste*, *Play* (1868) and *School* (1869). After years of frustration, success enabled him to recover his delightful nature, and he was later immortalised by Pinero as Tom Wrench in *Trelawny of the Wells*.

SARDOU, Victorien (1831–1908). French dramatist, almost as skilled a master of the well-made play as his mentor, Scribe, for all that Bernard Shaw rudely called his methods and influence 'Sardoodledum'. Though his imitators may have written poor, over-contrived pieces, his were brilliantly made. They include a number for Sarah Bernhardt, most notably *Fedora* (1882), *La Tosca* (1887) which now lives via Puccini, the famous spectacular, *Theodora imperatrice de Bizance* (1884) and *Cléopatre* (1890), etc: strong melodramas for a now legendary tragedienne. *Madame Sans-Gêne* (1893) was a historical romance – from washerwoman to duchess – which gave Rejane a colossal success, and which has lasted the best of his huge output of plays in many different genres.

BJORNSON, Bjornstjerne (1832–1910). Norwegian dramatist and novelist, more popular in his own day than Ibsen, though mainly remembered now as a great Norwegian patriot. His early plays are histories, including *King Sverre* (1861), *Sigurd the Wild* (1862) and *Mary Stuart in Scotland* (1864) the finest of them. Next came social dramas, including *The Bankrupt* (1875), a plea for decent business standards. His finest play is perhaps *Beyond Human Power* (1883) which, like his final dramas, was more concerned with spiritual than social matters. A sequel to it of the same name (1895) is about labour relations and anarchy.

GILBERT, W. S. (Sir William Schwenck, 1836–1911). English dramatist and humorist. His immortal collaboration with Sir Arthur Sullivan is not the concern of this book, though his reputation today relies entirely upon that. Before that he wrote a number of plays, and burlesques and fantasies encouraged, amongst others, by T. W. Robertson.

BECQUE, Henri François (1837–1899). French dramatist remembered for two major naturalistic plays in striking contrast to well-made plays by Scribe, etc. They are *Les Corbeaux* ('The Vultures', 1882) and *La Parisienne* (1885), photographic studies without comment of bourgeois life and love, written with devastating effect. Though his talent took a different form he was, with Zola, the leader of the French naturalistic movement: Zola was a theorist, Beque a remarkable and original practical dramatist.

DALY, Augustin (1838–1899). American dramatist and producer-director, who from 1869 ran a company renowned for its ensemble and realistic approach. His New York company visited London several times, and in 1891 Daly's Theatre opened in London, built for him by George Edwardes. His own plays include a London melodrama, *Under the Gaslight* (1867) and *Horizon* (1871), set in the West. His realistic dramas and melodramas peopled the stage with native Americans and were full of local colour.

HERNE, James A. (1839–1901). American dramatist and actor who, after collaborating with Belasco in *Hearts of Oak* (1878), etc., wrote several realistic dramas influenced by Ibsen, Zola and Tolstoy, including *Margaret Fleming* (1890).

GOLDFADEN, Abraham (1840–1908). Russian Yiddish dramatist who is regarded as the first major Yiddish playwright, and whose work at Jassy, Rumania, was the true beginning of the Yiddish theatre (1876). He wrote musical and historical plays, but after many successes, died in poverty in New York. His finest play is possibly *Shulamith* (1881), a historical piece first seen in Warsaw, as Russia's Yiddish theatres had been closed. Many of his musical plays, expressing the hopes and sufferings of the Jews, remain in Yiddish repertoires today. They include *The Two Kuni Lemels* (1880).

NAMIK KEMAL (1840–1888). Turkish dramatist and poet, author of idealistic and patriotic plays aimed at bettering and educating the people. His first, *The Fatherland or Silistria* (1873), helped start a revolution.

VERGA, Giovanni (1840–1922). Italian dramatist and novelist whose *Cavalleria Rusticana* (1884) gave Duse a whale of a part, and was later to become even more famous via Mascagni's opera. Neither *La Lupa* (1896) or his other plays are as fine as his novels. Most are set in his native Sicily.

ZOLA, Émile (1840–1902). French dramatist, major novelist and critic who aimed to destroy the well-made play and replace it with naturalism. His best play is *Thérèse Raquin* (1873), but he was never a true dramatist, thinking life and art were one and the same: his major influence as a playwright lay in his prefaces; others could give a 'slice of life' better than he on the stage.

HOWARD, Bronson (1842–1908). American dramatist, whose well-constructed plays range from social drama to farce and included businessmen and expatriots in their casts. They include *The Banker's Daughter* (1878) and *Aristocracy* (1892). Many regard *Young Mrs. Winthrop* (1882) as his best play: how a marriage is nearly destroyed by business and social life. He helped secure better copyright laws for dramatists.

JAMES, Henry (1843–1916). American dramatist and major novelist who lived much of his life in Britain. He longed for success as a playwright, but *Guy Domville* (1895) was a disastrous failure after earlier plays had been unproduced. Officially abandoning the theatre, he later had a success with *The High Bid* (1907) in which an American widow fights to save an estate from a grasping capitalist. Since his death, he has achieved the fame he sought in the theatre from adaptations of his novels, including *Berkeley Square* (from *The Sense of the*

Past), *The Heiress* (from *Washington Square*), *The Turn of the Screw, The Aspern Papers*, etc.

HARRIGAN, Edward (1844–1911). American dramatist, actor and manager, author of a number of loosely constructed but well characterised comedies of New York life, including *Squatter Sovereignty* (1882), set in a shantytown.

GIACOSA, Giuseppe (1847–1906). Italian dramatist whose early successes were verse dramas set in the middle ages, including *Il Trionfo d'amore* (1875) and 18th-century comedies. Then, in *Tristi Amore* ('Unhappy Love', 1887) and other plays, he switched to well-written bourgeois prose plays. He was one of Puccini's librettists for *Boheme, Tosca* and *Butterfly*.

STRINDBERG, August (1849–1912). Swedish dramatist and novelist, author of more than 50 plays and 'the fountainhead of virtually all of modernism in the drama' (Thornton Wilder). Allegedly a famous misogynist, he actually liked domesticity (with three wives) but his personality made for stormy relationships. After early historical and farcical rural plays – the best-known being *Lucky Peter's Travels* (1882) – an abrupt, devastating change came with *The Father* (1887); in this, an army officer is locked in a death struggle with his wife which ends with him in a straitjacket and dying of a stroke. Here for the first time we see Strindberg's battle of the sexes, a battle the women always win.

There followed the lethal *Miss Julie* (1888), *Creditors* (1888) and several one-acters – including *Playing with Fire* (1892) – ultra-realistic plays sometimes beyond theatrical realism. He returned to drama in 1898 with two parts of a huge symbolic play, *To Damascus*; then entered a period of colossal productivity, including no less than 15 Swedish history plays; one of the finest is *Erik XIV* (1899). Maeterlinck's influence was apparent in the delightful *Swanwhite* (1902), while symbolism and expressionism are in evidence in *The Dream Play* (1902), Part 3 of *To Damascus* (1904) and *The Ghost Sonata* (1907), one of Strindberg's 'chamber plays'; this last, peopled by grotesques, contrasts appearance with sordid reality.

He also returned to his earlier and savage style in *The Dance of Death* (1900), his best-known play, about a hate-filled marriage approaching its silver wedding, and with a male lead, Edgar, which is one of the most famous and taxing in modern drama;

a second part is less well-known and less successful. Another fascinating late play is *Easter* (1901), a morality whose heroine combines his sister, Christ and Balzac's Seraphita. The final plays are suffused with symbolism and realism, notably *The Storm* (1907) and *The Pelican* (1907), chamber plays written for a small theatre. His last play was *The Great Highway* (1909), written when he was strongly influenced by mysticism. It is a mixture of allegory, satire, myth and literary allusion, and Strindberg's farewell to the world and the theatre, for he died three years later of cancer, having shaken 'down the living stars from heaven' (Sean O'Casey). He had never stopped experimenting, exploring new subjects, and – in many plays – searingly examining the sex war; and he also examined both the mysteries of the universe and of the unconscious. His finest plays are never long out of the international repertoire.

JONES, Henry Arthur (1851–1929). English dramatist whose first big success was the classic melodrama, *The Silver King* (1882), with Henry Herman. He wrote an enormous number of plays, and came to be regarded as an Ibsenite, though he was more a fine craftsman who was prepared to handle social and moral topics and issues. *Michael and his Lost Angel* (1896) has a puritanical clergyman falling in love with a girl he has earlier condemned, while *The Liars* (1896) is a comedy of manners about marriage. His best known play today is *Mrs. Dane's Defence* (1900), with a famous court room scene.

PERETZ, Yitskhok (1852–1915). Polish-born Yiddish dramatist and poet and the 'father of modern Yiddish literature.' His plays are not over-suited to the stage, for all their brilliant moments. *Night in the Old Market* (1907), a dramatic poem in four acts, was later dramatised and given in Moscow in 1925. He lives as an inspiration more than as a playwright, and his fame rests on his short stories.

GREGORY, Lady Augusta (1852–1932). Irish dramatist who, with Yeats, founded the Irish National Theatre Society which became the Abbey Theatre. She wrote peasant comedies, tragedies, patriotic plays and fantasies, sometimes collaborating with Yeats. The best-known include *The Pot of Broth* (with Yeats, 1902) the patriotic *Cathleen ni Houlihan* (with Yeats, 1902), *Spreading the News* (1904) and *The Rising of the Moon* (1907), the last two being very fine one-acters. All her plays were written in the dialect of western Ireland.

BELASCO, David (1853–1931). American dramatist, producer and showman whose stagings were realistic to a degree, and who was the author or co-author of some 70 plays. He never looked back after *The Girl I Left Behind Me* (1893): a fort besieged by the Sioux is relieved by the U.S. Cavalry. Other hits included *Madame Butterfly* (1900), with John Luther Long (the origin of the opera), and *The Darling of the Gods* (1902). *The Girl of the Golden West* (1905) was also used by Puccini. From 1906 he produced everything from melodrama to Shakespeare at his Belasco Theatre.

GORDIN, Jacob (1853–1909). Russian-born Yiddish dramatist, author of 80 plays, including his best-known *The Jewish King Lear* (1892), *Mirele Efros* (1898), and *God, Man and Devil* (1900) partly based on Goethe's *Faust*. All these appeared after his emigration to America. His plays are serious, simple and well-characterised.

WILDE, Oscar (1856–1900). Irish dramatist, poet, novelist and wit who made his name in the theatre

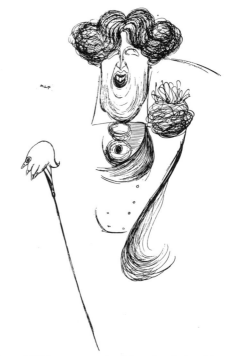

Oscar Wilde, as seen by Max Beerbohm (from the Author's Collection).

with *Lady Windermere's Fan* (1892), a very witty play which is also a social drama. *A Woman of No Importance* (1893) followed; then came a play which discarded the sentiment of his earlier ones, *The Importance of Being Earnest* (1895), an elegant high comedy equalling Congreve at his best and one of the glories of English drama and literature. He was imprisoned during its run. His over-ripe *Salome* (1892), an enjoyably extravagant one-acter, was written in French and is better known via Richard Strauss's opera.

PINERO, Sir Arthur Wing (1855–1934). English dramatist, famous in his own day for well-made emotional dramas and – remembered better today – broad farces, plus one sentimental but captivating glimpse of the theatre of a generation earlier, *Trelawny of the Wells* (1898). He made his name with his farce, *The Magistrate* (1885), still given today, as are *The Schoolmistress* (1886) and *Dandy Dick* (1887). A sentimental play, *Sweet Lavender* (1888) increased his popularity; then followed social dramas like *The Profligate* (1889) and the famous *The Second Mrs. Tanqueray* (1893), about a woman with a past who is led to suicide. Later successes included *His House in Order* (1906). Though he finally lost the public and has since been assailed, his reputation as a craftsman is secure, and his finest plays survive.

SHAW, George Bernard (1856–1950). Anglo-Irish dramatist, critic, publicist and one-man ginger group, and the most influential British playwright since Shakespeare. He is now a classic and the critics who have done their pigmy best to undermine his position have failed. Mountains cannot be felled by mice.

After spells as a critic of books, art, and, ineffably, music and, incomparably, the theatre (until 1897), he concentrated mainly on the stage. His first play, *Widowers' Houses* (staged 1892) about slum landlordism, at once proclaimed his debt to Ibsen (he wrote *The Quintessence of Ibsenism*), his brilliance in dialogue, and a gaiety that he was determined to put to practical use in getting his ideas across. *The Philanderer* is less compelling, but *Mrs. Warren's Profession* (1894) about prostitution is as interesting as his first success, *Arms and the Man* (1894), a satire on the romantic soldier. (*Mrs. Warren* was banned until the 1920s, though performed privately.)

The delightful, thoughtful and Ibsenish *Candida* followed (1895), and other plays in this amazingly

fruitful period included *The Man of Destiny*, a satiric view of young Bonaparte; the delicious comedy, *You Never Can Tell*; *The Devil's Disciple*, a thoughtful melodrama; and *Caesar and Cleopatra*, a major and entertaining historical play written in 1898.

Man and Superman (1901–3) saw Shaw developing his idea of the Life Force governing man and was a great success in Britain and America. In 1904, Shaw obtained a base at the Royal Court Theatre under a sympathetic management run by Granville Barker and Vedrenne and produced *John Bull's Other Island* (1904), *Major Barbara* and *The Doctor's Dilemma* (1906), as scintillating today as it was when the medical abuses it exposed were still active. More lightweight, but very entertaining are *Misalliance* (1910), *Androcles and the Lion* (1912) complete with a huge preface on Christianity – Shaw's prefaces are as important as they are highly readable and often provocative – and *Pygmalion* (1913) about the flower girl turned into a lady; incredibly, the classic musical *My Fair Lady*, did not harm its essence.

The Chekhovian *Heartbreak House* (1920) showed a new depth in Shaw's vision and is regarded as a masterpiece. *Back to Methuselah* (1922) has glorious moments but is not as good as Shaw thought, and one section of it *The Tragedy of an Elderly Gentleman* is second-rate. *St. Joan* (1923) is however, for most, another masterpiece. There followed a decline, though his political comedy, *The Apple Cart* (1929) is very fine. Of the later plays, perhaps only *Too True to be Good* (1932), *The Millionairess* (1936) and *In Good King Charles's Golden Days* (1939) have survival value. Yet, as all Shavians know, even his least inspired plays have much to offer, as well as his never-ending command of language. Shaw's ideas, expressed with steady wit and endless lucidity, survive long after the follies he exposed have been reformed – unless, as in *Geneva* (1938), the ideas are sub-standard.

Shaw's characters sometimes suffer at the expense of ideas, which also affect his construction; yet even in, say, *Getting Married*, an 'ideas' play about every aspect of marriage, in which the characters 'sit around' and discuss the subject endlessly, they are still credible. Many of his plays are regularly performed, few are totally forgotten. In the last resort he could write incomparably – and wittily. Shaw the clown, the orator, the politician is gradually being forgotten: Shaw the writer cannot be.

HEIBERG, Gunnar (1857–1929). Norwegian dramatist and poet whose satires and comedies include *The Balcony* (1894) and *The Tragedy of Love* (1904). He also wrote political plays and social dramas.

SUDDERMANN, Hermann (1857–1928). German dramatist whose successful realistic dramas of middle-class life were later abused by critics. Yet several of his 'problem plays' survive, most notably *Home* (1893), known as *Magda* in Britain and America.

THOMAS, Augustus (1857–1934). American dramatist, author of many plays about aspects of American life. His finest is *The Copperhead* (1918), about a civilian patriot in the American Civil War.

BRIEUX, Eugene (1858–1932). French dramatist, the most prolific of the naturalistic playwrights of his day, but too inclined to preach, partly because of his undoubted pity of humanity. His four finest plays are perhaps *Les Trois Filles de M. Dupont* (1897), exposing the miseries of dowry marriages; *La Robe Rouge* (1900), about the temptation to abuse authority; *Les Avaries* ('Damaged Goods', 1902), with its theme venereal disease, a sensation in Britain and the U.S.A.; and *Maternité* (1903), about abortion and birth control. Not a great artist or a wit, his career was still a worthy one.

COURTELINE, Georges (1858–1929). French dramatist whose farces often have a serious, realistic side. A number are still given. Some of his plays deal with army life, including his first, *Lidoire* (1886) and *Les Gaitiés de l'escadron* ('A Good Time in the Squadron', 1895). In *L'Article 330* (1901) he created Jean Phillipe La Brige, who could out-argue judges and lawyers; while in what many consider his best play, *Boubouroche* (1893) a bachelor, his mistress and her lover are convincingly shown.

MARTYN, Edward (1859–1923). Irish dramatist and novelist, 'the Irish Ibsen' according to some of his early admirers. His finest play is possibly *The Heather Field* (1899), in which the hero throws away everything including his sanity in trying to reclaim a submerged field, but survives undaunted.

SHOLEM ALEICHEM (1859–1916). Russian-born Yiddish dramatist and novelist who emigrated to America, where his plays were very successful. His gallery of characters was colossal and his fame continues to grow. The hit musical, *Fiddler on the Roof* (1964) was adapted from a novel of his about Tevye, who also appears in the play *Tevye the Dairy Man*

(1915). Other successes included *The Treasure* (1908) and *It's Hard to Be a Jew* (1914).

BARRIE, J. M. (Sir James) (1860–1937). Scottish dramatist and novelist whose *Peter Pan* (1904), despite an undercurrent of criticism from Shaw and lesser folk, remains *the* children's play. Of his many other plays, the best known are *Quality Street* (1902), *The Admirable Crichton* (1902), *What Every Woman Knows* (1908), *Dear Brutus* (1917), *Mary Rose* (1920), and his brilliant one-act thriller, *Shall We Join the Ladies?* (1922). Unfortunately, sentiment and whimsy often drowned his very real comic talent. But *Peter Pan* lives!

CHEKHOV, Anton (1860–1904). Russian dramatist and short-story writer, author of several supreme masterpieces. A small-town grocer's son, he studied medicine in Moscow, writing some short stories. Soon he was writing farce in the French fashion, but Russianised, including *The Bear* (1888), *The Proposal* (1889) and *The Wedding* (1890). His first major play was *Ivanov* (1887), a study of a man's misguided life and soured marriage. Neither it nor *The Wood Demon* (1889) was very successful, while *Platonov* from this period was not staged until the 1920s. His first great play *The Seagull* (1896) also failed – completely – the director and actors failing to understand it. The breakthrough came in 1898 when the directors of the Moscow Art Theatre, Nemirovitch-Danchenko and Stanislavsky, got permission to revive the play.

In this production Chekhov's blend of tragedy and comedy, and the lonely isolation of the beautifully drawn characters were understood and put over, the comedy and absurdity emphasising the tragedy as in all good Chekhovian performances. There followed *Uncle Vanya* (1899) which is a revised *Wood Demon, The Three Sisters* (1901) and *The Cherry Orchard* (1904). Then Chekhov died at the very height of his powers, as he was beginning to be understood.

That Chekhovians find his greatest plays eternally haunting, moving and entertaining does not mean that it is easy to analyse his appeal or, especially, his unique talent. His plots appear loosely drawn to the extent that some hardly allow them to be plots at all. Yet he worked at each one with exceptional care. He said to a novice: 'If a gun is hanging on the wall in the first act, it must be fired in the last.' Yet the effect of the characters on each

A scene from Chekhov's The Seagull, *produced at the Maxim Gorky Theatre in Moscow, with S. Korkoshko as Nina and L. Gubanov as Trigorin. (Photo: Novosti)*

other is the most significant part of a Chekhov plot. He was a kindly man who took his scientific and medical training seriously, and he believed that science could transform mankind, yet as J. B. Priestley said in his memorable short biography, 'Doctors have turned to writing both before and after his time, but not to writing like this.' And he notes his extreme literary sensibility. In addition to his laser-like eye, and his knowledge and humanity, Chekhov was a supreme master of atmosphere, character and situation, sketched with extraordinary economy. No one has known better what to include and what to leave out. Russians can detect in him a prophet of a coming, heroic future. Indeed, it would have been heroic if the world was peopled with Chekhovs: practical – more so than most of his characters – and humane. It was a stupendous genius who could make audiences care passionately and deeply about whether or not a cherry orchard should be sold, about three sisters longing for a Moscow they would never reach.

HANKIN, St. John (1860–1909). English dramatist whose Edwardian plays had far more substance than those of many of his contemporaries, and were given by the Stage Society and the Court. His best known are *The Return of the Prodigal* (1905) and *The Cassilis Engagement* (1907). To his gift for comedy he added detachment and notable pessimism.

HOYT, Charles (1860–1900). American dramatist, author of farces and satirical comedies about American life, which prepared the ground for later playwrights down to Kaufman and Hart. His best known play is *A Trip to Chinatown* (1891).

BRACCO, Roberto (1861–1943). Italian dramatist who tried to create an Italian theatre of ideas. Yet he was more successful portraying Neapolitan life in *Don Pietro Caruso* (1895) and in an intimate study of suffering in *Il Piccolo Santo* (1912).

TAGORE, Rabindranath (1861–1941). Indian dramatist, poet and philosopher whose plays drew inspiration from Sanskrit classical drama, Bengali folk drama and the theatre of the West. His range is enormous and his reputation grows. Towards the end of his life he concentrated more on dance dramas. Early plays include the sad, but very popular *The Post Office* and a symbolic work about non-violence, *Sacrifice* (1890). Many of his plays are written in lyric verse and are staged on a mainly bare platform, props often having symbolic significance.

FEYDEAU, Georges (1862–1921). French dramatist, perhaps the supreme master of bedroom – or some would say any kind of farce. His situations are brilliantly devised and pressure leads to danger, then panic, and (happily) he is no respecter of persons. Now a classic in France, a number of his plays have been successfully exported (including to British TV), notably *Occupe-toi d' Amélie* (1908), Coward's *Look after Lulu* being one version of it. Mistaken identities and physical deformities are among Feydeau's repertoire, both of which appear in *La Puce à l'Oreille* ('A Flea in her Ear', 1907); this was a hilarious success at Britain's National Theatre (1966), translated by John Mortimer.

HAUPTMANN, Gerhart (1862–1946). German dramatist, once hailed as the equal of Ibsen and Strindberg. His naturalistic *Vor Sonnenaufgang* ('Before Sunrise', 1889) was a success; then, after similar plays, he wrote a historical drama about a revolt of Silesian weavers in 1844, *Die Weber* ('The Weavers', 1892), one of the first plays in which a crowd was the hero and which had great influence on later playwrights. *Der Biberpelz* ('The Beaver Coat, 1893) is a brilliant comedy, and Hauptmann also mastered fantasy and symbolism. Among his other notable plays are the dramatic fantasy, *Hanneles Himmelfahrt* ('The Assumption of Hannele', 1893), *Die versunkene Glocke* ('The Sunken

Bell', 1896), also a fine comedy *Der rote Hahn* ('The Red Cock', 1901), *Rose Bernd* (1903) in which the heroine succumbs to her environment, and *The Rats* (1911) – a gloom-laden tragi-comedy set in a poor quarter of Berlin. *The Weavers* won him a Nobel Prize.

MAETERLINCK, Maurice (1862–1949). Belgian dramatist and poet who wrote in French. His symbolic dramas are concerned with the individual's inner conflict, not man fighting with his world: his people are the instruments of a hidden force. His first major success was the famous *Pelléas and Melisande* (1892), overshadowed now by Debussy's even more famous opera; it is a dream-like, eerie, poetic, mysterious piece, the characters more definite than many in Maeterlinck's plays, the theme being whether a girl tricked into an unsatisfactory marriage should give way to true love. His most successful play was – and is – *The Blue Bird* (1908), and it is also his most hopeful; a sequel, *The Betrothal* (1922), was less successful.

SCHNITLZER, Arthur (1862–1931). Austrian dramatist and novelist whose plays are lighthearted and elegant on the surface, but who looked at his characters with a cool, almost clinical cynicism, though with some compassion. His profession was medicine and he and Freud admired each other. His plays include *Anatol* (1893), sketches about the life of a man-about-town; *Lieberlei* (1895) in which a working-class girl kills herself after finding that her aristocratic lover has been playing with her affections; and *Reigen* (1902) about the merry-go-round of love (on which the film *La Ronde* was based). *The Green Cockatoo* (1899) is a savage, brilliant one-acter set in a tavern on the night the Bastile is stormed.

ANSKY, S. (1863–1920). Russian-born Yiddish dramatist, essayist and ethnologist, and author of the famous *The Dybbuk* (1920), a play which is more folk-lore than drama and deals with demoniac possession, pre-ordained relationship and redemption in death.

D'ANNUNZIO, Gabriele (1863–1938). Italian dramatist, poet and writer. His plays are strong on poetry, weak on humanity. They include the verse tragedies, *Francecsa da Rimini* (1901) and *La Fiaccola sotto il moggio* ('The Light under the Bushel', 1905); and the fine pastoral tragedy, *La Figlia di Iorio* ('Iorio's daughter', 1904). Eleonora Duse helped make his name by playing a number

Above: *The 1968 production by the English Stage Company of* Look Back in Anger *was transferred from the Royal Court to the Criterion in the West End.* Below: *The Royal Court, home of the English Stage Company, pictured in 1968. (Photos: Central Office of Information)*

of his heroines, including *La Gioconda* (1898)

WEDEKIND, Frank (1864–1918). German dramatist and actor, influenced by Hauptmann and tending towards Expressionism. His constant theme is sex and its effects, enough to get *Frühlings Erwachen* ('Spring's Awakening', 1891) banned in Britain in 1963. This and the earlier *Die Junge Welt* ('The World of Youth', 1890) concern adolescent problems. *Erdgeist* (1895) and *Die Büchse der Pandora* ('Pandora's Box', 1903) are about Lulu, later turned into an opera of that name by Berg. His later plays are more and more violent, a sort of prelude to 1914, but in his last, *Herakles* (1917) reality has finally given way to Expressionism. In his revolutionary frankness, exposure of middleclass hypocrisy and concentration on sex, also his accurate ear for language, he made his world more real than the naturalists, going to the very heart of the human comedy and tragedy.

HEIJERMANS, Herman (1864–1924). Dutch dramatist and novelist, author of many realistic dramas about human misery, including a number about the working classes. His masterpiece is *Op Hoop van Zegan* ('The Good Hope', 1900), about the exploitation of fishermen by their owners, which actually resulted in legislation. He also wrote about the middle class, as in his very popular *Schakels* ('Links', 1903), about a conflict between a self-made man and his family; and could turn to fantasy, as in *Uitkomst* ('The Way Out', 1907). This wide-ranging playwright is the greatest produced by Holland in modern times.

FITCH, Clyde (1865–1909). American dramatist whose sub-Ibsen plays – *The City* (1909), etc. – dealt with problems of the day, though he had made his name at home and abroad with romances and comedies: *Beau Brummell* (1890), *Captain Jinks of the Horse Marines* (1900), etc. He often wrote of women with a flaw – for instance kleptomania in *The Girl and the Judge* (1901).

HOUSEMAN, Laurence (1865–1959). English dramatist and novelist, best remembered for his *Victoria Regina* (1935) which, incredibly, ran into censorship trouble at first in Britain, before triumphing on both sides of the Atlantic.

YEATS, W. B. (1865–1939). Irish dramatist and poet, and a director of the Abbey Theatre, Dublin, from 1904. Beginning with Celtic-Twilight romanticism – *The Land of Heart's Desire* (1894), etc. – he moved to peasant drama, collaborating with

Lady Gregory in *Cathleen ni Houlihan* (1901) and later in poetic dramas. A period of Irish legend followed, including *Deirdre* (1905–6); then came a group of concise plays, including *The Only Jealousy of Emer* (1916). Even more austere are his final plays, notably *The Words on the Window Pane* (1930) about Swift, and *Purgatory* (1938). But it should be stressed that none of his plays rank with his work in helping create the Irish theatre and, particularly, his lyric poetry.

BENEVENTE, Jacinto (1866–1954). Spanish dramatist, author of many social comedies. His best plays are *Los malhechores del bien* ('The Evil Doers of Good', 1905) urging moral tolerance, *Los interes creados* ('The Bonds of Interest', 1907) a puppet show view of modern life, and a rural tragedy, *La mal querida* ('The Passion Flower', 1913).

GALSWORTHY, John (1867–1933). English dramatist and novelist, many of whose plays deal with social problems. His first, *The Silver Box* (1906), was produced at the Royal Court by the Barker-Vedrenne management. *Strife* (1909) is about a strike, *Justice* (1910) about prison and the law. Later plays included *The Skin Game* (1920) and *Loyalties* (1922) which touched on anti-Semitism, also *Escape* (1926). A scene in *Justice* exposing the facts about solitary confinement helped change the law.

PIRANDELLO, Luigi (1867–1936). Italian dramatist, the most important and widely known of modern times. His pessimistic plays explore reality, the difficulty of defining it and the pointlessness of man's efforts to create reality and find truth. His masterpiece and best known play is *Six Characters in Search of an Author* (1921) in which a number of people break into a theatre rehearsal and truth and illusion become memorably mixed; while the best known of his later plays is *Enrico IV* (1922), in which a young man is deluded into thinking he is the German Emperor Henry IV. His other most acclaimed play is *Right You Are If You Think You Are* (1918). Pirandello saw nothing but uncertainty, no true sanity, and his influence on post-war European drama was considerable. He proclaimed that appearance is reality, so accept what meets the eye. And it should be stressed for those who do not know his plays that despite his negative beliefs, his sense of theatre is remarkable.

CLAUDEL, Paul (1868–1955). French dramatist and poet who experienced a religious revelation at the age of eighteen. Religion was the basis of all his plays except his first, *Tête d'Or* (1889). His first to be performed was *The Tidings brought to Mary* (1912), a modern miracle play, six years after he wrote his famous *Partage de midi* ('Break of Noon', produced by Jean Louis Barrault in 1948); it is a tragic triangular drama.

L'Otage ('The Hostage', given at the Comédie Française in 1934, brought him prestige in France, after succeeding earlier in Britain), while *The Satin Slipper* (1919–24) is his best known, and biggest of his later work, a mighty story of Renaissance lovers separated by continents, but eventually attaining spiritual joy. Claudel's religious views and studies of human love and its relationship to divine love alienate non-believers, who yet realise his greatness.

GORKY, Maxim (1868–1936). Russian dramatist and novelist whose *The Lower Depths* (1902), set in a doss-house, was a triumph for himself and the Moscow Art Theatre and remains his best play. A man of the people, hailed by the Soviets, whose only other early play to approach his masterpiece is *The Enemies* (1907); his only remarkable later play is *Yegor Bulychev* (1932), and also perhaps *Dostigayev and the Others* (1932) – another part of an intended sequence about the fall of the old régime.

ROSTAND, Edmond (1868–1918). French dramatist and latter-day Romantic who wrote verse dramas with meaty parts for actors. By far his finest is *Cyrano de Bergerac* (1898), with its long-nosed poet-hero. Almost as famous, though far less dramatic and well-constructed, is *L'Aiglon* (1900), about Napoleon's young son, which gave Bernhardt a splendid part.

MOODY, William Vaughan (1869–1910). American dramatist and poet who hoped to write poetic dramas of contemporary life, but was forced to switch to prose, notably in two fine plays, *The Great Divide* (1906) and *The Faith Healer* (1909), the first about the battle between puritanism and freedom, the second between earthly and spiritual love. His early death is considered a major loss.

WYSPIANSKI, Stanislaw (1869–1907). Polish dramatist, poet and painter whose many plays cover a wide range. One of the most interesting is *Wesele* ('The Wedding', 1901), in which Romanticism is displayed as a force for evil.

ANDREYEV, Leonid (1871–1919). Russian dramatist, attacked by Tsarists and Soviet critics alike, especially for his *Life of Man* (1906), but now more valued. *He who Gets Slapped* (1916) is his best-known play, 'he' being an intellectual who tries to become ordinary, joining a circus as a clown. A deep pessimist, his star is in the ascendant.

QUINTERO, Serafin (1871–1938), and **Joaquin** (1873–1944). Spanish dramatists who wrote over 150 comedies and dramas set in Andalusia.

SYNGE, J. M. (1871–1909). Irish dramatist who helped found the Irish Theatre Movement. He wrote a number of very fine plays including *The Shadow of the Glen* (1903), a dark comedy; the one-act *Riders to the Sea* (1904), a tragedy of fisherfolk. There followed *The Well of the Saints* (1905) and *The Tinker's Wedding* (1907) about a couple on the roads. *The Playboy of the Western World* (1907) is Synge's masterpiece, a wonderful tragicomedy about the timid Christy Mahon, who is hero-worshipped for allegedly killing his tyrant of a father; it incredibly caused riots in Dublin because of 'insults' to Irish womanhood. His unfinished *Deirdre of the Sorrows*, about old Irish legends, is a poetic drama fine enough to make his early death particularly sad.

JARRY, Alfred (1873–1907). French dramatist and poet, remembered for a single, now mythical, symbolic farce *Ubu Roi* (1896). Ubu is a cowardly, monstrous clown who kills and replaces the King of Poland and rules with appalling cruelty. It is a grotesquely savage attack on the bourgeoisie and its abuse of authority, and influenced the Surrealists.

HOFMANNSTHAL, Hugo von (1874–1929). Austrian dramatist and poet, best known abroad for his very fine libretti for Richard Strauss. His methods were the very opposite of the naturalists, for his plays are deeply poetic and often full of inner conflicts, and set in a harsh, mysterious world, though he never gives way to despair: life is too enthralling. His first lyric plays were *Der Tor und der Tod* ('Death and the Fool', 1893) and *Der Tod des Tizian* ('The Death of Titian', 1893). He then explored classical, more robust themes, transforming rather than merely translating: *Elektra* (1903), *Oedipus and the Sphinx* (1905), *Venice Preserved* (1905), *Jedermann* ('Everyman', 1912) – a regular feature of the Salzburg Festival – Calderon's *Life is a Dream*, which became the inspiration for his first full-length play, *Der Turm* ('The Tower',

1925). He worked closely with the great director Max Reinhardt and, after a period of neglect, his reputation is now high again. As for his libretti (*Elektra, Der Rosenkavalier, Ariadne auf Naxos,* etc.), they are incomparable.

GHÉON, Henri (1875–1944). French dramatist, many of whose plays are about saints, including *Le Pauvre sous l'escalier* (1921) about St. Alexis – his masterpiece.

MAUGHAM, W. Somerset (1874–1965). English dramatist and novelist, and a very successful writer of comedies of manners and dramas. The former, his finest plays, reached their peak in the 1920s – notably *Home and Beauty, The Circle* and *The Constant Wife.* More serious plays included *The Letter* (1927) and *For Services Rendered* (1932). He gave up the theatre after the relative failure of *Sheppey* (1933). The most famous adaptation of one of his stories was the notorious *Rain* (John Colton and Clemence Randolph). In 1908 he had four plays running in the West End.

MacKAYE, Percy (1875–1956). American dramatist and poet inclined to pretentiousness in masques and pageant dramas, but not in his best serious play, the historical fantasy, *The Scarecrow* (1909) and his finest comedy, *Anti-Matrimony* (1910) – in which youngsters emancipated by Shaw and Ibsen are pleasantly mocked.

SANCHEZ, Florencio (1875–1910). Uruguayan dramatist, author of a number of naturalistic plays about life in the towns and country, including *La Gringa* ('The Immigrant Girl', 1904), about an old farmer who, fatally, cannot change his ways.

FITZMAURICE, George (1877–1963). Irish dramatist, whose reputation has risen sharply. His best-known play is *The Country Dressmaker* (1907), a lively peasant comedy.

BARKER, Harley Granville (1877–1946). See Chapter 6.

CROTHERS, Rachel (1878–1958). American dramatist and director whose plays often deal light-heartedly with women's rights. They include *Nora* (1903) and *Susan and God* (1937).

DUNSANY, Lord (1878–1957). Anglo-Irish dramatist whose plays for the Abbey Theatre – usually combining satire, fantasy and fable – include *The Glittering Gods* (1909) and *The Laughter of the Gods* (1919).

MAYNE, Rutherford (b. 1878). Irish dramatist and

a founder of the Ulster Theatre. Perhaps his finest play is the one-act *Red Turf* (1911), a peasant tragedy.

KAISER, Georg (1878–1945). German dramatist and a leading Expressionist. After a comedy, *The Jewish Widow* (1911), came the historical *The Burghers of Calais* (1914) in which his 'new man', universal and of limitless potential, appears. *From Morn to Midnight* (1916) portrays the horrors of modern civilisation and its robot-like men in the story of a bank clerk whose attempt at freedom ends in death. He then embarked on three plays which traced most pessimistically the rise of our industrial civilisation: *The Corral* (1917), *Gas I* (1918) and *Gas II* (1920). He never again equalled these achievements and, indeed, was persecuted for them in the 1930s. His *Colportage* (1923–4) is a slightly more optimistic view of the new man.

MOLNAR, Ferenc (1878–1952). Hungarian dramatist, author of *Liliom* (1909) which inspired the musical *Carousel,* and *The Guardsman* (1910), a serious farce.

STERNHEIM, Carl (1878–1942). German dramatist and author of biting satire on bourgeois attitudes, with comments on the position of the individual in a modern industrial and technological society, which apparently frees him – but does the opposite. He was one of the few modern German playwrights to achieve good comedies, albeit biting ones. His plays include *A Pair of Drawers* (1911), *The Snob* (1912) and *1913* (1915), a family trilogy.

EVREINOV, Nikolai (1879–1953). Russian dramatist and director who ridiculed realism in the theatre. His famous *The Theatre of the Soul* (1912), using the fact that we appear differently to different people, has several actors playing the different aspects.

ASCH, Sholem (1880–1957). Polish born Yiddish dramatist and novelist, author of some 20 plays, the best-known of which is *God of Vengeance* (1907), set in a brothel. Settling in America, he wrote a number of plays about outcasts and criminals, sympathetically drawn, and because the leading figure in Yiddish drama, raising its literary status.

HIRSHBEIN, Peretz (1880–1948). Russian-born Yiddish dramatist whose finest play is the idyllic folk comedy, *Green Fields* (1916). His plays abound with kindly, gentle characters.

O'CASEY, Sean (1880–1964). Irish dramatist, whose first play, *Shadow of a Gunman* (1923) is masterly, and whose second and third, *Juno and the Paycock* (1924) and *The Plough and the Stars* (1926), are masterpieces. All are set in Dublin of the Troubles (1916–22). Not since Jacobean England had a writer in English written tragedies of the highest rank, interspersed with comedy and farce, and written in prose that was poetic, realistic and utterly memorable.

Settling in England he wrote his last major play, a very fine anti-war drama, *The Silver Tassie* (1928), with a symbolic second act. It was rejected by the Abbey Theatre, which O'Casey abandoned as an outlet for his plays for many years. The best of his later plays are possibly *Purple Dust* (1940), a comedy; and the symbolic drama, *Red Roses for Me* (1943). His last works are full of vitality, but less convincing; his first three plays guarantee his immortality.

LONSDALE, Frederick (1881–1954). English dramatist, whose Society comedies of manners include *Aren't We All?* (1923), *The Last of Mrs. Cheyney* (1925) and *On Approval* (1927), all well-made, and none of them forgotten.

MARTINEZ SIERRA, Gregorio (1881–1947). Spanish dramatist whose masterpiece is *Cradle Song* (1911), set in a nunnery. A great optimist – and translator of Shaw's plays.

DRINKWATER, John (1882–1937). English dramatist, director and actor, the finest of whose verse plays is *Abraham Lincoln* (1919). He collaborated with Sir Barry Jackson at Birmingham Rep.

GIRAUDOUX, Jean (1882–1944). French dramatist, who worked with the great actor-director, Louis Jouvet. His plays, intelligent and elegantly written, include *Siegfried* (1928) a symbolic piece about Franco-German friendship, *Amphitryon '38* (1929) a light comedy set in classical times, *Judith* (1932), *Intermezzo* (1933), *Tiger at the Gates* (1935), *Ondine* (1939) and *The Madwoman of Chaillot* (1945). A master of the theatre and a believer in words, his plays are dubbed shallow and too cool by some, greatly admired by others.

BERGMAN, Hjalmar (1883–1931). Swedish dramatist and novelist, author of many plays and film scripts. Influenced by Maeterlinck, Ibsen, and later, Strindberg, he wrote folk comedies, superb studies of small-town life, and historical and romantic dramas; his best plays are very stylishly and opulently written. Among his best known are the one-act *Mr. Sleeman is Coming* (1918), *Sweden-*

hielms (1925) about the family of a Nobel Prize winner, and his dramatisation of an early novel, *The Markurells of Wadköping* (1929). Richard Vowles has vividly written that at his best Bergman's works often suggests a Noel Coward adaptation of Dostoyevsky, though his comic grotesqueness is all his own.

BRIGHOUSE, Harold (1883–1958). English dramatist, the best of whose realistic North Country plays is now a classic: the comedy, *Hobson's Choice* (1916).

ERVINE, St. John (1883–1971). Anglo-Irish dramatist and critic, who managed the Abbey Theatre for a time, where some of his early works were staged. His best known plays are *Jane Clegg* (1913) and *Robert's Wife* (1937), while perhaps his finest is *John Ferguson* (1915), a strong Irish tragedy.

FLECKER, James Elroy (1884–1915). English dramatist and poet, author of *Hassan* (1923).

LAWRENCE, D. H. (1885–1930). English dramatist, poet and major novelist, the merits of whose realistic plays only came to light in the 1960s, when the English Stage Company began to revive them. Set in the Nottinghamshire mining country, they include *A Collier's Night Out* (1906), *The Daughter-in-Law* and *The Widowing of Mrs. Holroyd*, all written before 1914.

WITKIEWICZ, Stanislaw (1885–1939). Polish dramatist whose plays anticipated Beckett and Ionesco, etc., and were 'discovered' in the 1950s. They include *The Pragmatists* (1918) a tragicomedy, and *The Madam and the Nun* (1923) dedicated to 'all the madmen of the world'.

ROBINSON, Lennox (1886–1958). Irish dramatist, director and manager, associated with the Abbey Theatre for many years. He wrote political and patriotic tragedies, but his biggest success was *The White-Headed Boy* (1916), a light comedy.

SHELDON, Brewster (1886–1946). American dramatist undone by 'sticky romanticism', according to Howard Taubman. This weakened his problem plays like *The Nigger* (1909) and *The Boss* (1911) The biggest success was *Romance* (1913) between a clergyman and an opera singer. Though crippled with arthritis he collaborated with and helped many younger dramatists.

ABBOTT, George (b. 1887). American dramatist, director, actor and play doctor whose plays include *Broadway* (1926) and *Coquette* (1927). He directed and wrote many musicals, including *The Boys from Syracuse* (1938) and *The Pyjama Game* (1954).

CAPEK, Josef (1887–1945). *See* **Capek, Karel** (1890–1938).

FERBER, Edna (1887–1968). American novelist whose *Showboat* was turned into a brilliant musical (1926). With George Kaufman she wrote a number of plays including a satire on the Barrymores, *The Royal Family* (1927).

ROSSO di SAN SECONDO, Pier (1887–1956). Italian dramatist and novelist whose wide-ranging finely written plays include *Marionette che passione!* (1918) about three puppet-like people confessing to and fighting with each other while swayed with fierce passions.

ANDERSON, Maxwell (1888–1959). American dramatist whose plays range from historical and verse dramas to social criticism and comedies. *What Price Glory?* (1924), with Laurence Stallings, is *the* American First World War play, while his historical dramas include *Mary of Scotland* (1933) and *Valley Forge* (1934). The Sacco-Vanzetti case inspired *Winterset* (1935), while other plays of the 1930s – his most productive period – include *High Tor* (1936) and *Key Largo* (1939); later successes include *Anne of the Thousand Days* (1951), about Anne Boleyn. A believer in poetic drama, his final position in the history of the American theatre remains uncertain.

BERNARD, Jean-Jacques (b. 1888). French dramatist and poet who, in reaction to over-wordy plays, conceived the Theatre of the Unspoken, emphasising characters' actions and reactions, rather than their words. His plays, often about love and the unspoken drama of the spirit, include *Martine* (1922) and *L'Ame en peine* (1926).

BRIDIE, James (1888–1951). Scottish dramatist (actually Dr. O. H. Mavor) who founded the Citizens' Theatre, Glasgow. A witty, prolific playwright, whose plots and construction are inconsistent, his first big success was *The Anatomist* (1930), about Dr. Knox of Burke and Hare notoriety. Other fine plays include *Tobias and the Angel* (1930) and *Mr. Bolfry* (1943), in which one of the best Devils in drama descends on a Scottish manse. *Mr. Gillie* (1950) is about a schoolmaster. Though his talent was diminished when not writing about Scotland, the whole British theatre benefited by his wit, vitality and intelligence.

ELIOT, T. S. (1888–1965). American-born English poet and dramatist whose attempts to revive poetic and religious drama were worthy and distinguished, though not very theatrical. In the later plays, it is hard to detect the verse. His first, possibly his most lasting play is *Murder in the Cathedral* (1935) about Becket. *The Family Reunion* (1939) is a modern situation inspired by Greek drama. His later plays, especially *The Cocktail Party* (1949), had much success but their future is uncertain. The others are *The Confidential Clerk* (1953) and *The Elder Statesman* (1958). In their time they gave the British theatre a much-needed quality.

LEIVICK, H. (1888–1962). Russian-born Yiddish poet, whose *The Golem* (1921), a historical play written in America, is his finest achievement.

O'NEILL, Eugene (1888–1953). American dramatist, now generally regarded as his country's leading and most influential playwright. He was the son of the popular leading actor, James O'Neill, who (as outlined in *Long Day's Journey*) sacrificed a great serious career to play the Count of Monte

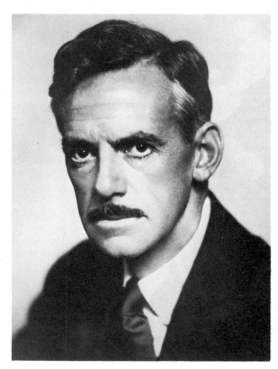

Eugene O'Neill, America's greatest dramatist. (Photo: Author's Collection)

Cristo for many years. The son's first success was *Beyond the Horizon* (1920), and 14 very productive years followed. In these were, amongst others, *The Emperor Jones* (1920) about a Black ruler, *Anna Christie* (1921) in which a 'fallen woman' is redeemed by love, *All God's Chillun Got Wings* (1924), and a tortured and highly emotional drama set on a New England farm in the 1850s, *Desire Under The Elms* (1924). *The Great God Brown* (1926), his best play to that date, was followed by a serene comedy satire, *Marco's Millions* (1928). Then came the very emotional and strong *Strange Interlude* (1928), the very long *Mourning Becomes Electra* (1931) which is the Oresteia set in New England after the Civil War, and the warm, nostalgic *Ah, Wilderness* (1933).

After a spell away from the theatre, O'Neill returned with the pessimistic, Gorky-like *The Iceman Cometh* (1946, but written earlier), set among derelicts. When revived in the 1950s, it marked his rise to his present fame. His last play in his lifetime was *A Moon for the Misbegotten* (1943, produced 1947); then, posthumously in 1956, came his masterpiece, *Long Day's Journey into Night*, now widely regarded as the finest of all American plays. A 'play of old sorrow written in tears and blood' about the Tyrone family, it is strictly autobiographical. Years of hate, love, torment and blame are condensed into one terrible day and night, with father, mother, Jamie and his younger brother Edmund (O'Neill himself) – all incomparably drawn.

O'Neill has been accused of poverty of language, with even an admirer like Brooks Atkinson claiming that he never wrote a quotable line. So great was his involvement with his finest characters and so memorably dark is his vision, that it could be claimed that lack of memorable language does not matter. He is no O'Casey, but there are moments of simple, monosyllabic glory. In the supreme scene where the penny-pinching Tyrone senior explains himself to Edmund he has the superb line: 'It was in those days that I learnt to be a miser.' And the mother at the play's end, after a mad scene no less, says, 'I fell in love with James Tyrone and was so happy for a time.' The curtain falls.

STODOLA, Ivan (b. 1888). Slovakian dramatist notably successful for his satirical comedies, including *Tea with the Senator* (1929). He helped develop Slovakian drama.

COCTEAU, Jean (1889–1963). French dramatist, novelist, poet, film-maker and designer whose plays are concerned with love and death and lovers being separated. They range widely and include the monodrama *La Voix Humaine* (1930), *La Machine Infernale* (1934, a version of the Oedipus story), the romantic costume drama *The Eagle has Two Heads* (1946), *The Knights of the Round Table* (1937, an Arthurian tragi-comedy), and the love story, *Renaud et Armide* (1943), written in couplets. A great theatrical showman, his best plays should survive changing tastes.

KAUFMAN, George S. (1889–1961). American dramatist and director, most of whose many successes were written in collaboration. They include *Beggar on Horseback* (1924) with Marc Connelly, *Dinner at Eight* (1932) with Edna Ferber, and two superb comedies with Moss Hart, *You Can't Take it With You* (1936) and *The Man Who Came to Dinner* (1939). A first-rate director, he was a supreme figure on Broadway.

LINDSAY, Howard (1889–1968) and **CROUSE, Russel** (1893–1966). American dramatists who wrote the colossal hit, *Life with Father* (1939) and the Pulitzer Prize-winning political comedy, *State of the Union* (1945).

TRAVERS, Ben (b. 1889). English dramatist and great farce writer, including three classics for the Aldwych, *A Cuckoo in the Nest* (1925), his masterpiece *Rookery Nook* (1926), and *Thark* (1927). Farce lovers should read his autobiography, *Vale of Laughter*.

ČAPEK, Karel (1890–1938). Czech dramatist who collaborated with his brother **Josef** (1887–1945), though each wrote separately, too. Their best-known play is *R.U.R.* (1921), a famous Expressionist drama in which robots take over the world. Almost as well known is *The Insect Play* (1921) perhaps more a revue, but a very theatrical and ironic view of humanity disguised as insects. *The Makropoulos Affair* (1923), better known abroad in Janacek's operatic version, is a counterblast to Shaw's *Back to Methusalah*, challenging his optimistic view of longevity. Karel's last play was the anti-fascist *Matka* (1938).

CONNELLY, Marc (b. 1890). American dramatist who collaborated with George Kaufman in *Merton of the Movies* (1922), *Beggar on Horseback* (1924), etc. and with other playwrights, but whose most famous play is *Green Pastures* (1930) – Biblical scenes expressed as Negro fantasy. Some might find it patronising, even offensive today, but it had a great effect.

WERFEL, Franz (1890–1945). Austrian dramatist and novelist, author of the influential *Goat Song* (1921) about a half man, half beast who leads a revolt and who symbolises humanity's bestiality. He also wrote a Faust triology, etc.

BULGAKOV, Mikhail (1891–1940). Russian dramatist and novelist who suffered at the hands of Soviet censors. Many of his plays were withdrawn after a few performances, including his most famous, *The Day of the Turbins* (1926), which dared to show White Russians as human beings instead of monsters.

CHRISTIE, Dame Agatha (b. 1891). English dramatist and prolific writer of detective stories. Her most famous play, *The Mousetrap*, is running in London 'for ever' (since 1952), but her best plays are *Ten Little Niggers* (*Indians* in the U.S., 1943) and *Witness for the Prosecution* (1953).

HOWARD, Sidney (1891–1939). American dramatist whose most famous work is *They Knew What They Wanted* (1924) – a lively, sentimental comedy drama about a mail order bride. His other plays include *Yellow Jack* (1934) about the conquest of Yellow Fever, and *Alien Corn* (1933).

LAGERKVIST, Par (b. 1891). Swedish dramatist and novelist, little known outside Scandinavia, where he is regarded as almost the equal of Ibsen and Strindberg. After demanding the fusion of realism and symbolism using the resources of the modern theatre, he wrote Strindbergian one-act plays, including the triptych, *The Difficult Hour* (1918), fusing expressionism and cubism. His later plays include *The King* (1932), a political allegory, *Victory in the Dark* (1939) and *Barabbas* (1953), but he is best known as a novelist.

BETTI, Ugo (1892–1953). Italian dramatist who was a successor to Pirandello. His finest plays, concerned with remorse, responsibility, guilt and identity, are *Corruption in the Palace of Justice* (1949), *Crime on Goat Island* (1950), *The Joker* (1951), *The Queen and the Rebels* (1951) and *The Burnt Flower-bed* (1953). The first is his masterpiece, and concerns an investigation into an adventurer's death.

MACLEISH, Archibald (b. 1892). American dramatist and poet whose *J.B.* (1958) is a modern Job play set in a circus tent.

OBEY, André (b. 1892). French dramatist whose

best-known plays were written for Copeau's Compagnie des Quinze, *The Rape of Lucrece*, *The Battle of the Marne* and *Noah*, all non-realistic in form and all produced in 1931.

RICE, Elmer (1892–1967). American dramatist whose first major play *The Adding Machine* (1923) was also his finest. It attacks regimented materialistic society. Other plays include *Street Scene* (1929), a sentiment-cum-violence Pulitzer Prize winner, and the strong anti-Nazi *Judgement Day* (1945).

BEHRMAN, S. N. (1893–1973). American dramatist, considered by many as the finest native playwright of the comedy of manners. His successes include *The Pirate* (1942) adapted from a play by Ludwig Fulda, *Amphitryon '38* (1938) from Giraudoux, *The Second Man* (1927) and *No Time for Comedy* (1939).

HECHT, Ben (1893–1964). American dramatist and novelist whose two best-known plays were written with Charles Macarthur (1896–1956): *The Front Page* (1928) a superb comedy-melodrama newspaper story, and the comedy *Twentieth Century* (1932).

MAYAKOVSKY, Vladimir (1893–1930). Russian dramatist and poet who worked with the director Meyerhold and whose plays, despite Lenin's disapproval, survive. They are *Mystery-Bouffe* (1918), a revolutionary vision of joy, *The Bed Bug* (1929), a satire about a bourgeois and a bed bug frozen and reawakened in a communist 1978, and *The Bath House* (1930), another satire – on corruption, bureaucracy and red tape.

TOLLER, Ernst (1893–1939). German dramatist whose success, *Masses and Men* (1921) is about a woman revolutionary. *The Machine-Wreckers* (1923) is about the Luddite Riots (1812–15), while *Brokenbow* (1923) looks at the marriage problems of a soldier returning impotent from the war. *Yippe, We're Alive* (1923) is even bleaker. Toller killed himself in New York, utterly disillusioned.

GREEN, Paul (b. 1894). American dramatist, author of Southern dramas, including *The House of Connelly* (1931). After the anti-war *Johnny Johnson* (1936) he switched mainly to regional and historical folk drama, the first being *The Lost Colony* (1937), set in North Carolina.

MORGAN, Charles (1894–1958). English dramatist, novelist and critic whose serious, worthy plays include *The Flashing Stream* (1938), *The River Line* (1952) and *The Burning Glass* (1954), all written in

A scene from Michael Blackmore's production of The Front Page *by Ben Hecht and Charles MacArthur at the National Theatre in 1972. Left to right are Alan MacNaughton as Walter Burns, Harry Lomax as Mr. Pincus and Denis Quilley as Hildy Johnson. (Photo: Sophie Baker)*

what John Russell Taylor has called 'self-consciously beautiful mandarin prose'.

PRIESTLEY, J. B. (b. 1894). English dramatist and novelist who made his name with the dramatisation (with Edward Knoblock) of his novel, *The Good Companions* (1931). There followed three plays about Time, all excellently made, *Dangerous Corner* (1932), *Time and the Conways* (1937) and *I Have Been Here Before* (1937) and, amongst others, *Eden End* (1934), *When We are Married* (1938), *Johnson over Jordan* (1939), *An Inspector Calls* (1946) and *The Linden Tree* (1947). His wide-ranging plays have usually been at least theatrically effective, his characterisations are vivid, his social comment often gets across, and he is a fine writer of comedy. After popularity, then some neglect, he is now being 're-discovered'.

ARTAUD, Antonin (1895–1948). See **Cruelty, Theatre of,** Chapter 6.

LAWSON, John Howard (b. 1895). American dramatist, Marxist and Expressionist whose finest play is *Processional* (1925), which he called 'a jazz symphony of American life' and in which the ordinary man is seen a victim of capitalism.

BARRY, PHILIP (1896–1949). American dramatist, author of the much-admired symbolic fantasy *Here Come the Clowns* (1938), and some pleasant comedies, notably *The Philadelphia Story* (1939).

MONTHERLANT, Henri de (b. 1896). French dramatist, novelist and essayist, author of eight plays between 1942 and 1954, including *La Reine Morte* (1942), a historical play with a theme of love versus politics; *Malatesta* (1943–4, produced 1950), *The Master of Santiago* (1945, produced 1948), and *Port-Royal* (1954). Their themes are Church-versus-State, nobility, violence and cruelty. His non-historical plays include *Tomorrow the Dawn* (1948, produced 1949). Though he officially gave up the theatre in 1954, he has continued to write plays since 1956.

SHERRIFF, R. C. (b. 1896). English dramatist and novelist, author of several plays including one masterpiece, *the* British First World War drama, *Journey's End* (1928), which affected and affects survivors, pacifists and neutrals alike.

SHERWOOD, Robert (1896–1955). American dramatist of great range, whose first play, *The Road to Rome* (1927), was a satirically comic comment on Hannibal's march and war. Other plays include the high comedy, *Reunion in Vienna* (1931); the gangster drama, *The Petrified Forest* (1935); the prophetic, ironic vision of the Second World War, *Idiot's Delight* (1936); and an excellent history play, *Abe Lincoln in Illinois* (1938). *There Shall be No Night* (1941), set in the invaded Finland of 1940, deeply stirred its audiences.

SOYA, Carl-Erik (b. 1896). Danish playwright and novelist, especially admired for his satirical plays, as in the anti-war *Corseting the Lion* (1950), and *Petersen in the Underworld* (1957), an adaptation of the Orpheus story.

WILDER, Thornton (1897–1971). American dramatist and novelist whose *Our Town* (1938) is a very successful evocation of small town life. *The Merchant of Yonkers* (1938) later became *The Matchmaker* and the musical *Hullo Dolly*, while *The Skin of Your Teeth* (1942), a 'history of the world in comic strip' and a tribute to man's powers of sur-

vival, had a great success. It and *Our Town* won Pulitzer Prizes.

BRECHT, Bertolt (1898–1956). German dramatist, director and theorist whose influence on the modern theatre has been colossal. This has been because of his theories. He asked that the actor should not 'live' a part but, while understanding it fully, be outside it enough to be able to make a comment on it. The audience, in turn, is expected to judge the character critically. This is 'alienation', more a guide for working than a rigid discipline. It, plus Brecht's subject matter, result in a theatre of debate, which in his early plays proclaimed communism as the correct goal. Yet his best work went much further than a mere party line. Brecht wanted the Epic Theatre, not in the usual meaning of 'epic', but plays which appealed mainly to an audience's reason more than its feelings. In Brechtian terms this means a clear presentation of incidents unencumbered by conventional theatrical construction, with a storyteller sometimes being used, and sometimes songs. His famous Berliner Ensemble had a tremendous influence on the British theatre when it visited London in 1956, many dramatists including Arden, Osborne, Whiting, Bolt and Shaffer, being inspired to use his precepts in varying degrees.

A scene from Brecht's Galileo staged in 1962 by the Piccolo Theatre of Milan, and directed by Giorgio Strehler. (Photo: Italian Institute, London)

His first major success was *The Threepenny Opera* (1928), a Marxist anti-bourgeois satire updating *The Beggar's Opera* of John Gay. The score was by the brilliant Kurt Weill. Their *The Rise and Fall of the City of Mahagonny* (1930) is a masterpiece. Brecht left Germany in 1933 and his greatest period was spent in the U.S.A.: *The Life of Galileo* (1937–9), *Mother Courage* (1938–9), *The Good Woman of Setzuan* (1935–41), *The Resistible Rise of Arturo Ui* (1941) – Hitler and his rise in terms of Capone's Chicago – *The Caucasian Chalk Circle* (1943–5), etc. He returned to Germany in 1949 and from the moment that the Berliner Ensemble gave *Mother Courage* with his wife Helene Weigel in the lead, his reputation at last soared. Interestingly, his Brechtian anti-heroine and profiteer and survivor of the Thirty Years' War is so indomitable and sympathetic that alienation is only partial. In this and his other masterpieces, Brecht's sheer theatrical honesty and flair undermines his rigid theories – which is why the best of them will live.

GHELDERODE, Michel de (1898–1962). Belgian dramatist who often combines magic, medieval Christianity and the comic and grotesque in his plays, which include farcical tragedies like *Pantagleize* (1929) and *Sire Halewyn* (1934). He became popular in Paris in 1949 when his *Fastes d'enfer* ('Chronicles of hell', 1929) created a scandal, and his reputation has steadily grown since.

LORCA, Federico Garcia (1898–1936). Spanish dramatist and poet, the most widely known of modern Spanish playwrights, whose death in the Civil War was a theatrical tragedy. He made his name with the 'popular ballad' *Mariana Pineda* (1927), about a revolutionary heroine of the 1830s, sacrificed in the name of liberty. After a number of farcical and poetic folk plays, including the 'violent farce' *The Shoemaker's Prodigious Wife* (1930) and other pieces, he ended his short career with three works which made him internationally famous. *Blood Wedding* (1933) is a grim, semi-symbolic, often savage drama of family feuds: a bride runs away with an ex-lover, who is murdered by her husband. *Yerma* (1934) is a passionate play about a childless wife, while *The House of Bernarda Alba* (1936) shows a brutal tyrant of a mother ruling over five frustrated sisters. Despite denouements which are totally defeatist, these plays, all of them peasant tragedies – and the last of them his masterpiece – are perhaps the most successful poetic plays of modern times.

MUNK, Kaj (1898–1944). Danish dramatist and priest whose best known play is *Ordet* ('The Word', 1932) about the power of God in an age of unbelief.

AUDIBERTI, Jacques (1899–1965). French dramatist, poet and novelist whose plays, written opulently, examine good and evil and the flesh and the spirit, using a mixture of satire, comedy, cruelty and philosophy in all of them. His major success was *Le Mal court* ('Evil Runs', 1947), an 18th-century tragi-comedy fairy story, full of both innocence and sensuality.

OLESHA, Yuri (1899–1960). Russian dramatist, and novelist who, having welcomed the Revolution, suffered from official attacks on his work, despite trying to adapt his ideals. His finest play, *A List of Assets* (1931), in which an actress finds neither East nor West capable of understanding Hamlet's nature and problems, was never allowed a production.

COWARD, Noël (1899–1973). English dramatist, composer, lyric-writer, novelist, entertainer and wit. His finest play is perhaps *Private Lives* (1930), the best high comedy in English since Wilde's *The Importance of Being Earnest*. Almost as fine are *Hay Fever* (1925) and *Present Laughter* (1943), while other notable plays are his first and scandalous success, *The Vortex* (1924) with a mother who has affairs and her son on drugs, the popular patriotic hit, *Cavalcade* (1931), *Design for Living* (1932) and *Blithe Spirit* (1941) in which a husband is deliciously haunted by his first wife. None of Coward's post-war plays were as good as these, though some had long runs. His finest musical is *Bitter Sweet* (1929), while his lyrics for shows, revues and cabaret include some which are part of the British heritage.

SALACROU, Armand (b. 1899). French dramatist whose use of a number of styles in a single play has been criticised, as has his easy way of solving serious problems, yet whose dramatic strength and originality has resulted in a number of successes. *The Unknown Woman of Arras* (1935) has a suicide reliving her life, while *La Terre est ronde* (1939), a portrait of a Savonarola, was given at the Comédie Française. More recently, *Sens Interdit* (1953) explores what might happen if time began going backwards.

VITRAC, Roger (1899–1952). French dramatist and poet, a disciple of Alfred Jarry. His *Victor* (1928) anticipates both the Theatre of Cruelty and the Theatre of the Absurd.

CARROLL, Paul Vincent (1900–1968). Irish dramatist, best-known beyond Ireland for *Shadow and Substance* (1937), set in a bigoted and ignorant village. His other plays include *The White Steed* (1939) and *The Strings My Lord Are False* (1942), a tribute to the bombed people of Glasgow where he was a schoolmaster for many years. Many of his plays were produced at Dublin's Abbey Theatre.

DE FILIPPO, Eduardo (b. 1900). Italian dramatist, actor and director, who was born into a theatrical family of Naples. He and his brother, **Peppino** and sister, **Titina**, established *The Company of the Humourous Theatre* (1932), Eduardo writing Neapolitan farces and comedies, and all three making their names as magnificent actors. In 1945, he founded his own company which is now world famous. His finest plays, which show his under-

Eduardo de Fillipo, Italy's greatest living dramatist and a famous director and performer. (*Photo: John Blau*)

standing of the people, and the suffering under the play-acting behind the Naples of legend, include *Napoli Millionaria* ('Millionaire Naples', 1945), *Filumena Marturano* (1946), in which the name-part is one of the finest female creations in Italian drama; *Questi fantasmi* ('These Ghosts', 1946) and *Saturday, Sunday, Monday* (1959), now in the repertoire of Britain's National Theatre.

POGODIN, Nikolai (b. 1900). Russian dramatist, author of a trilogy about Lenin, also *The Aristocrats* (1934), showing prison camps as educational institutions, and the patriotic drama, *Creation of the World* (1946).

ABELL, Kjeld (1901–1961). Danish dramatist whose seriocomic plays, he has said, owe much to Hans Christian Andersen. In one of them, *Days on a Cloud* (1947), a scientist is put into a mythological setting where a witty argument establishes his responsibilities to society.

HORVATH, Odon (1901–1938). Hungarian-born German dramatist, forced to flee from Germany after satirising the Nazis in his best plays, *Italian Night* (1930) and *Stories from the Vienna Woods* (1931) and later works, only to be killed by a falling tree in Paris. In these, and later plays like the comic drama, *Don Juan Returns from War* (1935), he revealed a deep sympathy with the 'little man', a fine sense of the absurd, and a flair for dialogue, all of which are now being rediscovered.

JOHNSTON, Denis (b. 1901). Irish dramatist, author of a number of plays, two of them famous: the satiric *The Old Lady Says No* (1929), and *The Moon on the Yellow River* (1931) about a revolutionary idealist who opposes the erection of a power plant. *The Dreaming Dust* (1940) is about Dean Swift.

VAN DRUTEN, John (1901–1957). Anglo-American dramatist whose many plays include a once-notorious school-story, *Young Woodley* (1928), *The Voice of the Turtle* (1943), *Bell Book and Candle* (1950), an underrated modern witchcraft comedy, and *I am a Camera* (1951), from Isherwood's stories, *Goodbye to Berlin*.

AYMÉ, Marcel (1902–1967). French dramatist and novelist. Though best known for his fiction he has written a number of plays, including a ferocious comedy, *La Tête des Autres* (1952), and the fantasy, *Les Oiseaux de la lune* (1955).

GRIEG, Nordahl (1902–1943). Norwegian dramatist, a Marxist and author of a number of controversial plays admired by Brecht, his finest being *Defeat* (1937), about the Paris Commune of 1871. He got Norway's gold reserves to Britain in 1940, then died in a bombing raid over Berlin.

STEINBECK, John (1902–1968). American dramatist and major novelist, whose finest play, *Of Mice and Men* (1937) is from his novel. He also wrote *The Moon is Down* (1942) and *Burning Bright* (1950).

TARDIEU, Jean (b. 1903). French dramatist and poet, whose usually short plays anticipated the Absurd and Ionesco, then mainly followed Absurdist lines. They include *Qui est la?* (1947), *Faust et Yorick, Conversation Sinfonietta*, etc. He has stated that the loftiest expression of language is silence and in *Les Amants du metro* (1960) he can state: 'I am nothing, you are nothing, there is nothing.' In another play there is no visible actor, just lights on objects – *Une Voix sans personne* (1960).

GREENE, Graham (b. 1904). English dramatist and major novelist whose plays are *The Living Room* (1953), a powerful study of suicide and despair; *The Potting Shed* (1957); *The Complaisant Lover* (1959); and *Carving a Statue* (64), a tragifarce. He and Basil Dean dramatised his *The Heart of the Matter* (1950), and Pierre Bost and Dennis Cannan, his *The Power and the Glory* (1956).

KING, Philip (b. 1904). English dramatist, author of two superb farces, *See How They Run* (1944) and *Sailor, Beware!* (1955), perhaps more a farcical comedy, with Falkland L. Cary. In the latter is the monumental creation, Emma Hornett, the ultimate mother-in-law.

HART, Moss (1904–1961). American dramatist. With George Kaufman he wrote three American comedy classics; *Once in a Lifetime* (1930), *You Can't Take It With You* (1936) and *The Man who came to Dinner* (1939) and other plays; while a later solo success was *Light up the Sky* (1948). He also wrote the book of the musicals, *Face the Music* (1941), and *Lady in the Dark* (1941) which he directed, as he did *My Fair Lady* and *Camelot*. His autobiography (of his early life), *Act I*, is a theatre classic.

HELLMAN, Lillian (b. 1905). American dramatist who has written several scalding, well-constructed dramas, including *The Children's Hour* (1934) about gossip and rumours of lesbianism, which was banned in Britain. Her other plays include the grand melodrama, *The Little Foxes* (1939), the

anti-Nazi *Watch on the Rhine* (1941), *Another Part of the Forest* (1946) and *Toys in the Attic* (1960), a torrid drama set in the South.

SARTRE, Jean-Paul (b. 1905). French dramatist, novelist and philosopher, and a major Existentialist. The theatre has never been his major love, but he has written several major plays: *The Flies* (1942) which has Orestes killing his mother on his own not Apollo's, initiative; *No Exit* (1944), with three characters trapped in a living room which is hell, Sartre's most brilliant play; and *The Condemned of Altona* (1959), set in a post-war German family, but a parable on the use of torture and the war in Algeria. Other plays include *Lucifer and the Lord* (1951), which stresses the absurdity of man and the absence of God, and a political comedy, *Nekrassov* (1955).

WILLIAMS, Emlyn (b. 1905). Welsh dramatist and actor, and author of a number of very fine commercial successes including one of the finest of all chillers, *Night Must Fall* (1935), and the semi-autobiographical *The Corn is Green* (1938).

USIGLI, Rodolfo (b. 1905). Mexican dramatist whose sharp attacks on his countrymen's character and attitudes resemble Bernard Shaw's plays. His two finest dramas are *Crown of Shadows* (1947), and *The Gesticulator* (1947), a searing exposure of the Mexican character and an attack on the way the ideals of the 1910 Revolution were corrupted.

BECKETT, Samuel (b. 1906). Irish dramatist and novelist whose most famous works have been written in French. His most influential play has been his first, *Waiting for Godot* (1953), the foundation stone of the Theatre of the Absurd. It is a tragi-farce about two tramps who await the coming of the mysterious Mr. Godot, who may or may not be God. The play is certainly a comment on man in our time, stranded on his own in what seems a meaningless universe.

Beckett's world is narrow in the extreme, if universal. His plays are poetic and static, also nihilistic, and they have steadily got shorter. After *Godot* came *Endgame* (1957), about a pitiful group living in dustbins in a tower sealed from a dead world, *Krapp's Last Tape* (1958) – he listens to a 30-year-old tape of his life – *Happy Days* (1962) in which a talkative woman is buried in a heap of earth, and *Play* (1963), a three-handed one-acter which is given twice in succession. Audience alienation may grow with the world; the above account may sound like parody, but Beckett's stature is immense.

KINGSLEY, Sidney (b. 1906). American dramatist, whose *Men in White* (1936), a hospital play, won a Pulitzer Prize. His finest play, *Dead End* (1935) is set in New York's slums in the Depression and was called by Brooks Atkinson a raucous tone poem of the modern city.

ODETS, Clifford (1906–1963). American dramatist whose first success, *Waiting for Lefty* (1935), electrified audiences; its six scenes in one act were set against the background of a taxi-drivers' strike, and it inspired American conscience drama. His other plays are *Awake and Sing* (1935), a portrait of a working-class Jewish family, and the famous *Golden Boy* (1937) produced, like the others, by the Group Theater, and with a theme of a young violinist forced into boxing. *The Big Knife* (1949) is an attack on Hollywood, *The Country Girl* (1950; *Winter Journey* in Britain) – is a fine backstage play. Odets disappointed many of his admirers, partly because too much was expected of him.

BUZZATTI, Dino (b. 1907). Italian dramatist and novelist whose *Un Caso clinico* (1953) is a successful Absurdist play.

FRY, Christopher (b. 1907). English dramatist and poet who, with Eliot, but more obviously and attractively, revived poetic drama in Britain after the Second World War. His plays include a delightful one-acter, *A Phoenix Too Frequent* (1946), *The Lady's Not For Burning* (1948), a spring-like medieval play enchanting to all except those who resent its lack of dramatic impetus, the autumnal *Venus Observed* (1950), the Mystery play *A Sleep of Prisoners* (1951) and several more. He has also translated plays from the French, including *Ring Round The Moon* (1950) and *Tiger at the Gates* (1955).

ADAMOV, Arthur (1908–1970). Russian-born French dramatist, at first obsessed with the impossibility of communication and the resulting alienation, which makes him a playwright of the Absurd. His plays from this period include *The Parody* (1947) and *Ping-Pong* (1954), though this shows a growing awareness of politics. His later plays have been influenced by Brecht, including *Paolo Paoli* (1957), which presents the causes of the 1914 war in terms of commerce: the trade on butterflies and ostrich feathers. *Spring 71* (1961) is about the Paris Commune.

ARBUZOV, Alexey (b. 1908). Russian dramatist, author of the very popular *The Irkutsk Story* (1960) and other plays, including *The Promise* (1966) – a moving drama of three adolescents in the siege of Leningrad.

SAROYAN, William (b. 1908). American dramatist whose pleasant one-act *My Heart's in the Highlands* (1939) was followed by his very well-known *The Time of Your Life* (1939), set in a San Francisco honky-tonk. His genial, sentimental optimism has appeared since in other plays, including *The Cave Dwellers* (1957) which is set in an abandoned theatre.

GELINAS, Gratien (b. 1910). French-Canadian dramatist who *Tit-Coq* ('Lil' Cock', 1948) was a landmark in French-Canadian theatre because of its truthful characters and atmosphere, rather than its plot. *Bousille and the Just Ones* (1960) is a popular family melodrama.

GENET, Jean (b. 1909). French dramatist whose years as a professional criminal and jailbird, allied to a bitter upbringing and homosexuality, have produced a number of plays which repudiate ordinary society in a most alarming and impressive way. Conveniently slotted into the Theatre of the Absurd or the Theatre of Cruelty, he is more rightly to be classed as a unique outsider. His world is one of ritual and dreams of fantasies of violence, sex, revenge and power. As for his characters, they reflect his own world. In *Deathwatch* (1947) a murderer dominates a prison cell; in *The Maids* (1947) despised servants turn to murder; in *The Balcony* (1956), the setting is a brothel, with the inmates enacting their fantasies by pretending to be a general, a judge and a bishop – which they become when revolution breaks out. *The Blacks* (1957) has Negroes ritually enacting their treatment at white hands, while *The Screens* (1966) gives Algerian peasants their chance to express their grievances.

ANOUILH, Jean (b. 1910). French dramatist, not only popular (except among some intellectuals) in France, but admired internationally, partly because of his sheer theatrical flair. For all his versatility, his pessimism is always present, not only in his fatalistic *pièces noires*, but in his *pièces grincantes* ('grating'), *pièces brilliantes* and even his *pièces roses*. A standard theme is innocence lost by experience, and many characters say 'No'. All this, plus (often) a romantic aura, has led to many successes. Among them are *Antigone* (black, 1942),

Ring Round the Moon (brilliant, 1947), *Colombe* (brilliant, 1951), *Ardèle* (grating, 1948) and *The Waltz of the Torreadors* (grating, 1952). *The Lark* (1953) is about Joan of Arc, while *Becket* (1959), well-known also as a film, is about Becket and Henry II. Yet another theme which recurs is a play within the play. His plays would, in fact, be very similar if it were not for his extreme inventiveness and skilled craftsmanship.

NAUGHTON, Bill (b. 1910). English dramatist, the most successful of whose regional comedies are *Alfie* (1963) and *Spring and Port Wine* (1964).

FABBRI, Diego (b. 1911). Italian dramatist, author of a number of plays inspired by his religious beliefs. They include *The Knot* (1935) frowned on by the Fascists and rewritten as *The Swamp* (1942), *Inquisition* (1950), *The Seducer* (1951) whose ending he was forced to change by Church pressure, and *Armed Watch* (1956).

FRISCH, Max (b. 1911). Swiss dramatist and poet whose plays are experimental in form, partly influenced by Shaw and Brecht, and usually symbolic, amusing parables – which he often revises. His first play was *Santa Cruz* (1944), a dream play about freedom and marriage. *The Chinese Wall* (1946) farcically shows man's refusal to learn by experience. *When the War was Over* (1949) is mainly a realistic epic set in Russian-occupied Berlin, while his other plays are *Count Oderland* (1951), *Don Juan* (1953), with the hero loving geometry more than women; and his two best-known pieces, *The Fire-Raisers* (1953) and *Andorra* (1962). All dates refer to first versions. *The Fire-Raisers* is a witty satire on bourgeois folly, a parable springing from Benes and the Czechs and Germans who allowed Hitler to thrive, while *Andorra* is a moving play about anti-semitism.

HOCHWALDER, Fritz (b. 1911). Swiss dramatist born in Vienna, whose best known plays include *The Strong are Lonely* (1943) and *The Public Prosecutor* (1949), both historical dramas.

RATTIGAN, Terence (b. 1911). English dramatist, author of a number of immensely popular, very well-made comedies and dramas. Critical attacks in the '60s made it seem that he would abandon the theatre, but he has returned – and his first colossal hit, *French Without Tears* (1936), was revived by the Young Vic (1973). Other plays include the excellent *Winslow Boy* (1946), based on the Archer-Shee scandal, *The Browning Version* (1948),

a one-act tragedy about a failed schoolmaster, and his most famous play, *The Deep Blue Sea* (1952), called by Tynan a 'searing study of the destructive zeal of love'. *Separate Tables* (1954) was another hit, and *Ross* (1960) is a successful study of Lawrence of Arabia; his most recent work is *In Praise of Love* (1973).

ROUSSIN, André (b. 1911). French dramatist whose comedies and farces include *The Little Hut* (1947) and *Nina* (1949).

WILLIAMS, Tennessee (b. 1911). American dramatist, whose first success was *The Glass Menagerie* (1945), a wistful autobiographical play. His next-produced play is his most famous, *A Streetcar named Desire* (1947), whose lyric qualities and searing ferocity proclaimed an exceptional talent. *Summer and Smoke* (1948) has a theme of loneliness, plus the Williams 'eternally baleful female' (Howard Taubman). This very creative writer continued with *The Rose Tattoo* (1951), *Camino Real* (1953) and *Cat on a Hot Tin Roof* (1955), a study of non-communication on a Southern plantation. *Orpheus Descending* (1957) was a reworking of *Battle of Angels*, set in a Southern lynching area; *Suddenly Last Summer* (1958) is horrifying and atmospheric; *Sweet Bird of Youth* (1959) is about an aging film star and a gigolo and has a castration as its climax. There followed the comedy, *Period of Adjustment* (1961) and the sultry, eerie *Night of the Iguana* (1962); then the authentic Williams genius did not reappear until *Small Craft Warnings* (1972). His plays are lyrical, often cruel, sensuous and sometimes savage, while his theatrical sense and atmospheric powers are usually masterly. Even when he sometimes repels, the effect is still hypnotic, and he ranks, with Arthur Miller, as the finest American dramatist since O'Neill.

DENNIS, Nigel (b. 1912). English dramatist, novelist and critic whose witty plays, in Shavian and Voltairean mould, have as some of their main targets religion and psychoanalysis. They include *Cards of Identity* (1956) from his novel, *The Making of Moo* (1957) in which a Colonial official invents a religion, and *August for the People* (1961) a study of power and publicity.

HOME, William Douglas (b. 1912). Scottish-born dramatist, author of many commercial successes, mainly comedies – *The Reluctant Debutante* (1955), etc. – but some serious, like his prison drama *Now Barabbas* (1960).

IONESCO, Eugene (b. 1912). Rumanian-born dramatist who writes in French, and who is a leading playwright of the Absurd, expressing it through absurd images. He moved to France in 1936 and the flat platitudes of an English primer inspired him to write a 'tragedy of language' about the difficulty of communicating in words. It was the one-act *La Cantatrice chauve* (1948), translated as *The Bald Prima Donna* (Britain) and *The Bald Soprano* (U.S.A.); in it, characters from an English language manual come to life in a very funny 'parody of a play'. *The Lesson* (1950) is another one-act language play in which a professor rapes and kills a pupil: now Ionesco was going in for shock tactics and extreme audience alienation. *Jack* (1950) is a one-act parody of bourgeois conformity, *The Future is in Eggs* (1951) a one-act attack on proliferation, while *The Chairs* (1951), again in one act, is a brilliant study in non-communication, with a husband and wife entertaining invisible guests on empty chairs.

After Victims of Duty (1952) Ionesco switched to full length plays including *Amédée* (1953) about a growing corpse which symbolises a couple's dead love. Several plays about a little man called Bérenger followed, including *Rhinoceros* (1958) in which all the townsfolk turn into these aggressive animals except Bérenger, in a fine symbol of the dangers of conformity. *Exit the King* (1961) has King Bérenger with only his fortitude left to him. He also appears in two later plays, *A Stroll in the Air* (1963) and *Hunger and Thirst* (1966). Ionesco has also written other one-act plays, and many consider his shorter pieces his finest because of the brilliant concentration on a single image. Yet the fortitude shown in *Exit the King* and *Rhinoceros* are in moving contrast to his earlier nihilism. His influence has been colossal.

RODRIGUES, Nélson (b. 1912). Brazilian dramatist and novelist who has moved from plays modelled on the Greeks, including a chorus, to often – searing studies of life in Rio de Janeiro. His *The Wedding Dress* (1943) in which he examined the subconscious mind of a guilt-stricken woman, made his name.

CAMUS, Albert (1913–1960). French dramatist, novelist, philosopher and major literary figure, born in Algiers, where he founded Le Théâtre du Travail. His plays include *The Misunderstanding* (1945), about the absurdity of existence – he was a founding father of the Absurd – and *Caligula* (1945)

based on the Roman monster emperor who is shown challenging the absurdity of existence by indulging in total immorality and cruelty with a chillingly mad sanity. *State of Siege* (1948) from his novel, *La Peste*, and created with Jean-Louis Barrault, was an allegory and an attempt at total theatre which failed; while *The Just Assassins* (1949) is a tragedy of conscience. He also adapted plays, including Dostoyevsky's *The Devils* (1958), as *Les Possedes*.

INGE, William (1913–1973). American dramatist whose atmospheric small-town dramas include *Come Back, Little Sheba* (1950), *Picnic* (1953), *Bus Stop* (1955) and *The Dark at the Top of the Stairs* (1957). All were filmed.

DAVIES, Robertson (b. 1913). Canadian dramatist, the most performed native playwright, whose plays include a one-act backwoods comedy, *Overlaid* (1948) and *At My Heart's Core* (1950), set in 1837 but with modern Canadian undertones.

ROZOV, Victor (b. 1913). Russian dramatist, many of whose successes have been about the problems of the young, notably *Uneven Combat* (1961).

SHAW, Irwin (b. 1913). American dramatist, author of two fiery plays, the anti-war *Bury the Dead* (1936) and *Siege* (1937), set in the Spanish Civil War. The 'fairy tale', *The Gentle People* (1939) has a racketeer overthrown by two old men.

DUNCAN, Ronaald (b. 1914). British dramatist and poet whose best-known play is the religious mansque, *This Way to the Tomb* (1945).

DURAS, Marguerite (b. 1914). French dramatist and novelist, author of several naturalist plays, notable for their dialogue and examination of feeling. *La Musica* (1966) showed the agony of parting, while *Days in the Trees* (1966) explores a love-hate relationship between a mother and her son, the strongly drawn mother being a superb part for a major actress. *Suzanna Andler* is a tremendous study of an unsatisfied woman, while *The Lovers of Viorne* is a searing study of the motive for a murder.

FIGUEIREDO, Guilherme (b. 1915). Brazilian dramatist whose plays include *Greve geral* ('General Strike', 1949), based on Lysistrata, and *Um deus dormiu là em casa* ('A God Slept There at Home', 1949), based on a classical theme and about Alcmene who is too sophisticated to believe in the gods. *The She Fox and the Grapes* (1952) is based on Aesop.

MILLER, Arthur (b. 1915). American dramatist, with Tennessee Williams the finest of the post-War years. His works reflect a strong social conscience, partly due to his having been brought up in the Depression era, and also explore personal and family relationships. He is greatly concerned with the individual's responsibilities, and his admiration of Ibsen is admitted and evident, as in his first big success, *All My Sons* (1947); this fine play examines war profiteering and personal guilt in a family setting.

Death of a Salesman (1948), his finest play and a great one, has as its pitiful hero Willy Loman, an aging salesman thrown aside because he is failing to sell. The construction, including use of flashbacks, is as masterly as it is lethal, and all the main characters are memorably drawn. Though Willy is a little man, sorry for himself, Miller turns his story into tragedy. Miller adapted *An Enemy of the People* (1950), then wrote *The Crucible* (1953) about the Salem witch hunts, but drawing modern parallels. There followed *A View from the Bridge* (1955), *A Memory of Two Sundays* (1955), *After the Fall* (1964) an autobiographical play about Miller's marriage to Marilyn Monroe, *Incident at Vichy* (1968) a very powerful look at the way the Nazi persecution of the Jews could happen, and *The Price* (1968) a study of two brothers which was more admired abroad than at home. Since then this master craftsman has almost abandoned the theatre except for one lesser play, *The Creation of the World and Other Business* (1972).

WHITING, John (1915–1963). British dramatist and actor who died just as he had reached major status. His early works include a farcical fantasy, *A Penny for a Song* (1951), set in Dorset in Napoleonic times, and *Saint's Day* (1951), on which he had worked many years, a symbolic piece about an old, self-exiled revolutionary, with a theme of self-destruction. *Marching Song* (1954) is another play on the same theme. His last play, *The Devils* (1961), based on Aldous Huxley's *The Devils of Loudon*, about demonic possession among 17th-century nuns, is his finest. An examination of superstition and conscience, it is literate, poignant and very powerful.

TANNER, Haldun (b. 1916). Turkish dramatist influenced by comic and satirical trands from the Greeks to Brecht. His plays, some of which ran into political trouble, include the popular *The*

Ballad of Ali of Keshan (1964).

WEISS, Peter (b. 1916). German dramatist, now living in Sweden, whose first full-length play was *The Persecution and Assassination of Marat as Performed by the Inmates of the Asylum of Charenton under the Direction of the Marquis de Sade* (1964); this violent, strange, comic example of the Theatre of Cruelty, a classic example of 'director's theatre', was followed by *The Investigation* (1965) an 'oratorio' about Auschwitz and responsibility for Nazi atrocities. A Marxist, Weiss followed this with *The Song of the Lusitanian Bogey* (1969) about the Portuguese in Angola.

LOWELL, Robert (b. 1917). American dramatist and poet, author of *The Old Glory* (1967), a trilogy of verse plays from stories by Melvile and Hawthorne, but with contemporary implications. *Prometheus Bound* (1971) is an adaptation of Aeschylus.

MOSSENSON, Yigal (b. 1917). Israeli dramatist and novelist, author of realistic, contemporary plays, including *Kazablan* (1954) about the relations between Western and Oriental Jews.

ASPENSTRÖM, Werner (b. 1918). Swedish dramatist and poet, author of modern allegories with social comment, notably *The Apes Shall Inherit The Earth* (1959); in this Apes take a look at what the world was like using projectors and tape recorders.

MARQUÉS, René (b. 1919). Puerto Rican dramatist whose themes include liberty and love of the land and preserving his country's heritage. His plays include *The Ox Cart* (1953).

SIMPSON, N. F. (b. 1919). English dramatist whose plays of the Absurd include *A Resounding Tinkle* (1957) and his finest, *One Way Pendulum* (1959), whose main theme is the tyranny of things; a famous feature is a character teaching weighing machines to sing the Hallelujah Chorus.

KARVAS, Peter (b. 1920). Slovakian dramatist, the most important to appear since 1945. A socialist thinker, his most successful play is *The Midnight Mass* (1959), part allegory, part realism, in which the heroism of the 1945 uprising is extolled and the rôle of the modern bourgeoisie deplored.

MEGED, Aharon (b. 1920). Polish-born Israeli dramatist and novelist whose two major plays, *Genesis* (1962) and *The Busy Season* (1967), use the Bible for modern themes.

VIAN, Boris (1920–1959). French dramatist, novel-

The Piccolo Theatre of Milan's production of Weiss's Marat-Sade in 1967, with Charlotte Corday about to strike. (Photo: Italian Institute, London)

ist, actor, etc., whose finest play is the Absurdist *The Empire Builders* (1959). A disciple of Alfred Jarry.

BORCHERT, Wolfgang (1921–1947). German dramatist, whose only play, *Draussen von der Tür* ('The Man Outside', 1947), was the first major German play written after the Second World War. It is an Everyman tragedy in surrealistic form and portrays the devastation of a country as it affects a returning infantryman.

DURRENMATT, Friedrich (b. 1921). Swiss dramatist and novelist, who admits to being inspired by the Greeks, Shakespeare and Swift. His plays are ambiguous, ironic and concerned with corruption, power and death, and are gloomy, detached and skilfully constructed. They include *Romulus the Great* (1949, revised 1957) a satire about the last Roman Emperor and decadence; also a black comedy of modern life, *The Marriage of Mr. Mississippi* (1952); and his two best-known plays, *The Visit* (1955) and *The Physicists* (1962). In the first, an old millionairess returns home and buys the villagers to be avenged on an old lover, the playwright achieving suspense while satirising greed, hypocrisy and the media, present in force for the death sentence. *The Physicists* has a leading character who hides in an asylum to prevent the secret of the hydrogen bomb leaking out. It is a statement on society and the problem of avoiding the consequences of discoveries. *The Meteor* (1966) is a portrait of an egotistical dramatist seeking death but not succeeding.

SHAMIR, Moshe (b. 1921). Israeli dramatist and novelist, whose mainly realistic plays include *The House of Hilliel* (1950) about kibbutz life.

USTINOV, Peter (b. 1921). English dramatist, actor, entertainer and talker, whose plays include *The Love of Four Colonels* (1951), a realistic piece turned fantasy, with hilarious pastiches of Shakespeare, Molière, Chekhov and American local drama, and *Romanoff and Juliet* (1956), a delightful political fairy story. The other plays of this versatile man of the theatre are never less than interesting, especially the amusing *The Unknown Soldier and his Wife* (1968).

KIPPHARDT, Heinar (b. 1922). German dramatist whose best-known documentary plays, owing something to Brecht, are *The General's Dog* (1962), about an unpunished crime; *Joel Brand: the History of a Deal* (1965), about Eichmann and his conse-

quences; and, internationally well-known, *In The Matter of J. Robert Oppenheimer* (1964) about 'the father of the atom bomb' and his suspension for security reasons.

LAWLER, Ray (b. 1922). Australian dramatist whose best play is *Summer of the Seventeenth Doll* (1955), a realistic, tough, understanding look at an aging sugar-cane cutter.

BEHAN, Brendan (1923–1964). Irish dramatist whose first play, *The Quare Fellow* (1954) is a powerful tragi-comedy set in an Ulster prison. *The Hostage* (1956) is a brilliant comedy set in a brothel which is an I.R.A. post.

CHAYEFSKY, Paddy (b. 1923). American dramatist whose plays include *The Latent Heterosexual* (1968), a serio-comic satirical look at a poet, which starts as a spoof on homosexuality and drugs, and ends as a comment on the effect of Big Business on people.

DAGERMAN, Stig (1923–1954). Swedish dramatist, whose plays include *The Condemned* (1947), about the absurd nature of justice, pictured in expressionist terms, and not unlike the styles of Strindberg and Kafka.

MORTIMER, John (b. 1923). English dramatist notable for his characterisation and dialogue, especially in *The Dock Brief* (1957) and *Lunch Hour* (1960), both one-acters. His most impressive play is the autobiographical *A Journey Round my Father* (1970), while his most amusing is *Collaborators* (1973).

BOLT, Robert (b. 1924). British dramatist and a master of the historical play, most notably, *A Man for All Seasons* (1960) about Sir Thomas More. Another success was *Vivat! Vivat Regina* (1970), a slightly less deep study of Elizabeth I and Mary, Queen of Scots. Other plays include *A Flowering Cherry* (1957), a study in failure; *The Tiger and the Horse* (1960) and *Gentle Jack* (1963). His *The Thwarting of Baron Bolligrew* (1966) is a rare example of a good play for children.

BOWEN, John (b. 1924). English dramatist and novelist whose plays include *After the Rain* (1967) from his novel, about flood survivors on a raft, and their re-enactment of history.

GATTI, Armand (b. 1924). French dramatist of politically slanted plays, including *Public Song for Two Electric Chairs* (1966), about the Sacco and Vanzetti case in the U.S.A.

ATAY, Cahit (b. 1925). Turkish dramatist whose plays of village life, notably the satirical, delightful *In Ambush* (1962).

SAUNDERS, James (b. 1925). English dramatist who, after being influenced by Ionesco, wrote *Next Time I'll Sing To You* (1963), *A Scent of Flowers* (1964) which is a moving tragi-comedy, *Neighbours* (1967) and *Games after Liverpool* (1972). His later plays have reminded some of Pirandello.

YUKIO, Mishima (b. 1925). Japanese dramatist, author of modern *noh* dramas, set in an urban mechanised world.

ALONI, Nissim (b. 1926). Israeli dramatist whose work is unusually experimental in form and theme by native standards. His *Emperor's New Clothes* (1961) is the Hans Andersen story in Theatre of the Absurd terms.

OWEN, Alun (b. 1926). English dramatist, whose plays include *Progress in the Park* (1959), a Liverpool love story against a background of parental hostility and racial and religious tension; and *The Rough and Ready Lot* (1959), an historical play about mercenaries in South America in the 1860s.

REANEY, James (b. 1926). Canadian dramatist, author of original and striking small-town Ontario dramas, notable for their imagery, though sometimes not entirely stageworthy. *The Killdeer* (1960) is one of his finest.

SHAFFER, Peter (b. 1926). English dramatist who made his name with the realistic family drama, *Five Finger Exercise* (1958). Since then, his plays have included *The Royal Hunt of the Sun* (1964) a fine epic about the conquest of Peru, the very funny *Black Comedy* (1965) and the fine, thought-provoking *Equus* (1973). His brother, **Anthony Shaffer** (b. 1926) wrote the masterly thriller, *Sleuth* (1970).

BILLETDOUX, Francois (b. 1927). French dramatist whose first full-length play was *Tchin-Tchin* (1959) about an adulterous couple who take to the bottle. *Chez Thorpe* (1961) examines the impossibility of love and communication, while *Il faut passer par les nuages* ('You Must Pass through the Clouds', 1966) is a striking study of a rich old lady.

GRASS, Günther (b. 1927). German dramatist and novelist whose early plays were Theatre of the Absurd. These include *The Wicked Cooks* (1961), a caricature glimpse of political leaders as cooks busily wrecking the world; also *The Plebians Re-hearse the Uprising* (1966), a sceptical look at Brecht and his company in relation to the East Berlin workers' uprising on 1953.

JELLICOE, Ann (b. 1927). English dramatist and director. Her first play was *The Sport of My Mad Mother* (1956), an emotional, violent, ritualistic and symbolic look at an East End gang of adolescents and their leader, and mother-figure, Greta. Her best known play is *The Knack* (1961) – of getting the girl. Other plays include *Shelley* (1965), a study of the poet.

NICHOLS, Peter (b. 1927). English dramatist who made his name with *A Day in the Life of Joe Egg* (1967), a comic but sensitive look at a marriage when the only child is a spastic. *The National Health* (1969) is a tragicomedy set in a hospital ward, while *Forget-me-not Lane* (1971) is semi-autobiographical look at the author's childhood in the war. *Chez Nous* (1974).

SIMON, Neil (b. 1927). American dramatist, author of many popular situation comedies, including *Barefoot in the Park* (1963), *The Odd Couple* (1965) and *The Prisoner of Second Avenue*, also *The Sunshine Boys* (1972), about an aging ex-vaudeville pair.

ALBEE, Edward (b. 1928). American dramatist who first became known with *The Zoo Story* (1958), a lurid, Absurdist one-acter. A wide-ranging satirist, after his *The Death of Bessie Smith* (1959) and the stunning *The American Dream* (1961), he moved to Broadway from Off-Broadway with his famous *Who's Afraid of Virginia Woolf?* (1962), a passionate study, as ferocious and intense as Strindberg, of a domestic conflict which Brooks Atkinson called a contemptuous cartoon of marriage. Other plays include *The Ballad of the Sad Café* (1963) from the story by Carson McCullers; *Tiny Alice* (1964) a difficult metaphysical melodrama with its leading part a mixture of Christ, Faust and Job; and *A Delicate Balance* (1966), a grim portrait of relationships which have crumbled, leaving only a display of polite manners. Albee's especial talents lie in his waspish dialogue and flair for dramatic incident.

MARCUS, Frank (b. 1928). English dramatist and critic, whose plays include the very successful *The Killing of Sister George* (1965), an amusing, tolerant look at relationships, as in *Mrs. Mouse, are you Within?* (1968). Like the others, *Notes on a Love Affair* (1972) centres around women.

MERCER, David (b. 1928). English dramatist, author of *Ride a Cock Horse* (1965), *Belcher's Luck* (1966), *After Hagerty* (1970) and *Flint* (1970). This controversial playwright has turned from Marxism towards concern for the individual in his plays, the most appealing of which to date is *Flint*, a farcical-comedy melodrama, with its improbable hero an agnostic, lecherous vicar. *Duck Song* (1974).

AGAOGLU, Adalet (b. 1929). Turkish dramatist whose *Let's Play House* (1964) was a breakthrough, farcically dealing for the first time about repressive Turkish sexual mores.

CAGAN, Sermet (b. 1929). Turkish dramatist, author of politically orientated plays of ideas, including his country's most Brechtian play, *The Feet and the Legs Factory* (1964).

FEIFFER, Jules (b. 1929). American dramatist and cartoonist whose best-known plays are *Little Murders* (1967), satirising man's fascination with violence and war; and *God Bless* (1968), set in 'the immediate future with America fighting on three continents'.

FRIEL, Brian (b. 1929). Irish dramatist whose finest work is perhaps *Philadelphia, Here I Come* (1964), about non-communication against the situation of a young man soon to emigrate to the U.S.A.

HALL, Willis (b. 1929). English dramatist who wrote the fine war play, *The Long and the Short and the Tall* (1958) and collaborated with **Keith WATERHOUSE** (b. 1929) in the very entertaining *Billy Liar* (1960).

LIVINGS, Henry (b. 1929). English dramatist and actor, author of a number of very funny, realistic and sometimes fantastical farces and comedies, usually about accident- and disaster-prone 'little men' who challenge and defeat Authority. They are usually North Country working class in background. His plays include *Stop it, Whoever You Are* (1960) about a lavatory attendant's adventures; *Big Soft Nellie* (1961) who is a mother's boy; *Nil Carborundum* (1962), an R.A.F. farce; *Eh?* (1964) about an underdog who wrecks a factory; and *Honour and Offer* (1969). He has also written short Lancashire folk comedies called *Pongo Plays* (1971).

OSBORNE, John (b. 1929). English dramatist whose *Look Back in Anger* (1956) brought about a still-continuing revival in British drama and 'saved the English theatre from death through gentility' (Angus Wilson). Its abrasive anti-hero, witty, brutal and eloquent, became a national figure. There followed an earlier-written play, *Epitaph for George Dillon* (1956), written with Anthony Creighton, and *The Entertainer* (1957) a very theatrical piece, with the central rôle a third-rate music hall comic, Archie Rice, and a central theme of England in decay. *Luther* (1961) was a big success, as was *Inadmissable Evidence* (1964) about a solicitor in the process of disintegrating. *A Patriot for Me* (1965) is a magnificent drama about an historical Austro-Hungarian homosexual officer blackmailed into spying, against a panoramic view of a period.

A constant sub-theme in most Osborne plays is nostalgia for a vanished – Edwardian – England, and this, plus a growing objectivity and disappearance of Porter-like rebels, has seen him under increasing critical attack. Yet *Time Present* (1968), *The Hotel in Amsterdam* (1968) and, especially, *West of Suez* (1971) evoke moods which many find enthralling. His theatrical flair and ability to write good parts for actors and, more than formerly, actresses, is undisputed by most. *A Sense of Detachment* (1972), a Pirandelloesque look at today's problems, had his critics out in force.

ARDEN, John (b. 1930). English dramatist, author of perhaps the finest post-1956 British play, the 'historical parable', *Sergeant Musgrave's Dance* (1959). Set in a mining town around 1880, and about deserters led by Musgrave who is determined to ram home his exposé of war's horrors by an atrocity of his own (a modern event in Cyprus inspired Arden), it typifies the author's hatred of violence, but also his refusal to load the dice too much on one side. Using Brechtian means (song and dance) he creates a believable world, but unlike too many Brechtians, he realises the complexity of man and his environment and times.

Arden's later plays include *Live Like Pigs* (1958) about life on a housing estate, *The Happy Haven* (1960), *The Workhouse Donkey* (1963) about power and corruption in local government, and *Armstrong's Last Goodnight* (1964), a political Border Ballad. *Left-Handed Liberty* (1965) concerns Magna Carta, and *The Hero Rises Up* (1968), with his wife, **Margaretta d'Arcy**, is about Nelson. Their *The Island of the Mighty* (1972) was a much criticised Arthurian play.

Harold Pinter's The Caretaker *with (left to right) Peter, Donald Pleasance and Alan Bates. (Photo: Michael Boys)*

DUBÉ, Marcel (b. 1930). French-Canadian dramatist, author of many plays including *A Simple Soldier* (1958), a comedy about a discharged soldier and his divided family.

PINTER, Harold (b. 1930). English dramatist, master of the pause, hidden menace, jockeying for position in relationships and the 'irrationality of dialogue', as Ronald Hayman has called it. Unlike other members of the Theatre of the Absurd into which he has been tidily slotted, his power over an audience is total. Unlike most writers, he does not claim to know everything about his characters, simply what happens to them on stage. His early plays are mainly about working class folk; his later ones, more sophisticated and more sexual, but all are in part ambiguous, disturbing, complex, simple and dreamlike, also often very funny.

His plays include *The Room* (1957), the more menacing *The Dumb Waiter* (1957), *The Birthday Party* (1958) now widely regarded as one of his finest plays, and *The Caretaker* (1960) with two famous characters, Ashton, who has been given shock treatment, and Davies, the tramp. *A Slight Ache* (1961) and the more realistic *A Night Out* (1961) followed, also *The Collection* (1962), the masterly *The Lovers* (1963), and the very successful *The Homecoming* (1965). Other plays include *Landscape* and *Silence* (1969), the first a husband and wife reminiscing, the second, a Beckettian trio in a void. *The Basement* and *The Tea Party* (1970) were transferred from television.

HOCHHUTH, Rolf (b. 1931). German dramatist, author of historical plays of fact, including *The Representative* (1963), an attack on Pope Pius's failure to protest about Nazi treatment of the Jews. His *Soldiers* (1968), with its main theme of the atrocity of large scale bombing, and a remarkable portrait of Churchill, became notorious for the author's allegations that Churchill connived at the death of his Polish ally, Sikorski. As Hochhuth refused to reveal his sources, his play's reputation suffered badly.

FUGARD, Athol (b. 1932). South African dramatist and director of a theatre group. *The Blood Knot* (1966) is a fine play about two Cape Coloured brothers, one of whom tries to pass as white. *People are Living Here* (1970). His company gave three more of his plays at the Royal Court (1974).

GELBER, Jack (b. 1932). American dramatist, author of *The Connection* about drug addicts. Other plays include *Square in the Eye* (1965).

TERSON, Peter (b. 1932). English dramatist, noted for writing convincingly, sympathetically and exuberantly about young people. His plays include *Zigger-Zagger* (1967), *The Apprentices* (1968) and *Good Lads at Heart* (1971), and most have been for Michael Croft of the National Youth Theatre and for Peter Cheesman, director of the Victoria, Stoke-on-Trent, who notes Terson's gift for writing 'in a way that is both very funny and profoundly serious at the same time'.

WESKER, Arnold (b. 1932). English dramatist who made his name with a trilogy about a Jewish family from 1936–59, *Chicken Soup with Barley* (1958), *Roots* (1959), his most famous play in which the family does not appear on stage, and *I'm Talking about Jerusalem* (1960). *The Kitchen* (1959) is the world and humanity in (brilliant) terms of a day in a restaurant kitchen, while *Chips with Everything* (1962) is the world in robot-guise in terms of an R.A.F. station, and is both powerful and funny. Later, more controversial, plays have included *The Four Seasons* (1965), *Their Very Own Golden City* (1966) and *The Friends* (1970), a disillusioned piece. *The Old Ones* (1972) is a warmly-drawn portrait of a Jewish family. Wesker's earlier – most famous – plays saw him almost too involved in his characters, though their idealism is convincing, and they are never one-dimensional. Not until *Chips with Everything* did detachment appear, though without loss of feeling and vigour.

WOOD, Charles (b. 1932). English dramatist, many of whose plays express a love-hate relationship with the Army, including *Cockade* (1963) and *Dingo* (1967) a violent, farcical attack on Jingoism and the effects of fighting and war on individuals, whose impact was diminished by the statement that the Second World War was fought 'for all the usual reasons'. *Fill The Stage with Happy Hours* (1963) is a grim backstage comedy. *H* (1969) is about Havelock's march on Cawnpore and Lucknow in the Indian Mutiny, which uses Brechtian methods and is all the better for not being one-sided. *Veterans* (1972) is an ironic glimpse of filming on location, inspired by Wood's work on *The Charge of the Light Brigade*. His great potential remains unfulfilled at the time of writing.

ARRABAL, Fernando (b. 1933). French dramatist, born in Spanish Morocco, whose experience of cruelty has helped him create a world full of it and of innocence. His plays include the anti-military satire *Picnic on the Battlefield* (1959), *The Car Cemetery* (1959) a very black comedy, and a 'shock-drama' *The Communicant* (1966). He is a most pessimistic writer of the Absurd. His best known play is *The Architect and the Emperor of Assyria* (1971), a tense and shattering two-hander set on a desert island, with the two protagonists acting out sado-masochistic fantasies.

ORTON, Joe (1933–1969). English dramatist, whose farces and black comedies make up for lack of characterisation by their brilliant dialogue and inventive, grisly plots. They include *Entertaining Mr. Sloane* (1964), *Loot* (1966), a black farce about a splendidly corrupt group of people, and *What the Butler Saw* (1969). Orton admitted to being influenced by a heady mixture, Strindberg and Ben Travers.

STOREY, David (b. 1933). English dramatist and novelist, whose wide-ranging plays are exceptionally and realistically detailed, but do not flaunt their themes. As he has written, 'all the options are open'. *The Restoration of Arnold Middleton* (1967), about a clowning schoolmaster who is going mad, has a recurring theme of mental trouble. *In Celebration* (1969) looks powerfully at the problem of the educated children of a working class family, while *The Contractor* (1969) dramatises work – erecting and dismantling a wedding reception tent. *Home* (1970) is, we gradually see, set in a mental home and may be about the decline of life and hope, or the decline of Britain, or both, while *The Changing Room* (1971) is an astonishing realistic tour-de-force about before, during and after a Rugby League football match. *Cromwell* (1973), an epic drama set in Cromwell's time but not about him, has themes of puritan idealism and spiritual hopes against a background of yesterday's – and today's – conflicts. *The Farm* (1973) is closer to *In Celebration* in its absorbing study of a family whose climax is a rejection by the son of the house of farm, family, society – and England? Opinions vary sharply as to Storey's stature, but none deny his major talent.

BENNETT, Alan (b. 1934). English dramatist and satirist, whose sharp, entertaining plays include *Forty Years On* (1968), *Getting On* (1971) and *Habeas Corpus* (1973).

SOYINKA, Wole (b. 1934). Nigerian dramatist, possibly the finest in Africa, whose plays are modern in subject, but ritually patterned. His finest is *A Dance of the Forest* (1963), a symbolic study of Nigeria past and present, written for the country's independence.

BOND, Edward (b. 1935). English dramatist whose plays include *Saved* (1965), *Early Morning* (1968), *Narrow Road to the Deep North Sea* (1968), *Black Mass* (1968), *Lear* (1971) and *The Sea* (1972). Apart from voicing beliefs shared by many about war, violence breeding violence and the grim situation of modern industrial man, he is obsessively convinced that all authority (Society, State, Church) is the ultimate evil, which seems like anarchy carried to extreme lengths. In *Narrow Road*, a play set in 17th-century Japan, he solves this by presenting man free of authority, naked, unafraid and re-born. Yet as his concept of mankind is at least partly a violent one, his outlook is bleak. He uses shock tactics (as in his re-working of *Lear*) but for some the result is counter--productive. His power however, and his major talent, was evident to many early in his career, especially abroad, some recognising that *Saved*, which uses

Ralph Richardson and John Gielgud in David Storey's Home. (*Photo: Peggy Leder*)

the language of the inarticulate and has a notorious baby-murder scene, has true compassion. If many consider his methods sometimes misfire, no one would deny the value of his work. In *Bingo* (1973) Bond looks at Shakespeare.

McGRATH, John (b. 1935). English dramatist, author of two notable plays, *Events while Guarding the Bofors Gun* (1966) and *Bakke's Night of Fame* (1968), and the striking triple-bill, *Plugged-in* (1972). A committed radical socialist playwright.

RICHARDSON, Jack (b. 1935). American dramatist who came of the fore Off-Broadway in the 1960s. Much more articulate than most modern playwrights, he has been characterised by Milton Levin as like Shaw in his wit, but closer to Giraudoux and Anouilh in his tone of ironic disenchantment. His plays include *The Prodigal* (1960) in which he uses the Orestes story, *Gallows Humour* (1961), two related prison plays, and *Lorenzo* (1963), set in Renaissance Italy and concerning strolling players caught up in a war.

TOPOL, Josef (b. 1935). Czech dramatist, a leading spokesman for the younger generation of his countrymen. His most-admired play is *The End of Shrovetide* (1963), in which major questions of life and death are discussed against a background of a small-town carnival. The socialist standard bearers are shown as complicated, less-than-perfect humans, not ideal people.

GRAY, Simon (b. 1936). English dramatist and novelist, whose plays include *Wise Child* (1967), *Dutch Uncle* (1968) and the witty, brilliant *Butley* (1971).

HAVEL, Vaclav (b. 1936). Czech dramatist whose *The Garden Party*, a satirical attack on middle-class relations and attitudes, was the first major drama of the Absurd in Czech.

ZINDEL, Paul (b. 1936). American dramatist, whose much-acclaimed *The Effect of Gamma Rays on Man-in-the-Moon Marigolds* (1970), a grim but compassionate picture of family life, won a Pulitzer Prize. It was followed by *And Miss Readon Drinks a Little* (1971).

STOPPARD, Tom (b. 1937). English dramatist whose entertaining *Rosencrantz and Guildenstern are Dead* (1966) is a *Godot*-like view of *Hamlet* with the vaguely-drawn pair as the heroes, and with their scenes with Hamlet incorporated into the play. *Enter a Free Man* (1968) and *The Real Inspector Hound* (1968) followed, then came a 'stark, raving sane' play (John Barber), *Jumpers* (1972) set in a crazy future and featuring an aging philosophy don and his ex-show business wife. It is a hilarious tribute to irrationality.

HAMPTON, Christopher (b. 1946). English dramatist whose plays include the very successful 'bourgeois comedy', *The Philanthropist*, and *Savages* (1973) a passionate, tense study of Brazilian politics, the treatment of her Indians and the meaning and effectiveness of liberalism.

HARE, David (b. 1947). English dramatist whose excellent *Slag* (1971) was followed by *The Great Exhibition* (1972) parodying all Royal Court plays and, with Howard Benton, *Brassneck* (1973).

Peggy Ashcroft as Queen Margaret and Donald Sinden as York in Peter Hall's production of The Wars of the Roses *at Stratford in 1963. (Photo: British Tourist Authority)*

79

CHAPTER 3
PLAYERS
i~English-Speaking

John Barrymore, whose virtual abandonment of the stage after his famous Hamlet helped kill the tradition of American classical acting. (Photo: Author's Collection)

ABINGTON, Frances (1737–1815). English actress, the first Lady Teazle. Reynolds painted her as Miss Prue in *Love for Love*.

ACHURCH, Janet (1864–1916). English actress and tragedienne, the first to play Ibsen's Nora in Britain. She excelled in Ibsen and Shaw.

ADAMS, Maude (1872–1953). Very popular American actress, renowned for her work in Shakespeare and Barrie. Triumphed aged five as Little Schneider in *Fritz*.

AINLEY, Henry (1879–1945). English actor, potentially a great one until drink took its toll, renowned for his looks and voice. His Hamlet and romantic leads were less interesting than his Malvolio – for Granville Barker (1912) – and Hassan (1923).

ALDRIDGE, Ira (1804–1867). Black American actor known as 'the African Roscius'. His parts included Lear, Macbeth and Othello, which he once played opposite Edmund Kean. He rarely acted in America, and was particularly successful in Britain and Germany.

ALEXANDER, Sir George (1858–1918). Popular English actor-manager who began with Irving. For many years he ruled the St. James's where he encouraged British dramatists including Wilde. His most famous success was in *The Prisoner of Zenda*, playing Rudolf and the King.

ALLEYN, Edward (1566–1626). England's first great actor, also a shrewd manager and the founder of Dulwich College. He starred in Marlowe's great rôles, including Tamburlaine, and was only excelled (one may assume) by Burbage.

ALLGOOD, Sara (1883–1950) Irish actress of Abbey Theatre fame, whose greatest rôle was Juno in *Juno and the Paycock* (1924) which she created.

ANDERSON, Dame Judith (b. 1898). Australian actress, mostly performing in the U.S.A., supremely good at playing evil rôles in classical and modern plays, including Medea, Lavinia in *Mourning Becomes Electra* (1932) and Mrs. Danvers in the film of *Rebecca*. D.B.E., 1960.

ANDREWS, Harry (b. 1911). Quite simply the best major Shakespearean supporting actor in Britain since 1945 at the Old Vic, Stratford and elsewhere: Bolingbroke, Kent, Buckingham in *Richard III*, Enobarbus, etc. The name-part in Edward Bond's *Lear* (1971).

ASHCROFT, Dame Peggy (b. 1907). Outstanding English actress whose career began at Birmingham Rep in 1926. She has played most of the great classical rôles, is regarded as perhaps the finest Juliet of the century (1932 and 1935), and her famous Duchess of Malfi has been seen twice, for Gielgud (1944–5) and for the Royal Shakespeare Co. (1960). Also for the R.S.C. was her epic Margaret in *The Wars of the Roses* (1963–4), from her teens to old age. Her commercial successes have included Hester in *The Deep Blue Sea* (1952), while her portrayal of the murderess in *The Lovers of Viorne* (1971) for the English Stage Co. was another triumph. D.B.E., 1956.

BANCROFT, Anne (b. 1931). Leading American actress of stage and screen, who first made her name as Gittel in *Two for the Seasaw* (1958) and Annie Sullivan in *The Miracle Worker* (1959). She has since played Mother Courage, Regina in *The Little Foxes*, etc.

BANKHEAD, Tallulah (1903–1968). American actress who was a major West End Star and personality in the 1920s, only rarely having a part worthy of her. In 1937 she was a notorious Cleopatra (as she agreed) and a splendidly vicious Regina in *The Little Foxes* in 1942.

BARRYMORE, Ethel (1879–1959). American actress, sister of Lionel Barrymore (1878–1954) who gave up the theatre for films, and John (see below). Ethel acted with Irving, played Portia, Lady Teazle, Juliet, and many commercial leads in which her beauty was a great asset, and, despite filming, served the theatre best of the three. A late triumph was as Miss Moffat in *The Corn is Green* (1940).

BARRYMORE, John (1882–1942). American actor, the most acclaimed Hamlet of his day (New York, 1922: London, 1925) and a notable Richard III. His non-classical performances included a very fine Falder in *Justice* (1916). Sadly, he virtually gave up the theatre after his last Hamlet, for films and high living.

BATES, Alan (b. 1934). English actor whose parts have included Richard III at Stratford, Ontario (1967), Petruchio at Stratford (1973), also the original Cliff in *Look Back in Anger* (1956) and a witty and scintillating performance in the title rôle of Simon Gray's *Butley* (1971).

BELLAMY, Anne (c. 1727–1788). English actress, Juliet to Garrick's Romeo, and not too outshone by Mrs. Siddons as a tragedienne, though considerably less respectable, to the extent of adversely affecting her career.

BENSON, Sir Frank (1858–1939). Major Shakespearean actor-manager, among whose finest performances was Richard II. His famous touring company of 'Bensonians' existed from 1883–1933 and brought simple, direct Shakespeare to millions. A fine trainer of actors, he was in advance of his time in insisting on physical fitness (about which there were many jokes which now seem flat). See *Benson and the Bensonians* by J. C. Trewin.

Thomas Betterton, the greatest of English Restoration actors and a famous Shakespearean. (From the Author's Collection)

Edwin Booth was believed by many to be America's greatest actor. His brother assassinated Lincoln. (From the Mansell Collection)

BENNETT, Jill (b. 1931). Leading English actress who has recently been particularly striking in her husband, John Osborne's plays, especially as Pamela in *Time Present* (1968).

BETTERTON, Thomas (*c.* 1635–1710). The leading actor of Restoration England, also a manager and a less lethal adapter of earlier plays to the public's taste than some of his contemporaries. A rare case of an actor great in tragedy and comedy, his finest rôles were Hamlet and Sir Toby.

BLAKELY, Colin (b. 1930). Irish-born actor who made his name in major performances at the National Theatre, including Kite in *The Recruiting Officer* (1963) the lead in *Hobson's Choice* (1963) and a tough, ultimately moving Pizzaro in *The Royal Hunt of the Sun* (1964), etc. Has had many other successes since.

BETTY, William (1791–1874). English child actor who took London by storm as Hamlet, etc., aged 12, but had little success later.

BLOOM, Claire (1931). English actress who made her name with a much-acclaimed Juliet at the Old Vic (1952) and has played many classical rôles since.

BOOTH, Edwin (1833–1893). The greatest of a family of Anglo-American actors, the most notorious being the wretched John Wilkes, his brother, who shot Lincoln. Edwin surpassed his father, Junius Brutus Booth, to become possibly America's greatest Shakespearean actor: Hamlet, Sir Giles Overreach, etc. He alternated Othello and Iago with Irving (1881) in London, as his father had with Edmund Kean.

BRACEGIRDLE, Anne (c. 1663–1748). The creator of Millimant in *The Way of the World*, Mrs. Bracegirdle began as Betterton's pupil and retired in 1707 at the top, the leading actress of the day.

BRAITHWAITE, Dame Lilian (1873–1948). English actress and wit, whose most famous parts included Florance Lancaster in *The Vortex* (1924) and Abby in *Arsenic and Old Lace* (1942). D.B.E., 1943. Her daughter is the actress, Joyce Carey.

BUCHANAN, Jack (1890–1957). Scottish-born actor and revue artist, Britain's leading song-and-dance man between the wars.

BURBAGE, Richard (c. 1567–1619). English actor who almost certainly created Richard III, Hamlet, Othello, Lear and other great rôles. He outstripped Alleyn in critical estimation, and was clearly that rarest of beings, a great actor. His father James built the first English playhouse, The Theatre, in 1576, and with his brother Cuthbert built the Globe in whose fortunes Richard, like Shakespeare, was closely bound up. Apart from Shakespeare, he also played in Kyd, Webster and Jonson, and in *Bartholomew Fair* Jonson referred to him as 'your best actor'.

BURTON, Richard (b. 1925). Welsh-born actor who in the 1950s appeared destined to reach the pinnacle of the profession, his parts at the Old Vic including Hamlet, Coriolanus, Othello/Iago (with John Neville), Henry V, etc. Since then, films have mainly kept him out of the theatre, though parts have included a record-breaking Hamlet on Broadway (1969). Blessed with presence, fire and voice, his long absences from the theatre have saddened his admirers.

CAMPBELL, Mrs. Patrick (1865–1940). Remarkable English actress and wit, whose most famous parts included Paula in *The Second Mrs. Tanqueray*, Magda and the first Eliza Doolittle (1914), also Shakespearean and Ibsen rôles and Mélisande in French opposite Bernhardt as Pelléas. A glorious, impossible woman. See *The First Night of Pygmalion* by Richard Huggett.

CARNOVSKY, Morris (b. 1898). Leading American actor, one of the few in this century to become a major Shakespearean, especially as Lear (1956). Earlier associated with the Group Theater.

CLEMENTS, Sir John. See page 142.

CLIVE, Kitty (1711–1785). Outstanding English actress in comedy and farce, who fell out with Garrick partly because he (rightly) prevented her appearing in tragedy, for which she was unsuited.

COMPTON, Fay (b. 1895). English actress whose parts have included major Shakespearean rôles – Ophelia opposite Barrymore (1925), Volumnia at the Old Vic (1954), etc. – and Mary Rose (1920).

COOKE, George Frederick (1756–1811). English actor, famous in Britain and America almost as powerful as Edmund Kean as Richard III, etc. Drink killed him.

COOPER, Dame Gladys (1888–1971). English actress who graduated from the chorus and picture postcard fame to stardom on both sides of the Atlantic. Her two most famous parts were Mrs. Cheyney (1925) and Leslie in *The Letter* (1927).

CORNELL, Katharine (b. 1898). Major American actress, who, with her husband, the director, Guthrie McClintic, did much to raise the standards of the American theatre between the wars on Broadway and on tour. During 1933–4, at the height of the Depression, she toured 75,000 miles, playing Juliet, Candida and Elizabeth in *The Barretts of Wimpole Street*, one of her most famous rôles.

CUMMINGS, Constance (b. 1910). American actress in Britain since 1934, and an Old Vic Juliet and St. Joan in 1939. As a National Theatre Player, she has crowned her career with a magnificent Mary Tyrone in *Long Day's Journey into Night* (1972).

CUSHMAN, Charlotte (1816–1876). Leading American actress famed for her Lady Macbeth. She once played Romeo to her sister Susan's Juliet.

DENCH, Judi (b. 1935). English actress, one of the

Gerald du Maurier, an actor-manager whose masterly underplaying inspired many less-gifted imitators. (Photo: Author's Collection)

two or three finest younger actresses in Britain, most notably in Shakespearean rôles: Juliet, Viola, Hermione/Perdita, etc. Also as the Duchess of Malfi and Grace in *London Assurance* (1970).

DEWHURST, Coleen. American actress, outstanding in the classics and moderns, including *Moon for the Misbegotten* (1974).

DRAKE, Alfred (b. 1914). American actor and singer, whose career has included the original Curly in *Oklahoma* (1943), Hajj in *Kismet* (1953) and a fine Iago at Stratford, Connecticut (1964).

DREW, John (1853–1927). The finest of a family of American actors, much admired on both sides of the Atlantic in Shakespeare. His Petruchio was a particular success and, later, his Major Pendennis in a dramatisation of Thackeray's book.

DU MAURIER, Sir Gerald (1873–1934). English actor renowned for his skilled underplaying which some of his imitators did not do so well. His most famous parts were Bulldog Drummond and Lord Dilling in *The Last of Mrs. Cheyney* (1925). The first Captain Hook.

DUNNOCK, Mildred. American actress, the original Linda in *Death of a Salesman* (1949). Her many other successes have included Big Mama in *Cat on a Hot Tin Roof* (1955).

ELLIOTT, Denholm (b. 1922). English actor who has given many excellent performances since his award-winning Edgar in Fry's *Venus Observed* (1949).

EVANS, Dame Edith (b. 1888). English actress whose incomparable career in the classics and the commercial theatre has included one of the supreme performances of the century, Millimant in *The Way of the World* (1924), 'a city in illumination' according to James Agate. Two other definitive performances have been her Lady Bracknell (1939) and her Nurse in *Romeo* on several occasions. Also much admired was her Rosalind and her playing in Shaw, while her many commercial triumphs have included her superb portrait of a dominating woman, Mrs. Lancaster in *Waters of the Moon* (1951). D.B.E., 1946.

EVANS, Maurice (b. 1901). English-born American actor, the first Raleigh in *Journey's End* (1928), who, after Hamlet, Richard II, etc., at the Old Vic, became resident in America in 1935. He swiftly rose to be her leading classical actor, playing Hamlet, John Tanner, Dick Dudgeon, etc., also commercial leads including Tony Wendice in *Dial 'M' for Murder* (1952).

FERRER, José (b. 1912). Puerto Rican-born American actor and director, whose classical parts have included Iago opposite Robeson (1943), Cyrano, Richard III and Lord Fancourt Babberley in *Charley's Aunt*. Modern parts have included Jim Downs in *The Shrike*, which he also directed, and the title-rôle in *Edwin Booth*.

FFRANGCON-DAVIES, Gwen (b. 1896). English actress, whose many classical and modern parts have included Elizabeth in *The Barretts of Wimpole Street* (1930), Lady Macbeth (1942) and a very moving Mary Tyrone in *Long Day's Journey into Night* (1958).

FINLAY, Frank. English actor whose parts have included the title-rôle in *Sergeant Musgrave's Dance* (1959), Willie Mossop in *Hobson's Choice* at the National (1964), where he also played Iago, Dogberry, etc. Currently (1973-4) giving an excellent performance as Peppino in *Saturday, Sunday, Monday* at the National.

FINNEY, Albert (b. 1936). English actor who made his name at Birmingham Rep and at Stratford, where he went on for Olivier as Coriolanus with great success (1959). His Victor and Poche in *A Flea in Her Ear* (1966) at the National was widely praised. Modern parts of this brilliant and inventive actor have included the title-rôle in *Luther* (1961) and the husband in *Alpha-Beta* (1972).

FONTANNE, Lynn. See LUNT, Alfred.

FORBES-ROBERTSON, Sir Johnston (1853-1937). English actor-manager, generally regarded as the finest Hamlet of his time. His most famous modern rôle was the Stranger in *The Passing of the Third-Floor Back* (1908). His daughter **Jean** (1905-1962) was a notable Shakespearean (especially Viola) and Ibsen player, and the perfect Peter Pan (nine seasons), boyish, eerie and completely convincing.

FORREST, Edwin (1806-1872). Major American tragedian who cured early ranting to triumph in the great rôles, including Lear and Hamlet.

GARRICK, David (1717-1779). English actor and manager (Drury Lane, 1747-1776), who, after triumphing as an unknown as Richard III, rapidly became the greatest actor of his day, excelling in both tragedy and comedy. Renowned for a more natural style than his predecessors, he was a famous Hamlet, Macbeth, Lear, Benedick and Abel Drugger, etc., also a theatre reformer who banished the audience from the stage, concealed stage lighting from the audience, used de Loutherbourg as a designer (who painted naturalistic back-drops), and saw to it that most leading actors played at Drury Lane. He used a number of Shakespearean texts 'improved' during the Restoration period, while his best known play is *The Clandestine Marriage* (1766), written with George Colman. He was a pupil of Dr. Johnson and went to London from Lichfield with him.

GIELGUD, Sir John (b. 1904). English actor and director, a leader of his profession for a generation, and the most famous Hamlet of modern times (from 1930). Combines a noble voice and powerful presence with intelligence, emotional approach and sheer dedication to his art, and the result has been a memorable career and a number of great performances. He established himself as a classical player at the Old Vic (1929-31), his parts including Hamlet, Richard II, Romeo and Macbeth, while his most famous modern part at that time was the title-rôle in *Richard of Bordeaux* (1932). He alternated Romeo and Mercutio with Olivier (1935) and ran a season at the Queen's (1937-8) which is regarded by some as laying the foundations of English ensemble acting. The summit of the season, with an exceptionally strong cast, was *The Three Sisters*, directed by Michel St. Denis, and with himself as Vershinin.

Later parts included Lear and Prospero (1940), leads in an incomparable season he ran at the Haymarket (1944-5), and a cold, fanatical Angelo at Stratford (1950), also Cassius, Lear and Benedick. Commercial rôles have included Thomas Mendip in

The Lady's Not For Burning (1949), while a recent and moving triumph was in *Home* (1970). Prospero (1974) at the National. Knighted, 1953.

GORDON, Ruth (b. 1896). American actress who has played in Ibsen and Chekhov, and also as Mrs. Pinchwife in *The Country Wife* at the Vic (1937), a classic comedy performance later given in New York. Her many commercial successes have included Mrs. Levi in *The Matchmaker* (1954). Her husband is the skilled dramatist and director, **Garson KANIN** (b. 1912), author of *Born Yesterday*, etc.

GREENWOOD, Joan (b. 1921). English actress with a delectable creamy voice and comedy technique to match, whose parts range from Hattie in *The Grass is Greener* to Hedda.

GORING, Marius (b. 1912). English actor, who has played leads at Stratford and the Old Vic, acted Hamlet in French in France, and acted in German in Germany. Modern parts have included the lead in *Sleuth* (1971).

GRIMALDI, Joseph (1778–1837). Anglo-Italian actor, singer, dancer, mime and master of the harlequinade, and the greatest of all theatre clowns, who ruled Covent Garden for many years. The lead clowns in circuses are called 'Joeys' after him.

GRIMES, Tammy (b. 1934). American actress whose successes have included Molly in *The Unsinkable Molly Brown* (1960) and Amanda in *Private Lives* (1969).

GRIZZARD, George (b. 1928). American actor, whose Broadway rôles have included Hank in *The Desperate Hours* (1955) and Nick in *Who's Afraid of Virginia Woolf* (1962), and who has played Hamlet, Henry V, etc., at the Guthrie Theatre, Minneapolis, also a very fine Dauphin (1964).

GUINNESS, Sir Alec (b. 1914). English actor, exceptionally versatile, including many fine film performances. A modern dress Hamlet at the Old Vic (1938), which he rejoined after the war giving, amongst other parts, the finest Lear's Fool in memory. From the 1950s his stage appearances have been rare. Highlights have included the Cardinal in *The Prisoner* (1954) and the Father in Mortimer's *A Voyage Round My Father* (1971). He is renowned for his authority, dedication, cool naturalism and high intelligence. Knighted, 1959.

GWYNN, Nell (1650–1687). English actress included for her charm and fame, rather than (theatrical) talent. She retired from the stage in 1669.

HAGEN, Uta (b. 1919). German-born American actress, whose classical parts have included a fine Desdemona (1942), and whose modern ones include Blanche in *A Streetcar Named Desire* (1948) and Martha in *Who's Afraid of Virginia Woolf?* (1962).

HAIGH, Kenneth English actor, and the original Jimmy Porter in *Look Back in Anger* (1956). His many other parts in London and on Broadway have included the title-rôle in *Caligula* in both capitals, Mark Antony at Stratford (1963) and Laurie in *A Hotel in Amsterdam* (1969).

HARDWICKE, Sir Cedric (1893–1964). English actor, the leading Shavian of his day from his time at Birmingham Rep, and an occasional Shakespearean. A famous commercial part was Edward Moulton-Barrett in *The Barretts of Wimpole Street* (1930). A season at the Old Vic (at the New) in 1948–9 resulted in one major success, his Gaev in *The Cherry Orchard*. Much of his later career was devoted to film parts which were not worthy of his talents. His son Edward gave one of the finest comic performances of the '60s as Camille in *A Flea in Her Ear* (1966) at the National Theatre.

HARDY, Robert English actor who made his name at the Old Vic and Stratford in the 1950s, including a superb Prince Hal at the Vic. Parts in the '60s included the Count in Anouilh's *The Rehearsal* (1961). More lately he has been regularly on TV.

HARE, Robertson (b. 1891). Famous and adored English farceur, especially in farces by Travers and Vernon Sylvaine. His fruity tones, bald plate and timing, plus his flair in losing his trousers, has cheered up audiences for decades. A pillar – after a minor part in *Cuckoo in the Nest* (1925) – of the Aldwych farces, with Ralph Lynn and Tom Walls.

HARRIS, Julie (b. 1935). Notable American actress of wide range, whose parts have included Frankie in *The Member of the Wedding* (1950) and Ann Stanley in *Forty Carats* (1968).

HARRIS, Rosemary (b. 1930). English actress turned Broadway star, who played leads at the Vic in the '50s, Ilyena at the National in 1963, many classical parts in America, including Mme. Arkadina, and Eleanor in *The Lion in Winter* (1966) in New York, also Kate in *Old Times* (1972) and other rôles. She has won awards on both sides of the Atlantic.

HARRISON, Rex (b. 1908). English actor, a supremely good light comedian, famous since the first night of *French Without Tears* (1936). His

Edwin Forrest, a major American tragic actor and Macready's bitter rival. (From the Author's Collection)

Helen Hayes in her most famous rôle, Queen Victoria in Victoria Regina. (*From the Author's Collection*)

Platonov (Chekhov) at the Royal Court (1960) was widely admired, but his most famous rôle has undoubtedly been Higgins in *My Fair Lady* on stage and screen.

HAWTREY, Sir Charles (1858–1923). English actor-manager and a very fine light comedian.

HAYES, Helen (b. 1900). American actress, regarded by many as her country's leading actress, whose 'masterpiece' (Brooks Atkinson) was Victoria in *Victoria Regina* (35–8). Other parts have included Shaw's Cleopatra, Mary in Maxwell Anderson's *Mary of Scotland* (1934) and Amanda in *The Glass Menagerie* (London, 1948). Starred with James Stewart in a delightful revival of *Harvey* (1970). Her husband was Charles MacArthur, co-author of *The Front Page*.

HELPMANN, Sir Robert (b. 1909). Australian actor and dancer who, even while still at Sadler's Wells, made his name in the theatre as Oberon (1937), Hamlet (1944), etc. Now a leading director and choreographer, one of his greatest successes was Flamineo in *The White Devil* (1947). Played many leading classical rôles at Stratford and elsewhere in the 1950s, including Richard III. Knighted, 1968.

HEPBURN, Katherine (b. 1909). American actress of stage and screen fame, whose parts have included a much acclaimed Rosalind (1950) and an equally admired Lady in *The Millionairess* (1952). One of her noted modern parts was Tracy Lord in *The Philadelphia Story* (1937). The lead in the musical *Coco* (1969).

HICKS, Sir Seymour (1871–1949). English actor, director and dramatist, and an excellent comedian. He was one of the authors of London's first revue, *Under the Clock* (1893). His wife was the actress and beauty, Ellaline Terriss, daughter of the actor-manager, William Terriss, who was murdered by a madman outside the Adelphi stage door. Knighted, 1935.

HILLER, Wendy (b. 1912). English actress best known for her work in Shaw and in emotional parts. A famous Eliza Doolittle on stage and screen.

HORDERN, Michael (b. 1911). Very fine English actor, whose leading parts at Stratford and the Old Vic included a frightening Macbeth (1958). A noted and inventive comedian, he excelled himself in *Jumpers* (1972) at the National. A master of timing, frenzy and benevolence.

HOPKINS, Anthony (b. 1937). Welsh-born actor who made his name in the late 1960s at the National after going on for Olivier in *The Dance of Death* (1967). Macbeth (1972).

IRVING, Sir Henry (1838–1905). English actor-manager and the first British actor knight (1895). After a rugged beginning, which included 429 parts in 782 days in Edinburgh, he made a success in London in 1866. He became a theatre immortal in 1871 on the first night of *The Bells*, his Matthias transforming a good melodrama into great art. His Hamlet, a gentle, controversial interpretation three years later, made him the head of his profession. Criticism never ceased from a vocal minority about his mannerisms of movement and speech and his reluctance to perform new plays (the main reasons for Shaw's often fatuous attacks on him). In fact, in his early days as actor-manager there was precious little good drama about and, later, he was set in his ways, concentrating on Shakespeare, melodrama, and building up a strong company, which he trained magnificently. His hold on audiences was total and his striking personality and dynamic power to surprise made him always fascinating, sometimes great. His most famous parts included Shylock, Malvolio, Iachimo (which even Shaw liked), Becket in Tennyson's play, Hamlet (for many) and, of course, Matthias. His Macbeth ended 'like a famished wolf' (Ellen Terry, his great leading lady). His elaborate productions were later abused, but were right for their time, and he was chiefly responsible for bringing the middle classes back to the theatre. He was also an experimentor in lighting and décor. Lives of him by Gordon Craig and his grandson, Laurence Irving, are strongly recommended.

JEFFORD, Barbara (b. 1930). One of the finest younger English classical actresses, whose most famous part in London and New York has been St. Joan. Another major success was her Imogen at the Old Vic (1956).

JOHNSON, Celia (b. 1908). Very popular English stage and screen star in classical and modern rôles. The latter have included Sheila in *The Reluctant Debutante* (1955), the former, St. Joan at the Old Vic, Olga in *The Three Sisters*, Gertrude, etc.

KEACH, Stacy (b. 1941). American actor whose wide range of parts have included Falstaff in New York (1968), Buffalo Bill in Arthur Kopit's *Indians* (1969) and a much-admired Hamlet at New Haven (1972).

KEAN, Edmund (1787–1833). One of the greatest and, possibly, the most thrilling of all English actors, who died of drink when he should have been at the height of his powers. His Shylock in a half empty Drury Lane in 1814 made his name (via Hazlitt) and other stupendous, magnetic performances included Richard III, Iago, Othello and Sir Giles Overreach in *A New Way to Pay Old Debts*, in which he sent Lord Byron into a convulsion. He had nothing in his favour but striking eyes and genius. Yet Leigh Hunt spoke of his 'exceeding grace, his gallant levity, his measureless dignity: for his little person absolutely becomes tall . . .' This scandal-haunted romantic produced a respectable actor-son Charles (1811–1868), who had a distinguished career, but whose Shakespearean productions, for all their remarkable attention to detail, were slowed down by settings which were monuments of architectural accuracy. His *Dream* actually showed Athens in all its glory in Scene I.

KEMBLE, John Philip (1757–1823). The most famous male member of a family of English actors – Siddons was his sister – a stately, graceful actor whose technique (and behaviour) was very different from the more violent methods of Kean, a far greater player. He improved greatly, his finest part being Coriolanus. He managed first Drury Lane and then Covent Garden.

KING, Dennis (1897–1971). British-born Broadway star of plays and musicals, including François Villon in *The Vagabond King* (1925), Richard of Bordeaux, Higgins, Jasin in *Medea*, etc.

LAHR, Bert (1895–1967). American actor and comedian and star of musicals. His performance in *Du Barry Was a Lady* (1939) had a "spluttering violence and leering impudence that makes him one of the best comedians in the world" (Richard Watts, Jnr.). One of the Tramps in *Waiting for Godot* (1956).

LANG, Matheson (1879–1948). English actor-manager whose most famous performance was the title-rôle in *The Wandering Jew*. From 1907 he ran his own company giving romantic melodramas and Shakespeare, and it was he who directed the first Shakespeare season at the Old Vic in 1914, also acting in it. Earlier he had acted in Ibsen and Shaw at the Royal Court under Granville Barker.

LAUGHTON, Charles (1899–1962). English actor who, before going to Hollywood, was the finest character actor in Britain, his famous parts including Harry Heegan in *The Silver Tassie* (1929), Tony Perelli in *On The Spot* (1931) by Edgar Wallace, and the murderer in *Payment Deferred* (1931). Only one of his classical performances was a complete success, his frightening Angelo at the Old Vic (1933). His widow is the actress, Elsa Lanchester.

LAWRENCE, Gertrude (1898–1952). English actress and a star of plays, revue and musicals in Britain and America. The original Amanda in *Private Lives* (1930), also playing opposite Coward in *Tonight at 8.30* (1936). A superb Eliza Doolittle in New York (1946), which she first stormed in 1923. Two of her musical hits were as Kay in Gershwin's *Oh, Kay* (1926) and Anna in *The King and I* (1951). A superstar before the word was coined.

LAWSON, Wilfred (1900–1966). English actor who wrecked a potentially great career by drink. He excelled in Shaw, Priestley, Strindberg, etc.

LE GALIENNE, Eva. See page 149.

LEIGH, Vivien (1913–1967). English actress and beauty, for many years the wife of Laurence Olivier. Her finest performances were, perhaps, Jennifer in *The Doctor's Dilemma* (1942), Sabina in *The Skin of our Teeth* (1945) and Blanche in *A Streetcar named Desire* (1949) – also Scarlett O'Hara. More controversial in classical rôles, her Lady Macbeth at Stratford (1955) had as many admirers as detractors.

LEIGHTON, Margaret (b. 1922). Major English actress who made her name at the Old Vic (at the New) in 1944–7 – Yelena in *Uncle Vanya*, Regan, Roxane in *Cyrano*, etc. – and was later an unforgettable Masha in *The Three Sisters* (1951). A much-admired Cleopatra at Chichester (1969), her modern parts have included Celia in *The Cocktail Party* (1950), and Hannah in *The Night of the Iguana* on Broadway (1961).

LILLIE, Beatrice (b. 1898). Canadian actress and comedienne who first reached stardom in the Charlot revues of the '20s. *An Evening of Beatrice Lillie* (1954) was one peak in her career, which included *Aunt Mame* (1958), a straight rôle in London and New York, in both of which cities she was a major star.

LUNT, Alfred (b. 1892) and **FONTANNE, Lynn** (b. 1887). An incomparable husband and wife partnership, he being American, she English-born. Their technique has been the joy of audiences and the delight and despair of actors from the early

Edmund Kean, the most thrilling of all British actors, as Sir Giles Overreach, the part in which he sent Lord Byron into a convulsion. (Photo: Victoria and Albert Museum, Crown Copyright)

1920s. Excelling in Coward, Sherwood, Behrman, etc., they also played in more serious drama, especially for the Theater Guild (1925–9): *The Brothers Karamazov, Marco's Millions, etc.*, also, later, *There Shall be no Night* (1940) and Durrenmatt's *The Visit* (1958). Lunt has also been a fine director, while Fontanne was considered by Brooks Atkinson to be the finest of all Eliza Doolittles.

LYNN, Ralph (1882–1964). The supreme English farceur of modern times. His 'business' in Aldwych and later farces is now theatre legend.

McCOWEN, Alec (b. 1925). Wide-ranging English actor, whose notable performances have included an electric Mercutio at the Old Vic (1959), a sad, moving Fool in *Lear* (1962) and the lead in *Hadrian VII* (1968).

McEWEN, Geraldine (b. 1932). English actress whose many fine comedy performances at the National Theatre and elsewhere did not prepare audiences for her powerful, bitter Alice in *The Dance of Death* (1967) and other serious rôles.

McKELLEN, Ian (b. 1939). English actor who, after a successful Coriolanus for Guthrie at Nottingham (1963), made his name as Edward II and Richard II at the 1969 Edinburgh Festival. Since then he has been the begetter of the Actors' Company (1972), a splendid ensemble of major players.

McKENNA, Siobhan (b. 1923). Irish actress, the most acclaimed St. Joan since Sybil Thorndike, and a notable player in parts ranging from Pegeen in *The Playboy of the Western World* (1960) to Mme. Ranevsky (1968).

McKERN, Leo (b. 1920). Australian actor, whose notable parts have included Iago, Volpone, Peer Gynt and several of the great Clowns for the Old Vic, etc.

MACKLIN, Charles (*c.* 1700–1797). Irish actor, the first 'real' Shylock of his day. 'This is the Jew, That Shakespeare drew' (Pope).

MacLIAMMÓIR, Micheal (b. 1899). Irish actor, director, designer and dramatist, whose most famous parts have included Hamlet, Othello and Oscar Wilde in his own *The Importance of Being Oscar* (1960), also Robert Emmet in *The Old Lady Says No!* He has written a theatre classic, his autobiography, *All for Hecuba*, and he helped make the Gate the most adventurous theatre in Ireland between the wars.

MacMASTER, Anew (1895–1952). On his night, the greatest Irish Shakespearean of modern times.

Alas, this erratic genius only played one season in England: Stratford, 1937.

MACREADY, William (1793–1873). Great English actor who had the misfortune to dislike his profession and endure it at a time when the theatre and its audiences were at a very low ebb. His finest rôles included Hamlet, Macbeth and Lear, and he was one of the first to return to Shakespeare's actual texts minus later 'improvements'. As a manager he was efficient and ambitious to try and improve the state of the theatre by bringing in major writers and poets, but his only successes in this line were with Bulwer Lytton's *The Lady of Lyons* and *Richelieu*. His frank, rather pompous and humourless *Journal* is essential reading for students of his period. In his younger days a real rival to Edmund Kean, he escaped from his hated profession in 1851. The English theatre lost greatness in acting until Irving's sensational successes in the 1870s. See *Mr. Macready* by J. C. Trewin.

MANSFIELD, Richard (1857–1907). Major American actor in melodramas and great classical rôles, including Richard III, first given in London (1889). Though a romantic actor, he was prepared to give the new drama: *Peer Gynt* starring himself (1906), and America's first Bluntschli (1894) and Dick Dudgeon (1897). He also presented *A Doll's House* (1889), with his wife, Beatrice Cameron, as Nora.

MARTIN, Mary (b. 1913). American actress and singer, star of a number of musicals, including *The Sound of Music.* Her greatest rôle, which made her a theatre immortal, was Ensign Nellie Forbush in *South Pacific* (New York, 1949: London, 1951).

MARTIN-HARVEY, Sir John (1863–1944). English actor-manager who began with Irving, then entered management in 1899, playing his most famous rôle, Sydney Carton in *The Only Way.* His classical and romantic career touched greatness in 1912 with his Oedipus Rex, but after the 1914–18 war he was too often forced to revive Carton on his tours: his style and plays were out of fashion in post-war London. He was the last major link with the Victorian stage.

MARCH, Frederic (b. 1897). American actor of stage and screen, the first Mr. Antrobus in *The Skin of our Teeth* (1942) and the manificent creator of James Tyrone in *Long Day's Journey into Night* (1956), playing opposite his wife, **Florence ELDRIDGE** (b. 1901) who has often acted with him.

MASSEY, Raymond (b. 1896). Canadian actor, whose notable parts have included Harry Van in

Idiot's Delight (1938) and Lincoln in *Abe Lincoln in Illinois* (1940). Anna and Daniel Massey are his children by his second wife, the actress, Adrienne Allen.

MATTHAU, Walter (b. 1920). American actor, now a major film star, but a very successful Broadway player, notably as Benjamin Beaurevers in *A Shot in the Dark* (1961) and Oscar in *The Odd Couple* (1965), both of which won awards.

MATTHEWS, Jessie (b. 1907). English actress and dancer, a major star of musicals between the wars.

MERMAN, Ethel (b. 1909). Trumpet-toned American actress and singer, a star in Cole Porter's *Anything Goes* (1934), but after her Annie in *Annie Get Your Gun* (1946), an American Institution. Later triumphs have been in *Call Me Madam, Gypsy* and *Hello, Dolly*.

MICHELL, Keith (b. 1928). Australian actor who ranges from classical to musical parts and is now Director of the Chichester Festival Theatre (1974). Early successes included Petruchio at Stratford (1954), while his Antony two years later at the Old Vic was a very fine performance. His successes in musicals have included Nestor/Oscar in *Irma La Douce* (1958) and Don Quixote in *Man of La Mancha* (1968).

MILLER, Marilyn (1896–1936). American star of musicals, stardom coming to this delectable artist in *Sally* (1920). Other successes included *Sunny* (1925) and *As Thousands Cheer* (1933). The first to sing 'Look for the Silver Lining' and Kern's 'Who'.

MILTON, Ernest (b. 1890). American-born English actor, a magnificent Hamlet and an equally fine Lear, and a legendary figure, partly because of his wit.

MORE, Kenneth (b. 1914). English actor, renowned for his comedy technique on stage and in films, but who made his name with his superb Freddie in Rattigan's drama, *The Deep Blue Sea* (1952).

MORLEY, Robert (b. 1908). Hugely popular English personality actor on stage and screen. Perhaps his most memorable rôle has been his Arnold Holt in *Edward, My Son* (1947), by himself and Noel Langley.

NAZIMOVA, Alla (1879–1945). Russian-born American actress, famed for her Ibsen and Chekhov performances and, especially, for her Christine in *Mourning Becomes Electra* (1931).

NEVILLE, John (b. 1925). English actor who made his name at the Old Vic in the 1950s as one of the finest classical actors in Britain, graceful and romantic in the Gielgud tradition. Outstanding rôles were his Richard II, Pistol, Romeo and Hamlet, and he alternated Othello and Iago with Burton. He directed Nottingham Rep excitingly from 1963–8, since when he has played a number of classical parts, including Macheath in *The Beggar's Opera* at Chichester (1972).

NOVELLO, Ivor (1893–1951). Hugely popular actor, composer, dramatist and matinée idol, whose musical romances, *Glamorous Night, Careless Rapture, Crest of the Wave* and *The Dancing Years* dominated Drury Lane from 1935–9. Later successes included *Perchance to Dream* and *King's Rhapsody*. His plays included *The Rat* (1924), and he played Henry V at Drury Lane (1938). He starred in most of his shows, but his most famous song was not in any of them – 'Keep the Homes Fires Burning'.

OLIVIER, Sir Laurence, later Lord (b. 1907). English actor, director, manager and the first Director (1963–73) of the National Theatre. After Birmingham Rep and West End leads, alternated Romeo and Mercutio with Gielgud (1935), then in 1937 joined the Old Vic to play a range of parts that included Hamlet, Sir Toby and Coriolanus, an especially fine performance. After films and war service, he became with Richardson and John Burrell, a co-director of the Old Vic at the New Theatre, where his Richard III, a sardonic Satan rampant from his spidery first entrance to his writhing dance of death, ushered in a re-birth of great acting in the Kean and Irving tradition. Other parts in this period included Astrov, the ideal Hotspur, Oedipus and Mr. Puff, also a grandly conceived, desolate Lear which, for some, lacked the final emotional impact.

After a quieter period as an actor-manager, in which he acted Fry, Rattigan, and Caesar and Antony opposite his then wife, Vivien Leigh, he played Macbeth, Malvolio and Titus Andronicus in an historic season at Stratford (1955). There followed his famous Archie Rice, a thrilling Coriolanus (1959), etc., then the Chichester Festival as Director (1962–5), and the National, where his most acclaimed rôles have been Astrov, the Captain in *The Dance of Death*, Brazen in *The Recruiting Officer*, Tattle in *Love for Love* and, except for a dissenting minority, Othello and Shylock. In 1972 he added a superb James Tyrone in *Long Day's Journey*. He is married to the actress, Joan Plowright (see below).

Olivier's prime assets are striking eyes, a commanding, thrilling voice, looks which when younger made him the ideal Heathcliff (on film), sheer magnetism, and a sense of danger that makes for theatrical electricity. A born comedian, he made himself a tragedian though some find him lacking in 'heart'. By any standards, he ranks as head of his profession in Britain, possibly in the world. Knighted, 1947. Life Peer (the first actor peer), 1970.

O'TOOLE, Peter (b. 1932). Stage and screen actor, whose Hamlet opened the National Theatre. A Stratford Shylock and Petruchio (1960) and a fine King Magnus in *The Apple Cart* at Bristol Old Vic (1973).

PAGE, Geraldine (b. 1924). American actress whose range and strength have resulted in notable performances including Lizzie in *The Rainmaker* (1954) and Alexandra in *Sweet Bird of Youth* (1959), and many later rôles.

PASCO, Richard (b. 1926). English actor, whose many fine classical performances have included Richard II and Bolingbroke (Stratford, 1973) alternating with Ian Richardson (see below).

PLOWRIGHT, Joan (b. 1929). English actress, the wife of Olivier. Her first big success was Marjery Pinchwife in *The Country Wife* at the Royal Court (1956), and she was the first Beatie in *Roots* (1959). Her parts at the National have included particularly successful Chekhov performances: Sonya and Masha.

PLUMMER, Christopher (b. 1929). Canada's leading actor who has played many of the great rôles at Stratford, Ontario, including (from 1956) Henry V, Hamlet, Richard III, Sir Andrew, etc. King Henry in *Becket* in London (1961). With the National (1971), his finest performance was as Danton in *Danton's Death*.

PORTER, Eric (b. 1928). One of the strongest modern English actors, his parts have included Bolingbroke (1952) and, for the Royal Shakespeare Co. since 1960, Antonio in *The Duchess of Malfi*, Barabas in *The Jew of Malta*, Shylock, Macbeth and Lear, etc.

PORTMAN, Eric (1903–1969). English stage and screen actor who, after work at the Vic, became perhaps the most moving and powerful actor in the West End of the '40s and '50s, most notably his Crocker-Harris in *The Browning Version* (1948), the Governor in *His Excellency* (1950) and Mr. Martin and Major Pollock in *Separate Tables* (1954).

QUAYLE, Anthony (b. 1913). English actor and director, Director at Stratford from 1948–56. His finest classical performances have been Falstaff, Iago, Othello, and Aaron in *Titus* (1955). The first English James Tyrone in *Long Day's Journey* (1958) and the first Andrew Wyke in *Sleuth* (1970).

QUILLEY, Denis (b. 1927). English actor and singer – Candide (1959), etc. – whose performances at the National, including Jamie in *Long Day's Journey*, Hildy Johnson in *The Front Page*, and Macbeth, have been greatly admired.

QUIN, James (1693–1766). English actor whose declamatory style was eclipsed by Garrick, yet who played most of the great classical rôles to the admiration of many.

REDGRAVE, Sir Michael (b. 1908). English actor, director and dramatist, intelligent, stylish and subtle, who, apart from a period in the '40s when he was alleged to be too intellectual and unable to play comedy (Agate), has been greatly admired. His Berowne for the Old Vic (1949) put an end to the criticism, and among his finest performances since were a trio in 1953 at Stratford which lifted him to the peak of the profession: Shylock, Lear and Antony, this last the most successful in modern times. His many modern successes include Frank Elgin in Odets's *Winter Journey*, known as *The Country Girl* in the U.S.A. (1952). His daughter **Vanessa** (1937), has been the most admired Rosalind since the war (1962) and an enchanting Imogen, both for the Royal Shakespeare Co., also Nina in *The Seagull*, Jean Brodie, etc., and Cleopatra in a bizarre Bankside production (1973). His wife, **Rachel Kempson**, and other children, **Lynn** and **Corin**, are also distinguished players.

REDMAN, Joyce (b. 1918). Irish-born actress, the best Wendy (1942), whose classical parts for the Old Vic and National have included Solveig, Sonia, an unexcelled Mrs. Frail in *Love for Love* and an emotional and powerful Juno. She has also worked at Stratford, in the West End and on Broadway.

RICHARDSON, Ian (b. 1934). English actor who made his name at the Royal Shakespeare Co. (1960–70), his parts including Angelo, Prospero, Marat in *Marat-Sade*, etc. He returned in 1973 to alternate with Richard Pasco as Richard II and

Bolingbroke.

RICHARDSON, Sir Ralph (b. 1902). English actor, the greatest Falstaff of modern times, and blessed with personality, range, comic gifts and emotional power. Renowned for playing 'ordinary' men, he is an extraordinary actor. Aside from many West End successes, especially in Priestley, Dr. Sloper in *The Heiress* (1949), Doctor Farley in *Day by the Sea* (1953), Cherry in *Flowering Cherry* (1957), etc., his classical parts at the Old Vic and Stratford have ranged from Shakespeare to Chekhov. In the legendary Old Vic seasons at the New (1944–8), where he was a co-Director with Olivier and John Burrell, as well as Falstaff he was memorable as Peer Gynt, Vanya, etc. Two much-admired recent performances have been as Jack in *Home* (1970) and Wyatt Gillman in *West of Suez* (1971). Some find his mannerisms intrusive; his many admirers treasure them. His wife is Meriel Forbes.

ROBERTS, Rachel (b. 1927). Welsh actress, whose notable performances have included Anna in *Platanov* (1960), the lead in *Maggie May* (1964) and a searing performance in Whitehead's *Alpha-Beta* opposite Albert Finney (1972). Currently (1973). she has made a very successful début for the Phoenix company in New York in Feydeau and Dürrenmatt.

ROBARDS, Jason (b. 1922). American actor of authority and power, the first – and award-winning – Jamie in *Long Day's Journey* (1956), and an award winner for his Manley Halliday in *The Disenchanted* (1958) and Julian Berniers in *Toys in the Attic* (1960). A later performance for 'the theatrical memory book' (T. E. Kalem) was his Frank Elgin in *The Country Girl* (1972).

ROBESON, Paul (b. 1898). Black American actor and singer, who made his name as Jim Harris in *All God's Chillun Have Wings* (1924), Brutus Jones in *The Emperor Jones* (1924), Joe in *Show Boat* in London (1928), etc. Though he was a famous Othello, twice in Britain, once on Broadway, some found he lacked vocal variety and the technique and fire which the part needed, but others were greatly moved. One of the great voices of the century.

ROBEY, Sir George (1869–1954). English music hall artist, 'the Prime Minister of Mirth', who later excelled in revue and as Falstaff (1935). Knighted, 1954.

ROBSON, Dame Flora (b. 1902). English actress famous for her emotional power in modern and classical parts. The former have included Olwen in *Dangerous Corner* (1932), Alicia in *Black Chiffon* (1949) and her award-winning Tina in *The Aspern Papers* (1959), while her classical rôles and at the Old Vic and elsewhere have included a magnificent Lady Macbeth (1934), a memorable Paulina in *The Winter's Tale* (1951) and equally memorable work in Ibsen. D.B.E., 1960.

ROGERS, Paul (b. 1917). English actor who became a leading Shakespearean in the 1950s at the Old Vic, including very fine performances as Falstaff and Touchstone, and a highly-praised Macbeth (1954), in which he ended like a 'starved grey wolf' (J. C. Trewin). He played Falstaff again at Stratford (1966) and won an award for his Max in *The Homecoming* on Broadway (1965), both for the Royal Shakespeare Co.

RUTHERFORD, Dame Margaret (1892–1972). Adored English (to the core) actress, famed for her eccentrics, most notably her Madame Arcati in *Blithe Spirit* (1941). A noted Miss Prism and, later, Lady Bracknell, and a character superstar in films. D.B.E., 1967.

SCOFIELD, Paul (b. 1922). English actor, the finest to appear since the war, who made his name at Birmingham and Stratford (1946–8) in an astonishing range of parts including a famous Don Armado and a most moving, tormented Hamlet. His many West End successes have included the Twins in *Ring Round the Moon* (1950) and the whiskey priest in *The Power and the Glory* (1954), also, and most memorably, his More in *A Man for All Seasons* (1960). The most famous of many classical performances has perhaps been his Lear (1962) for Brook at the Royal Shakespeare and elsewhere – an astonishing, earthy, primitive, detailed pathetic and magnificent portrayal. Performances for the National included a Voigt in *The Captain of Kopenick* (1971), not only witty, but in which he grew from a whining ex-convict to what Ronald Bryden called a captain who 'at once seems two feet taller'. Scofield has magnetism, a flexible, unique voice which he is prepared to make ugly if the part requires it, deep seriousness and the gift of surprise. Some have found his delivery too still and flat on occasion; others prefer this 'working actor', as he describes himself, to any other.

Sarah Siddons, England's greatest tragedienne, called by Dr. Johnson a 'prodigious fine woman'. (Photo: Author's Collection)

SIDDONS, Sarah (1755–1831). A great, possibly the greatest, English tragedienne, born into a family of successful strolling players as Sarah Kemble. She married William Siddons when she was 18, a moderate actor who later managed her. After successes in the provinces, especially at Bath, she conquered London at her second attempt, creating a sensation unequalled by a British actress in Southern's *Isabella* at Drury Lane (1782). Reynolds and Gainsborough painted her, and Johnson called her a 'prodigious fine woman'. Her greatest rôles included Lady Macbeth and Volumnia, also Belvidera in *Venice Preserved*. 'She was tragedy personified,' wrote Hazlitt, but she avoided comedy, knowing it was not for her. She was unfairly accused of meanness: having known poverty she believed in taking care of her family responsibilities, not frittering her money away. Apart from a brief return for a benefit in 1819 she retired in 1812. Her best known relative was her brother, John Philip Kemble (see above).

SIM, Alistair (b. 1900). Scottish actor, famed for his performances in Bridie, etc., for his Hook, his rolling eyes and quizzical look, and for masterpieces of comic acting in Pinero's *The Magistrate* (1969) and *Dandy Dick* (1973), both of which have been seen in Chichester and London, and both of which are likely to be theatrical legends.

SINDEN, Donald (b. 1923). English stage and screen actor who has combined major classical and commercial work as few actors have managed to do. His most famous parts, all for the Royal Shakespeare Co., have been York in *The Wars of the Roses*, Malvolio, and Sir Harcourt in *London Assurance*, characterised by Harold Hobson as 'Oscar Wilde simultaneously playing George IV and the Apollo Belvedere'.

SMITH, Maggie fine English actress who made her name in revue and later at the National, not only in comedy, in which she excels – Silvia in *The Recruiting Officer* (1963), Myra in *Hay Fever* (1964) – but as a dignified, touching Desdemona. Her Mrs. Sullen in *The Beaux Strategem* increased her reputation, as have rôles like Amanda in *Private Lives* (1973). Married to Robert Stephens (see below).

SMITHSON, Harriet (1800–1854). English actress who is remembered as the wife of Berlioz, an unhappy match, and as the actress who 'revealed Shakespeare to France' on tour with Macready in 1828, her parts being Desdemona and Ophelia. The Romantics took her and her dramatist to their hearts.

SPRIGGS, Elizabeth (b. 1929). English actress who in the late 1960s sprang to fame with the Royal Shakespeare Co., most notably as the Nurse, a prim Edinburgh Maria, a lively Lady Gay Spanker in *London Assurance* and as the alcoholic Claire in Albee's *A Delicate Balance* (1968).

STEPHENS, Robert (b. 1931). English actor, the first George Dillon (1956) and later a very successful National Theatre player, his finest rôles being Plume in *The Recruiting Officer* (1963) and Atahuallpa in *The Royal Hunt of the Sun* (1964). Married to Maggie Smith (see above), with whom he acted in *Private Lives* (1973).

STANLEY, Kim (b. 1925). American actress whose most famous rôles have been Millie in *Picnic* (1953), Cherie in *Bus Stop*, and (in London) Margaret in *Cat on a Hot Tin Roof*. Her Masha in *The Three Sisters* (1964) was widely admired in New York, but the production was ill-fated in London.

STAPLETON, Maureen (b. 1925). American actress whose 'earthy vitality' (Taubman) as Serafina in *The Rose Tattoo* (1951) has been followed by many other fine performances, including Carrie in *Toys in the Attic* and three parts in *Plaza Suite* (1968), etc.

TANDY, Jessica (b. 1909). Anglo-American actress, a very fine Viola at the Old Vic (1937), and Lady Macbeth at Stratford, Conn., who has also played classical leads at the Tyrone Guthrie, Minneapolis. Her most famous Broadway rôle has been as the first Blanche in *A Streetcar Named Desire* (1947), a brilliant performance which won her major awards. She is married to the distinguished Canadian-born actor, Hume Cronyn.

TARLETON, Richard (?–1588). The most famous Elizabethan clown and, possibly, the inspiration of Yorick in *Hamlet*.

TAYLOR, Laurette (1884–1946). American actress remembered for her famous Peg in *Peg O' My Heart* (1912) and her 'deathless' (John Mason Brown) Mother in *The Glass Menagerie* (1945).

TEARLE, Sir Godfrey (1884–1953). English Shakespearean actor who spent much of his career in the West End when Shakespeare was out of fashion there. Blessed with voice and presence, he was a magnificent Antony in 1946, and a famous Othello at Stratford (1948).

TEMPEST, Dame Marie (1864–1942). English actress and singer whose 'small, exquisite talent (Agate)' was put to its most famous use as Judith Bliss in *Hay Fever* (1925), written by Coward for her.

TERRY, Dame Ellen (1847–1928). English actress, possibly the most adored of all, but also a magnificent one, the finest of a very talented family until her nephew, John Gielgud, rivalled her. She became Irving's leading lady in 1878, and some of her best rôles were Beatrice, Portia, Olivia, Desdemona, Viola, Cordelia, also Lady Teazle, the first being considered her masterpiece. Her Lady Macbeth divided opinion, but many admired it. Later, she became a manager playing in Ibsen and Shakespeare directed by her brilliant son, Gordon Craig (see page 142). She also created Lady Cicely in *Captain Brassbound's Conversion* (1900). Her correspondence with Shaw is as delightful as it is informative, as are her Memoirs. Her brother **Fred Terry** was a very popular romantic actor who

played in many productions with his wife Julia Neilson. His most famous part was *The Scarlet Pimpernel*.

THESIGER, Ernest (1879–1961). English actor, witty, clever and with a gargoyle-sharp face, one of the supreme Shavians: he was the first Dauphin, the first Charles II in *In Good King Charles's Golden Days*, etc. To Ken Tynan's chagrin, his Polonius in Moscow (1955) was 'annoyingly restrained'.

THORNDIKE, Dame Sybil (b. 1882). English actress and tragedienne, the first British and greatest St. Joan (1924), a famous Medea (1920) and notable as Judith in *Granite*, Volumnia, Miss Moffat in *The Corn is Green* (1938), etc., and in many classical and modern parts. In the first Old Vic Company (1914), she went on to play nearly all Shakespeare's heroines and Prince Hal (owing to shortage of men in the war). D.B.E., 1931. With her was her brother, **Russell THORNDIKE** (1885–1973), the first English Peer Gynt (1922), later Smee in *Peter Pan*, etc., and also a novelist – the Dr. Syn stories. Her husband was **Sir Lewis CASSON** (1875–1970), a distinguished actor and director, with whom she toured extensively, including the Welsh coalfields, in the Second World War, and who helped Shaw direct *St. Joan*, in which he played de Stogumber. Knighted, 1945. Their daughter **Ann CASSON**, another St. Joan, married the actor **Douglas CAMPBELL** (b. 1922), for many years a pillar of the theatre in Canada.

TREE, Sir Herbert Beerbohm (1853–1917). English actor-manager, whose Shakespearean productions were both elaborate and realistic, culminating in the notorious live rabbits in his *Dream*. His most famous non-Shakespearean part was as Svengali in *Trilby* (1895), and he was the first Higgins in *Pygmalion* (1914), about whose incredible origins, rehearsals and opening the reader should consult Richard Huggett's *The First Night of Pygmalion*. Tree was an erratic romantic actor, at his best in character parts. His wife Helen was a fine comedienne and major wit. Tree built His Majesty's Theatre (1897). He was the half-brother of Max Beerbohm.

TUTIN, Dorothy (b. 1930). English actress who made her name with her powerful Rose in *The Living Room* (1953). Her most famous parts include Sally Bowles in *I am a Camera* (1954), Hedvig in *The Wild Duck* (1955), Viola and Cressida at Stratford and her strong, tormented Jeanne in

The Devils (1961) for the Royal Shakespeare Co. performances in the '70s have included a striking Kate in *Old Times* and an utterly convincing, vigorous yet remote, Peter Pan.

VALK, Frederick (d. 1956). German actor who reached Britain via Czechoslovakia. His titanic Othello (1942) and fine Shylock (1943) for the Vic, was followed by Othello (1946) opposite Wolfit as Iago, the acting equivalent of Waterloo and Stalingrad. The Desdemona, Rosalind Iden, just survived.

VOSPER, Frank (1899–1937). English actor and dramatist whose short career was studded with masterly character performances, including Henry VIII in *The Rose Without a Thorn* (1932) and Dulcimer in *The Green Bay Tree* (1933). He brilliantly adapted a Christie short story for his *Love From a Stranger* (1936) in which he played the killer, and wrote *People Like Us* (1929), a moving drama about the Thompson–Bywaters murder. He was drowned at sea.

WALLACH, Eli (b. 1915). American actor, the first Alvarro in *The Rose Tattoo* (1951) and Kilroy in *Camino Real* (1953). A very successful Sakini in *The Teahouse of the August Moon* in London and New York. Recent parts have included Charles in *Staircase* (1968).

WALLER, Lewis (1860–1915). English actor-manager, a very popular romantic actor with a huge female following. His trumpet voice made him an ideal Henry V. Monsieur Beaucaire was his most famous romantic part.

WARNER, David (b. 1941). English actor best known for two major performances with the Royal Shakespeare Co., a moving Henry VI in *The Wars of the Roses* (1963–4) and a much admired, though unprincely Hamlet in Peter Hall's production (1965), also for his film rôles.

WELLES, Orson (b. 1915). American theatre and film giant whose Shakespearean rôles have included Hamlet, Mercutio, Lear (in a wheel chair perforce), Brutus and Othello. Also see Mercury Theater, page 129.

WILLIAMSON, Nicol (b. 1938). Scottish actor of striking power and talent, whose finest performances have included Bill Maitland in *Inadmissable Evidence* (1964) – 'sour eloquence and rancid fury'

(Michael Billington) – a controversial but much admired Hamlet (1969), and a scorching Coriolanus (1973) for the Royal Shakespeare Co.

WOFFINGTON, Peg (c. 1714–1760). Dublin-born actress and beauty whose famous *menage à trois* with Garrick and Macklin, and prowess in breeches parts, especially Sir Harry Wildair in *The Constant Couple*, should not be allowed to overshadow her excellence in comedy in general and as high-born ladies in particular, including Millimant. Her harsh voice kept her away from tragedy. Her Sir Harry, better than Garrick's, was the toast of London.

WOLFIT, Sir Donald (1902–1968). English actor-manager, the greatest Lear of modern times (1944), whose touring company brought Shakespeare to hundreds of thousands in Britain and overseas. Other famous parts, in a career which first became notable at the Old Vic and Stratford in the '20s and '30s (Cassius, Claudius, Kent, etc.) were Richard III, Touchstone, Iago, the Master Builder, Volpone, etc. His actor-managerial career, indeed his whole life, can only be understood by reading Ronald Harwood's critical, but affectionate biography, *Sir Donald Wolfit*. A rare performance as leader of a strong ensemble was his Tamburlaine at the Old Vic (1951) for Guthrie, with Wolfit a Mongol horde in himself and magnificent until, later in the run, he fell back on actor-managerial tricks in the old tradition. Later rôles included Oedipus Rex, Hook, leads in Ibsen and in Montherlant, as well as recitals with his talented wife, **Rosalind IDEN** (b. 1911), who was a fine Viola, Portia and, especially, Rosalind.

WOOD, John fine English actor, whose performances in the early '70s with the Royal Shakespeare Co. have lifted him to the front rank of contemporary actors: Sir Fopling in *The Man of Mode*, Brutus, Yakov Bardin in *Enemies*, Richard Rowan in *Exiles*, Sherlock Holmes (1974) to the manner born.

WORTH, Irene (b. 1916). American actress, mainly in the British theatre. Major performances have included a 'Truly tragic . . . the best' Desdemona (Darlington) at the Old Vic (1951), a magnificent Hedda (1970) and many fine modern rôles, including her Alice in *Tiny Alice* (1964) which won her the New York Drama Critics Award.

ii~Non-English-Speaking

ACKERMANS. A German acting family of the 18th century, founded by **Konrad Ernst Ackermann** (1710–71), whose company played at the new German National Theatre when it opened in 1764. His second wife was the actress, **Sophia Schröder**, and his stepson was the great **Friedrich Schröder**. The Ackermanns did much to raise the level of German theatre. Also see EKHOF and SCHRÖDER.

BARRAULT, Jean-Louis (b. 1910). Leading French actor, director and mime, who married the actress **Madeleine RENAUD** in 1940, joining the Comédie-Française that year. They left in 1946 to form their own company, having startled the august institution, partly by Barrault's speed of delivery, partly by extending the repertoire. His productions of *Antony and Cleopatra* and Claudel's *Le Soulier de Satin* were especially notable. The Compagnie Renaud-Barrault was soon famous at home and abroad, playing Claudel, Offenbach, *Hamlet* in Gide's translation, with Barrault as Hamlet, in his own (with Gide) adaptation of Kafka's *The Trial*. In 1959, he became director of the Théâtre de France, France's second theatre.

BASSERMAN, Albert (1867–1952). German actor, son of August Bassermann, and his country's finest Ibsen player. Driven out by the Nazis.

BELL, Marie (b. 1900). Major French actress who has combined light rôles and film stardom with great parts at the Comédie-Française, including Esther, Bérénice, Phèdre and Agrippine, also the Madame in Genet's *The Balcony*.

BÉJART family. A French acting family, closely linked with Molière. **Madeleine Béjart** was his mistress and played his witty maids, as well as managing his company's finances, and Molière later married her adopted daughter (or daughter) Armande, who was to create his later heroines.

BERNHARDT, Sarah (1845–1923). The most famous, internationally as well as nationally, French actress of her day who, after making her name in Coppée's *Le Passant* (1869), became first the star of the Comédie-Française after her Cordelia and the Queen in *Ruy Blas*, then, travelling and in her own Paris theatres, even more famous in a wide number of rôles. These included Phèdre, Hamlet, the King of Rome in *L'Aiglon*, and the leads in Sardou's melodramas, *La Tosca*, *Fédora* and *Théodora*. She stormed London in 1879 with Phèdre, New York in 1880 with Adrienne Lecouvreur. A slim beauty in her youth, she retained her unique 'golden bell' of a voice to the end, long before which she was a legend.

BIANCOLELLI family. A famous Italian 17th-century family of *commedia dell'arte* players.

BOCAGE, Pierre Francois (1797–1863). French Romantic actor, especially famous in Dumas rôles.

BRASSEUR, Pierre (1905–1972). French actor who, after playing Lemaître in the film, *Les Enfan. du Paradis*, became a flamboyant latter-day Lemaître for whom Sartre wrote *Kean* in 1958.

CASARÈS, Maria (b. 1922). French tragedienne who, after playing Deirdre of the Sorrows (1943) leads in Camus plays, etc., joined the Comédie-Française in 1952, playing the Step-Daughter in *Six Characters in Search of an Author* and a wide range of parts. Her performance in Merimée's *Le Carrosse du Saint-Sacrement* proved that this intense actress was also a comedienne. Since then she has had major successes including Lady Macbeth and Phèdre, and in Marivaux's comedy, *Le Triomphe de l'amour*.

COQUELIN, Constant-Benoit (1841–1909). The best-known of a French acting family, creator of Rostand's *Cyrano de Bergerac* and author of two major books on acting, *L'Art et le comédien* (1880) and *Les Comédiens par un comédien* (1882).

DEBURAU, Jean Gaspard (1796–1846). French

Edwige Feuillère, the renowned French actress whose most famous rôle has been the Lady of the Camelias. (Photo: David Sim)

mime who originated the famous Pierrot in the floppy white costume. He became the star attraction at the Funambules and was re-born via Jean-Louis Barrault in the film, *Les Enfants du Paradis*.

DE FILIPPO. See page 65 .

DELYSIA, Alice (b. 1889). French actress and singer, enormously popular in Britain in Cochran revues.

DEVRIENT family. A German acting family from the 18th century to the present, founded by **Ludwig Devrient** (1784–1832), a magnificent Falstaff who preferred himself in tragic rôles like Richard III and Shylock.

DUSE, Eleonora (1859–1924). Incomparable Italian actress, Bernhardt's main rival internationally, but far more subtle and thoughtful, if less obviously exciting. She was the mistress of Boito, Verdi's great librettist, and, later, of D'Annunzio, in whose plays she shone (*La Gioconda*, etc.), as she did in

Sardou (*Tosca*, etc.) and as Marguerite in *La Dame aux Camélias*. Gordon Craig directed her in *Rosmersholm* at Florence (1906).

EKHOF, Konrad (1720–1778). German actor, not only a major player, but one who did much to raise the status of his profession. He was with the Ackermann company for some years, and excelled in comedy and tragedy.

FEUILLÈRE, Edwige (b. 1907). French actress who became famous in Becque's *La Parisienne* and in *La Dame aux camélias*, both in 1937. Since then she has had major successes creating rôles in Giraudoux's *Sodome et Gomorrhe* (1943), Cocteau's *The Eagle has Two Heads* (1946) and Claudel's *Partage de midi* (1948), etc. Her Phèdre (1957) was considered un-classical.

FRESNAY, Pierre (b. 1897). French actor who made his name at the Comédie-Française (1914–26), then had a huge success in the title-rôle of Pagnol's *Marius* (1929), which he later played in the film. With his wife, the delightful actress and singer, **Yvonne PRINTEMPS**, he played in Coward's *Conversation Piece* in London (1934); a later success, which he also produced, was Anouilh's *Léocadia* (1940). A major film actor.

GRUNDGENS, Gustav. See page 143 .

GUITRY, Sacha (1885–1957). French actor and dramatist, son of Lucien Guitry, the actor, dramatist and manager. He starred in many of his own gossamer plays, often with his then wife, **Yvonne Printemps.** They include *Mozart* (1926) and *Frans Hals* (1931), and he also made successful films. A major comedian, actor and man-of-the-theatre.

JOUVET, Louis. See page 147 .

LECOUVREUR, Adrienne (1692–1730). French tragic actress, who joined the Comédie-Française in 1717, playing the title-rôle in Crebillon's *Electre*, and who banished the stilted methods of her predecessors. The mistress of Marshal Saxe, her story inspired Scribe and Legouvé's (inaccurate) *Adrienne Lecouvreur*.

LEMAÎTRE, Frédérick (1800–1876). A supreme French Romantic actor, superbly equipped to shine in melodrama and the great classical rôles: Hamlet, Othello, etc. More disciplined than Edmund Kean, he played the British genius in Dumas' *Kean, ou Désordre et Génie* (1836) and Hugo's *Ruy Blas* (1838), two of his finest achievements. Though his influence on the French theatre was great, he never played at the Comédie-Française, for which his methods might have been too powerful.

LENYA, Lotte (b. 1901). German singer and actress, the wife of Kurt Weill, and the incomparable creator of rôles by him and Brecht in *Mahagonny* (1927), *The Threepenny Opera* (1931) and *The Seven Deadly Sins* (1933), etc.

MARS, Anne Françoise Hippolyte (1779–1847). A famous French actress of the Comédie-Française. at home in tragedy and comedy: Molière, Dumas, Hugo, etc.

MODJESKA, Helena (1844–1909). Poland's most famous actress, a major tragedienne, first in Warsaw, then, from 1876 when she emigrated to America, as an international artist.

MONTDORY, Guillaume (1594–1651). One of the first great French actors, who first produced *Le Cid* (1636) and played the lead in it, Rodrigue.

PAXINOU, Katina (1900–1973). The greatest Greek actress of her day, who formed her own company with Alexis Minotis, her husband. As well as the supreme Greek rôles, including Medea, she played in O'Neill – Abbie in *Desire Under the Elms* – Lorca and Ibsen. Her most famous parts are Mrs. Alving in *Ghosts* and Bernarda Alba in *The House of Bernarda Alba*. She often acted in English on stage and screen.

PHILLIPE, Gérard (1922–1959). French actor internationally famous in films, but a major stage player from the 1940s. Camus' Caligula (1945), the lead in *Le Cid* (1951) for Vilar, etc. A very fine heroic actor.

RACHEL (1820–1858), whose real name was Elisa Felix, was a poor Jewish girl street singer who became perhaps the greatest of all French tragediennes. Joining the Comédie-Française in 1838, she was soon the supreme exponent of classical rôles like Phèdre and Hermione and also sensationally successful in modern parts, including Adrienne Lecouvreur. She toured Europe and visited America (1855), dying of consumption and overwork. Like the actress-singer Malibran, whose slightly earlier career was remarkably similar, she stirred her contemporaries as no one else did, and remains a thrilling, legendary name.

RAIMU (1883–1946), whose real name was Jules Muraire, was a supreme French character actor on stage and screen, excelling especially in Pagnol's *Marius* (1929) and *Fanny* (1931) and at the Comédie-Française in *L'Avare* and *Le Malade Imaginaire*.

RÉJANE (1857–1920), whose real name was Gabrielle Charlotte Réju, was a superb light comedian, her most famous rôle being Madame Sans-Gêne. She was internationally known.

RISTORI, Adelaide (1822–1906). Great Italian actress in Shakespeare, Schiller, etc., at home and abroad. Mrs. Kendal considered her greater than Sarah Bernhardt because Ristori managed to triumph without sex appeal.

ROSCIUS, Quintus (?–62 B.C.). The most famous Roman comic actor of his day who was making the equivalent of more than half a million pounds a year at the height of his popularity. His name has been used as a synonym for a major actor, e.g. The American Roscius, Ira Aldridge.

SALVINI, Tommaso (1829–1916). Italian actor, one of the most thrilling and volcanic of all Othellos at home and abroad.

SHCHEPKIN, Mikhail (1788–1863). A great Russian actor realistic but passionate, whose supreme triumphs were in the comic rôles of Shakespeare, Schiller and Gogol (*The Inspector General*). A major influence on Russian acting.

SCHRÖDER, Friedrich (1744–1816). A supreme figure in German theatre history, and the actor who introduced Shakespeare to Germany (though he tagged happy endings on to *Hamlet, Lear*, etc.). A subtle actor who believed in ensemble, he was particularly associated with Hamburg, where he worked with the Ackermanns, and with the Burgtheatrer in Vienna. As well as acting, he directed and managed.

TALMA, François Joseph (1763–1826). Great French actor of the Comédie-Française, much admired by Napoleon. He helped improve diction by increased naturalism and costumes by insisting on historical accuracy. A tragedian rather than a comedian, who triumphed despite much poor material.

WEIGEL, Helene (1900–1972). German actress, Brecht's wife and a famous interpreter of his major rôles – in *Mother Courage, The Caucasian Chalk Circle*, etc. She took over the direction of the Berliner Ensemble after Brecht's death.

ZACCONI, Ermete (1867–1948). Outstanding Italian actor in the great Shakespearean rôles, Tolstoy, Ibsen, etc., the first Oswald in *Ghosts* in Italy. A very versatile actor, his finest performances were as Hamlet and the title rôle in Testoni's *Il Cardinale Lambertini* (1905).

The theatre at Delphi, originally built in the 4th century B.C., but renovated in Roman times. It seated some 5,000 spectators. (Photo: Mansell Collection)

CHAPTER 4
THE PHYSICAL THEATRE

i~Theatre Architecture

GREECE

The earliest theatres known to us existed in Greece. They can be classified under three headings: Classical, Hellenistic and Graeco-Roman.

Classical

Greek theatre arose from the religious festivals celebrating the worship of the god Dionysius. Vast congregations were involved in the worship, so the physical conditions necessary for the celebrations were vast. The first audiences stood on a hill slope and looked down at the rhythmic dancing of a chorus. The chorus, made up of some fifty dancers, was sited at the bottom of the hill slope on a comparatively level piece of ground. This piece of ground was marked out in the form of a circle and was called the orchestra. In the centre of the orchestra, was an altar erected to the god. The movements of the chorus were accompanied by music.

From this situation, an actor evolved, and later a second and a third. The actors moved independently of the chorus and might play more than one part. They performed on a level strip of ground behind the orchestra. Where necessary, the hillslope was cut level for the actors.

With the establishment of a form of theatre separate from the earlier religious celebrations, the audience was provided with seats. These were built in tiers up the hillside. They were of wood and in consequence very little of the earliest theatres exists today. In the theatre of Dionysius at Athens, only a few stones of the first theatre can be traced, the present structure being of a much later period. In 499 B.C., a serious collapse of some of the wooden seating led to its replacement by permanent stone seating.

Until 465 B.C., there were no scene buildings. The actors performed against a background of open countryside or sea. In consequence, the earliest plays were set against backgrounds of open desert with no buildings in sight. Examples are *The Suppliants* (490 B.C.), *The Persians* (472 B.C.) and *Prometheus Bound* (c. 460 B.C.) by Aeschylus.

By 425 B.C., the skene had become so firmly established that it was set on a permanent stone base. It had become considerably more elaborate, and instead of being a simple small building against a background of open country, it had grown to become the whole of the background. It consisted now of a long front wall with a wing at each end. These wings projected towards the audience. Between them, a low stage was built, about a foot in height. On this stage, between the two wings and against the background of the skene, the actors gave their performances. Immediately behind the stage and in front of the skene was a structure of columns known as the proskenion, from which the word 'proscenium' is derived.

By the end of the 5th century B.C., the skene had become a permanent building, frequently made of stone. It had an upper storey – the *episkenion* – which was used for the operation of theatrical machines. The earlier convention of a desert back ground had now been superseded by a palace background, and three conventional doors had become established as part of the building. In tragedy, the doors had an individual significance: the centre door led directly into the palace and was reserved for royal persons; the left door (viewed from the audience) was used by secondary characters; the right door led to open country.

The orchestra in the theatre of this period was still a complete circle and the audience was seated round it in more than a semi-circle. A passageway called a *parados* existed at either end of the skene between the scene building itself and the audience. In time, these *paradoi* were closed by highly deco-

About 465 B.C., a significant change took place. A *skene* was erected behind the acting strip. This skene was first a simple, utilitarian building in which the actors could change. It meant, however, that the audience now saw a building as part of the background, and dramatists began to incorporate this skene into the action of their plays. In time, it became an established feature of the drama and action was set against a temple or palace – represented by the skene – instead of against an open landscape.

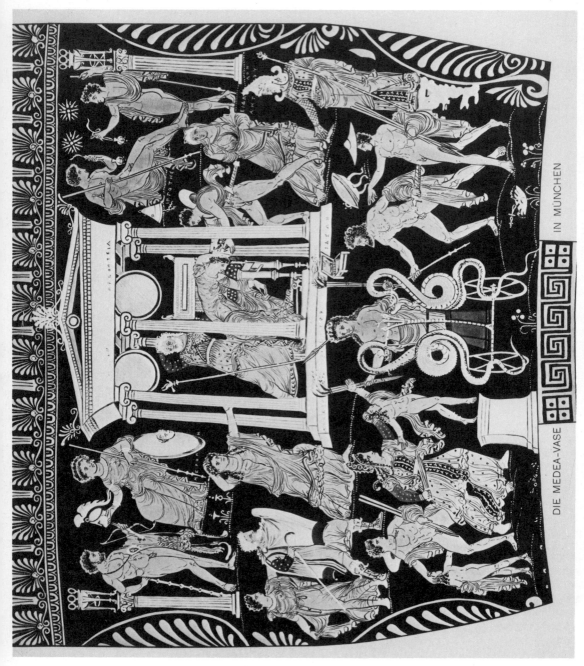

Medea's Revenge. The legend is the one used by Euripedes, but the scenes are not necessarily from any one version of the story. The vase painting dates from the 4th century B.C. (Photo: Mansell Collection)

rated gates. The original theatre at Epidaurus was an example of the skene and auditorium of this period.

Hellenistic

The Hellenistic theatre developed in the 4th century B.C. In some cases – the Dionysian theatre in Athens, for example – it was simply a reconstruction of existing earlier theatres. Other examples of Hellenistic theatres are at Epidaurus, Eretria, Oropos, Delos and Priene.

The typical Hellenistic theatre had a circular orchestra and an auditorium arranged round it in rather more than a semi-circle. The skene was rectangular and had three rooms, one of which was quite large. In the first storey of the skene –the episkenion – there were doorways. Some eight or nine feet in front of the skene was a series of columns which varied in height, according to the particular theatre, from ten to thirteen feet. These columns supported the stage. Ramps ran down from the two ends of the stage to the gateways of the paradoi.

The result was to isolate the actor completely from both chorus and audience. One of the reasons for this may have been to make the actor more clearly visible to the enormous audience, by raising him high above the ground.

Graeco-Roman

This last form of Greek theatre was developed under the growing influence of Rome, and the stage and stage buildings were of prime importance. Examples can be seen at Patara, Ephesus, Tralles, Myra, Magnesia, Sagalassos and Termessos.

The typical theatre had an auditorium that was still more than a semi-circle, but the orchestra was no longer a complete circle because of the encroachment of the stage buildings into it. The stage front, below the acting level, was highly decorated, as was the front of the scene building above the stage level. The stage depth was increased from the earlier eight or nine feet to something nearer twenty feet. The height of the stage was some two or three feet lower than in the Hellenistic theatre.

Costume

The tragic actor of Classical Greece was a well-thought-of member of the community. To a large extent this was the result of the religious origin of the theatre. As the theatre developed further and further from its religious sources, the social status of the actor declined.

The size of the auditorium dwarfed the actor. To overcome this he wore boots with raised wooden soles – the cothurnus – and a massive headdress – the onkos. These two devices increased his height to about seven and a half feet. To counterbalance this he wore padding, so that the appearance of his body was in proportion to his height. Over this padding he wore the dress of the period – the chiton and the cloak. The chiton was painted and ornamented according to the character the actor was playing. The colour of the cloak had a symbolic significance. Royal characters wore purple, for example, and characters in mourning wore dark colours. Rags indicated poverty, crowns indicated royalty, a crutch was symbolic of infirmity.

The tragic actor also wore a mask. This was formed in such a way that it made his speech more clearly audible in the vast theatre. The mask also bore the essential features of the character, showing age, station in life and general mood. It also showed the sex of the character, since all actors were male and female parts were therefore played by men.

The mask was made of linen, cork or wood and there were more than thirty different types available to the actor in tragedy. Apart from the general type of mask, there were special ones for particular purposes – the blind mask, the mask with a single eye or with a number of eyes, for example.

The costume for the comic actor was a parody of tragic costume. The padding was grotesque and the comic actor wore an exaggerated phallus. The comic actor was masked, and the mask revealed the status of the character, its sex and general nature.

Machines

Machines were used in both tragedy and comedy from comparatively early times. There were some fifteen or twenty machines in use, each capable of producing a special effect. A crane device was available, for example, to lower 'gods' from the top of the episkenion – the deus ex machina effect. A section of the stage could revolve to reveal the victims of a murder, since murder itself was not allowed to be shown.

Tall platforms were also used, together with low platforms on rollers. There were trap doors which

STRODE'S COLLEGE

A scene from Peter Brook's already legendary production of A Midsummer Night's Dream *for the Royal Shakespeare Company. Bottom (David Waller) is in the process of being 'translated'. (Photo: Camera Press, London)*

could be used for surprise entrances and exits, and thunder and lightning machines to suggest storms.

ROME

The Theatres
Initially, only wooden theatre buildings were allowed by the Senate and when a stone theatre was built in 154 B.C., the Senate ordered it to be pulled down. Later, this attitude changed and during the period 55–52 B.C., the first stone theatre was built on the instructions of Pompey. Many examples of Roman theatres still exist in the area once covered by the Empire. Those at Aspendos and Orange are particularly good examples.

The typical Roman theatre was sited on level ground, with the auditorium built up to improve lines of sight. The auditorium and scene buildings were conceived as a whole rather than as two separate units. In consequence, the paradoi of the Greek theatre were replaced by covered passages. The auditorium was exactly a semi-circle. The orchestra was also a semi-circle and was constructed in such a way that it could be flooded for the miniature naval battles that were so popular. Sometimes it was used for gladiatorial spectacles.

The stage was much deeper than it had been in the Greek theatre, and the height was about five feet. There were doors in the *hyposcenium* – the stage wall – and steps connected the stage with the orchestra. The hyposcenium was decorated with carved reliefs. The *frons scaenae* – the wall at the back of the stage, corresponding to the episkenion of the Greeks – was decorated with a number of doors and openings. In some theatres, a roof projected from the top of the frons scaenae over the stage.

In the later theatres a curtain – the *auleum* – was used. It was housed in a recess near the front of the stage and was lifted upwards instead of being dropped as in the modern theatre. Awnings could be drawn over the top of the *cavae* – the auditorium – to protect the audience from excessive heat from the sun, and rosewater was sprinkled into the air by slaves, to cool the atmosphere.

The actors and their costumes
The religious festivities out of which the Greek theatre arose, did not exist as far as the Roman theatre was concerned. The actors were mostly troops of slaves, trained by a manager to give particular performances. They usually had no social status, but could become very famous. See ROSCIUS in the preceding chapter.

The costumes worn by the actors were modelled on the earlier Greek costumes. *Buskins* – the cothurni of the Greeks – increased the height of the actor. Wigs and masks were worn and the colour of costumes took on a more detailed symbolism: white for old men, purple for young men; parasitic characters wore grey and courtesans yellow. Again, white hair indicated age, black hair youth, and red hair indicated a slave.

Initially, the comedy of Rome followed that of Greece. Later it degenerated. The *mimus* appeared, a type of knockabout farce with crude stock characters – stupid old men, faithless wives, slick seducers, braggarts. The mimus was highly bawdy and in them women appeared on the stage for the first time. The *pantomimus* was an even more vulgar type of farce, accompanied by licentious singing and dancing.

As the Christian church grew stronger, it increased its opposition to the theatres. In the 6th century A.D., Justinian ordered the theatres closed. Similar pressure from the church in Byzantium resulted in the closure of the theatres in the east in the 7th century A.D.

EARLY EASTERN THEATRE

India
A form of theatre had appeared in India by the first century A.D. It took place in palaces and temples and was religious in essence. Such stages as the players set up inside the buildings they were using, were carefully consecrated before any performance on them took place.

Performances took the form of complex dances, with symbolic gestures. The themes of the dramas were highly romantic and were concerned with the lives of royalty and the gods. This form of theatre reached its zenith between the 3rd and 8th centuries A.D. and then declined.

The actors in these dramas were professional and itinerant. Their stages were erected for each performance and dismantled afterwards. There was no permanent stage building in India until the British built one in 1776 in Calcutta.

China
Forms of theatre in China appeared very early. There were theatrical elements in the religious festivals in the 7th century B.C. But the main tra-

dition of Chinese theatre began in the 8th century A.D., under the emperor Ming Huang. The plays were usually comedies, based on well-known stories. They were performed inside the palace, usually by two actors.

Later, with the growing complexity of the plays, performances were given publicly on festive occasions. The stage used for theatrical performances – whether given in palaces, temples or in public – was a temporary construction. A typical theatre was a platform raised on wooden stilts, with a roof over the top. The platform contained a small acting area and room for musicians. Properties were available which had a symbolic significance for the audience. There was a dressing room behind or to one side of the main structure. Occasionally, the building had a second storey. Such scenery as existed was symbolic – a banner painted with waves, for example, symbolised the sea.

Japan (1)
Early theatre elements which existed as part of Buddhist festivities from early times, had developed into a recognisable theatre form by the 8th century A.D. But not until the 14th century was the classic *noh* theatre established. Since then, this form has hardly changed.

The *noh* stage was a platform some eighteen feet square, raised a few feet from the ground. The audience was placed round three sides of the stage. A passage – the *hashigakari* – led to the stage from the dressing room on the left (audience viewpoint). Three small pines were attached to the hashigakari and were of conventional significance. At the back of the stage was a painted background of woods and in front of it the orchestra sat. On the right of the stage was a chorus.

Two to six actors usually appeared in the play. The principal actor, the *shite*, and his companion, the *tsure*; a secondary character, the *waki*, and his companion. Sometimes a child – the *korata* – appeared, and also a further actor, the *ahi*.

The actors were all men, trained for their work from an early age. They wore highly coloured costumes of great richness. The shite and the tsure wore beautifully worked masks. The themes of the plays were well-known folk legends. The acting was so highly conventionalised that it had – and has – little significance for an uninitiated spectator.

MEDIEVAL THEATRE IN EUROPE
European theatre in the Middle Ages rose from two sources – the relics of the Roman mimus perpetuated by wandering players, and, especially, the celebrations of the Christian church.

Wandering Players in the Dark Ages
Contrary to legend, the knockabout farce of the Roman mimi did not die with the official closure of the theatres in the 6th and 7th centuries A.D. It was preserved by itinerant actors who gave performances in halls and courts as well as at markets and fairs. They went by many names – *mimi, histriones, jongleurs, ministri, ministralli.* Their performances included mime, music, singing, dance and acrobatics. Their costumes were contemporary and their properties rudimentary. Their stages were sometimes raised platforms, sometimes simply open spaces on the ground. They wandered Europe in groups, giving performances wherever they were invited.

The Church
From the 10th century A.D. onwards, small dramatic scenes began to appear in churches as part of the Christian celebrations of Christmas and Easter. The scenes depicted the birth and crucifixion of Christ. The actors were priests and the setting was the church itself. In the Easter play, for example, a cross was set against the north wall of the nave to symbolise the high altar. On the left (audience viewpoint) was set the Sepulchre and Heaven, and on the right Prison and Hell. Those characters in the Passion associated with Heaven, stood on the left; those associated with Hell stood on the right.

The popularity of the performances made it necessary to move them outside the church so that the growing audience could be accommodated. The arrangement remained substantially as it had been inside the church, with a central cross, Heaven to the left and Hell to the right. These various positions were arranged in a line in front of the audience and were known as 'mansions'. The action took place in front of them in turn.

Costumes became more elaborate and such set pieces as Hell's Mouth became highly decorated. The church introduced a ban which forbade the clergy to take part in the plays any longer, and the actors became members of the local population, and at times the professional wandering players.

Secular Control
With the withdrawal of the church from the plays,

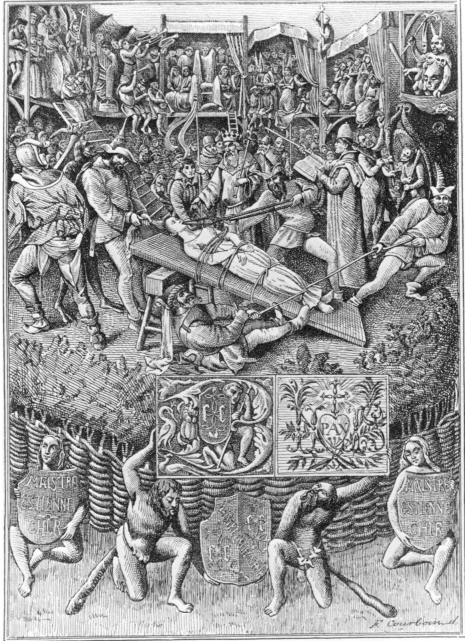

This is the only picture to show a Mystery play in performance. The drama is The Martyrdom of Saint Apollonia *and the original painting was drawn by Jean Fouguet (1415-83). Note the director with a wand and the prompt book. Is it a public dress rehearsal? (From the Mansell Collection)*

109

their organisation was taken over by secular authorities, usually the trade guilds. The texts of the plays were elaborated and sequences of plays, known as Mystery Cycles, were created. These were performed by members of the guilds, sometimes with a stiffening of the wandering professional actors.

Two forms of setting evolved, a static and a mobile one. The static setting evolved in France. A series of mansions were erected, facing an open square. They were arranged in a straight line or in a semicircle. The earlier convention still obtained, whereby Heaven and its associated mansions lay to the left of the centre line, and Hell to the right. This method of setting became known as *décor simultané* or 'multiple setting'.

The mansions became increasingly elaborate. Some had two storeys. Hell was singled out for particularly detailed treatment, with a gaping mouth into which the wicked were pitched. Steps led down from the mansions to the level square in front of them. The square was used as an acting area. It represented no fixed location. When Herod appeared on it, it became his palace courtyard: when the disciples used it, it might become the Garden of Gethsemene.

The mobile setting evolved in England and the Low Countries. Each guild was responsible for a particular scene, where possible a logical one – the Shipwrights and the Building of the Ark, etc. – and it mounted this scene on a 'pageant' or cart. The pageant stopped at certain places in a town during the celebration of Corpus Christi, and played its scene before an audience. It then moved to the next stop and replayed the scene before a new audience. A considerable number of pageants made up the whole Mystery Cycle. Most pageants were in an upper and lower section. The lower section was used for changing costumes, and the upper section – together with the street itself – was used for acting.

Since a pageant was a showpiece of the guild that had produced it, considerable care was taken in its construction and decoration.

Machinery and Effects

The machinery and effects of the Mystery Cycles showed a great deal of ingenuity. Hell's Mouth was depicted as the mouth of a massive beast. It could often close by means of a hinged jaw. It was lavishly and terrifyingly painted, and it could emit smoke and fire.

Trapdoors in some of the mansions and pageants allowed devils to descend into Hell. Earthquakes and thunderbolts were produced, and the activities of the devils were accompanied by the explosion of fireworks.

Costumes

Costumes were elaborate. Demons appeared in the skins of wolves and domestic animals. They wore the horns of bulls and rams and carried bells. Animal heads, masks, beards, wigs, were all worn by actors in the Cycles.

Adam and Eve sometimes wore white leather to suggest nudity. Persons of high birth wore highly elaborate dress.

The costume, except where it was to have a special significance, was the ordinary dress of the day. Colours had conventional meanings: Cain was dressed in red, Abel in white. White was also associated with Mercy. Green signified Truth, black Peace, and red Pity.

The Actors

The actors were usually the members of the guild responsible for the play. They were paid a token fee for their work – in 1483 in Hull, God was paid sixpence; in 1494 his pay had risen to tenpence. All the actors were men, and the 'mechanicals' scenes in *A Midsummer Night's Dream* give an idea of how some of them might have worked.

It seems likely that the professional performers, still wandering Europe and preserving the last remnants of the mimi of Rome, were used to play the more important parts in the Cycles. Their influence on the development of the comic scenes, and particularly of the Fool tradition, must have been considerable.

In France, this professional element was stronger than elsewhere. In 1402, for example, the *Confrèrie de la Passion* established the first permanent theatre at the *Hôpital de la Trinité* in Paris.

The acting style in the Cycles was highly realistic. Bladders were filled with animal blood, so that stabbing and tortures might appear real. Real instruments of torture were employed and actors sometimes endured actual pain. In one play, Christ almost died on the cross before being taken down. On another occasion, the Judas lost consciousness when he was hanged too realistically.

The Mysteries embraced the Bible from the

Creation to the Last Judgement. In the 15th century they were joined by the Moralities, played on fixed stages, in which virtues and vices and conditions – Mischief, Mercy, Good Deeds, Fellowship, Goods, etc. – were personified, often more dramatically and entertainingly than they sound. The most famous English example, *Everyman*, dates from the 1470s and is probably from the Dutch. The borderline between amateur and professional was now very blurred.

The Interlude

In France in the 14th century, and a little later elsewhere in Europe, the Interlude appeared. It was a brief, farcical play that is directly related to the Roman mimi. It was played as part of a banquet in the hall of a nobleman. The stage was very simple – a raised platform at the end of the hall, with a curtained background. The setting and costumes were also simple. Essential properties consisted of such things as a throne, a stool, a table. The actors playing in interludes were professionals, specially hired for the occasion.

RENAISSANCE ITALY

The performance of Mystery Cycles continued unchanged throughout Europe until the mid-16th century. The Renaissance – the revival of interest in classical Greece and Rome – brought with it new forms of theatre to Italy and France. Performances of the plays of the Roman playwrights, Terence and Plautus, in the late 14th century were given in improvised theatres based on the Roman pattern. But the scenic arrangement of separate rooms for the various characters, derives from the *décor simultané* of the Mystery Cycles.

In 1486, the *De Architectura* of Vitruvius was published. The work, originally written about 15 B.C., gave detailed information to the Italians on the form and nature of the classical Greek theatre. The information had a considerable effect on their views on theatre buildings and set. Independently of the work of scholars investigating the theatre of Greece and Rome, there were developments in art and architecture. One of these was concerned with the use of perspective. The first recorded use of perspective in the theatre was at Ferrara in 1508. A backcloth was used depicting a landscape with buildings and giving the illusion of great depth and distance.

In 1551, the Italian architect Sebastiano Serlio published *Architettura*, containing his ideas on theatres. He visualised a semi-circular auditorium on the Roman pattern, with a rectangular stage. The stage was in two parts. The forepart was level and was to be used for acting. The rear part was raked upwards towards the back, and was to be used for setting scenery. A backcloth was sited behind the raked stage, on which were painted scenes in perspective, and in front of the backcloth there were to be houses and other buildings, made out of wood and canvas to create the illusion of reality. All the acting was to take place in front of this complex set. The concept was an imitation of many of the principles of the classic theatre, with the addition of such features of the Medieval drama as the multiple set.

Between 1580 and 1584, the *Teatro Olimpico* was built in Vicenza by Palladio and Scamozzi. It was a permanent building with a semi-circular auditorium and a highly elaborate stone wall behind the raised acting area. In this wall were three doors, and behind each door were painted perspective views.

In 1618, the earliest proscenium arch appeared in the *Teatro Farnese* in Parma, and a curtain of the Roman type was used. The actors now used the whole depth of the stage instead of only that part in front of the scene buildings. The design of the Teatro Farnese has had a profound influence on all later theatres in the western world.

Machines and Effects

Permanent structures like the theatres at Vicenza and Parma, made the most complex and spectacular effects possible. Scenery could be changed to indicate changes of location, by sliding one painted piece in front of another. Backcloths could also be changed. Winches and rollers were used to produce effects like moving seas. Trapdoors were used and chariots and clouds could be made to appear and disappear by being lowered or raised from above.

Lighting was introduced for the first time as a part of the theatrical effect, and not simply to illuminate. Lanterns and candles were placed so as to contribute to the atmosphere of the action.

Commedia del' Arte

Relics of the old Roman mimi persisted, side by side with the new theatres. They were preserved

The historic Teatro Olimpico at Vicenza, built between 1579 and 1582 by Palladio and his pupil, Scamozzi. (Photo: Italian Institute, London)

by the professional itinerant companies. In 16th-century Italy, the *Commedia del' Arte* arose out of this tradition. The actors in the Commedia companies played stock characters – Arlecchina and Arlecchino, Pulcinella, Pantalone, etc. They wore distinctive costumes and improvised the dialogue during the course of the action. They usually played on the simple stage of the period, with a raised platform and a backcloth, but at times they also played in the new permanent theatres.

ELIZABETHAN AND STUART ENGLAND

Four main theatrical types can be distinguished in the period:

Court and University Theatre
Theatre performances began to take place at Court and in the Universities during the early part of Elizabeth I's reign. They were given in rectangular halls, and the elaborateness of the setting varied according to the size of the hall and the facilities available. Records of a performance in 1566, for example, show that stages very like those advocated by Serlio were in use, with multiple sets, and some use of perspective.

The actors were amateurs – they might be choirboys, or members of the Court or University. John Lyly, the playwright, had a company of boy actors who played at a hall in Blackfriars. An interesting feature of these performances was the introduction of a curtain suspended from rings, which could be drawn and opened to hide or reveal the stage.

The Public Theatres
The first public playhouses were converted inn yards. But the critical attitude of the London authorities to the professional theatre, made the companies decide to move outside their control. In 1576, James Burbage built *The Theatre* at Shoreditch for his company, the Chamberlain's Men, and followed this with *The Curtain*. In 1587, Philip Henslowe built *The Rose* in Southwark for his company, the Lord Admiral's Men. In 1595 *The Swan* was built in Southwark, and in 1599 *The Globe*. We know sadly little about any of them, but the following generalisations may serve in a short account:

The theatres were anything from round to octagonal, with galleries for the audience built one above the other. A large, raised stage jutted out from one wall of the theatre into the orchestra or

pit, which was open to the sky. The wall behind the stage was decorated in a way that suggested the Teatro Olimpico. The wall was pierced by three openings, the central one larger than the other two. Two further openings existed in the side walls.

The stage has a canopy over it, supported by columns, the ceiling being painted blue and decorated with golden stars. It was sometimes called 'the heavens'. Above the stage, were windows which were used by both actors and, some allege, the audience. There were in effect two stages, that which existed in front of the rear wall, and an inner stage which could be seen through the central doorway of the rear wall. The inner stage, which was used as a room or simply as a background, could be isolated from the outer stage by a curtain. (Not everyone agrees that this inner stage existed.)

Unlike the stage in the multiple set theatre, the stage in the Elizabethan public theatres could be made to represent any location. The location might be established by pieces of scenery which made the location clear. Frequently the text indicated the location – 'But till the King come forth, and not till then, Unto Southampton do we shift our scene.' (*Henry* V, II i)

The theatres were 'sumptuous', according to the reports of Continental visitors, with elaborately carved and painted interiors. Machinery such as cranes and trapdoors were widely used. Costumes still had some symbolic significance. The cloak of invisibility was an example. An audience accepted the convention that any character wearing it could not be seen by his fellows. The actors, who were professionals, were all male. They were not 'rogues and vagabonds', as Puritan propaganda alleged, and the audiences of all classes, apart from being very receptive, were a good deal more intelligent, probably, than legend and sneers by disappointed dramatists allow. Performances began around 2 p.m. to catch the light, a trumpet sounding from the tower, which housed machinery, to mark the start. A flag flew throughout, and audiences of some 2,000 seem to have been the rule.

The Private Theatres
The Private Theatres continued the traditions of the hall stages. They were covered, rectangular buildings lit by large candelabra. An example was the *Blackfriars*, built in 1576 and acquired in 1596 by Burbage as the winter quarters of the Chamberlain's Men. Other examples were *The Cockpit* in

Drury Lane, the *Whitefriars* and the *Salisbury Court*.

The Court Masques

The Masque had points in common with the Interlude. It was comparatively short, took place in a covered hall and, in Jacobean times, increasingly used scenery and scenic effects.

Inigo Jones was the principal driving force behind the development of the Masque. He was widely travelled and had visited the Italian theatres at Vicenza and Parma. In 1605 he mounted, in collaboration with Ben Jonson, *The Masque of Blackness*, in which he introduced such scenic ideas as a moving sea, revealed by removing a painted landscape placed in front of it. He experimented with a series of periaktoi – a three-sided Greek device with a scene painted on each side – which he turned to change an entire background. He used side wings, painted on both sides and mounted on pivots so that they could be turned through 180 degrees, to produce an almost instantaneous change of scene.

The later masques were put on in halls where almost half the available floor space was raised as a stage. The stage was arranged not only for acting but for the mounting of complex sets. At the back was a painted cloth which could be raised to reveal a change of scene. In front of the cloth were flats of painted canvas on wooden frames. They could be slid into and out of view in wooden tracks. Above the stage were cloud effects and machinery allowed figures to descend and ascend.

In front of the stage was a special seating block reserved for the principal members of the audience – the sovereign and certain members of the court. On either side were tiers of seats for less distinguished members of the audience.

Highly imaginative and lavish costumes were used in the masques, and special music was composed for them. Elaborate costume of the period was used, together with exotic Indian and Oriental designs. The actors who played in the masques were amateurs – members of the Court or other privileged bodies, who enjoyed taking part in the performances. As they were private, women could take part.

JAPAN (2)

From an early period, puppet theatre had existed in Japan, but in the 17th century it reached a new popularity in the form known as *Joruri*. The productions given in the puppet theatre were very elaborate. The puppets themselves were about two-thirds life size and were fully articulated. Some of them required more than one manipulator.

The puppeteers worked in full view of the audience and wore black to establish a convention of invisibility. Where necessary, a short puppeteer would wear wooden 'lifts' to raise him to the necessary height. The actions of the puppets were accompanied by music and song.

Kabuki also became an independent theatre form during this period, separating from the *noh* theatre and becoming more essentially popular. The actors were not masked, as in *noh*, and wore highly decorated costume and, in some cases, very elaborate make-up. Female parts were always acted by males. The elaborate scenery was changed by stage hands in full view of the audience. Conventionally, the stage hands were regarded as invisible. It is still a more popular form today than *noh*.

FRENCH AND ITALIAN SPECTACLE

The scenic ideas first put forward by Serlio, continued to be exploited in Italy and France. In sheer spectacle, Italian theatre and opera dominated Europe throughout the 17th and 18th centuries. Lavish sets were used, and the most ingenious methods of set-changing devised.

Machinery grew infinitely complex and such realistic effects as storms and shipwrecks became almost commonplace. The most famous name of the period in connection with set design was that of the Bibiena family. They dominated the field from the early 17th until the late 18th centuries. See page 140.

An important feature of the Italian and French theatres was that the actors ceased to work exclusively in front of the proscenium arch. Certain interior scenes – those which took place in rooms, for example – were played behind the proscenium, with the arch itself forming a frame for the action.

Theatres grew in size to accommodate the increasingly elaborate sets required not only by the drama but also by the opera. Vigarani's *Salle de Machines* theatre, for example, built in Paris in the 1660s, had a proscenium opening of 32 feet and a stage depth of 132 feet. Such theatres and the spectacles they mounted, influenced the whole of Europe, though their influence in England was less strong than elsewhere.

A whole literature has been built round this picture of the Swan Theatre as it is the only extant drawing of an Elizabethan theatre know to xist. Unfortunately it is a copy by Arend van Buchell of the original rawing made by a Dutch visitor to the heatre in 1596, Johann de Witt. (From he Author's Collection)

ENGLAND IN THE RESTORATION

In 1642, public theatre performances in England were banned during the commonwealth. Between that date and the restoration of the monarchy in 1660, no legal public performances of plays took place. In the provinces, some theatre performances continued, particularly of 'drolls' – condensed versions of Elizabethan plays. Attempts were made in London to circumvent the law by the introduction of plays with music. In 1656, for example, Sir William Davenant – Poet Laureate and producer of masques during the reign of Charles I – gave a performance of *The Seige of Rhodes*, a play with music. The performance took place in his own home before an invited audience.

With the return of Charles II to the throne, the ban on theatrical entertainment was lifted. Only two companies of performers, however, were authorised – the King's Men under the management of Thomas Killigrew, and the Duke's Men under Davenant. For the first time, women could perform on the stage.

The first performances after the Restoration took place in the old enclosed halls such as *The*

Cockpit. For three years, Killigrew's company used a converted tennis court until the first *Theatre Royal* had been built in Drury Lane in 1663. This theatre followed the Italian pattern with a pit in front of the stage and almost circular tiers of boxes. Particular attention was paid to scenic effects, after the style laid down in France and Italy.

In 1671 Davenant's company moved to the *Dorset Garden* theatre – possibly designed by Christopher Wren. The pit was almost surrounded by two tiers of seven boxes each, with an open gallery above them. On either side of the stage were two doors, used by the actors for entering and leaving the stage. Balconies over the doors could be used either by audience or actors. The acting took place in front of the proscenium arch, using the lavish scenic effects as backgrounds.

The Drury Lane theatre burnt down in 1672, but was rebuilt by Wren and opened again in 1674. The new theatre had three galleries, one above the other, almost surrounding the pit. The lower gallery was made up of boxes, with a royal box placed centrally. The theatre's scenic area took up half the available space of the building. A special room under the stage was available for the machinery necessary for the elaborate effects and set-changes.

The audiences in these theatres were mainly of the upper class. They attended the performances as much to be in the fashion as to see the plays. Pepys has left us unforgettable glimpses of the Restoration Theatre in his *Diary*.

The two authorised theatre companies merged in 1682 and came under the management of Christopher Rich, who thus had a monopoly of all theatre performances in London.

ENGLISH THEATRE IN THE EIGHTEENTH CENTURY

The early years of the 18th century saw the gradual decline of the rabid puritanism that had closed the theatres in the previous century. This led to a wider type of audience than had existed in the period immediately following the Restoration, with less bawdy, but distinctly less brilliant, plays, and a move towards more spectacular entertainment, musical entertainments and pantomimic displays.

In 1728, John Rich and John Gay produced *The Beggar's Opera*. The work was to establish a long line of Ballad Opera in England.

In 1732, the first Covent Garden theatre was opened under the management of John Rich, and in 1737 the Licensing Act came into force, by which only Drury Lane and Covent Garden were authorised to produce plays in London. The Act was evaded to some extent by arguing that musical entertainments were outside it. The Italian opera, for example, came to the Queen's Theatre in the Haymarket, and from there Handel continues to exert his considerable influence. Not until 1843 was the Act repealed. One way round it had been the Burletta.

During the later years of the century, both Drury Lane and Covent Garden were rebuilt or altered on a number of occasions. In 1746, David Garrick became joint manager of Drury Lane, and remained in control of the theatre for thirty years. Garrick was followed by the playwright, Richard Brinsley Sheridan, who mounted his own play *The School for Scandal* as his first production.

In 1794, a rebuilt theatre was opened, in which five tiers of boxes and a considerably bigger pit appeared. Some attention was paid to the safety of the audience – a sheet iron curtain could separate stage from auditorium, and four water storage tanks were built into the roof in case the building caught fire. William Capon broke with the classic convention and designed scenery based on such locations as the Tower of London and the Palace of Westminster. The Alsatian artist, Loutherbourg, designed naturalistic outdoor scenes and invented transparent scenery. He used built-up scenery rather than flat painted scenes. He removed the footlights, which had developed through the earlier years, and introduced scenes lit only from above and from the sides.

Certain conventions continued. Costume could be contemporary, but there were also conventional Eastern costumes and conventional Roman ones which paid little attention to historical accuracy. The convention of doors leading directly on to the stage in front of the proscenium arch continued, and did not finally disappear from English provincial theatres until the 20th century. David Garrick managed to remove spectators from the stage, a pernicious habit that had started in Elizabethan times.

The theatres remained fashionable meeting places. After the enlarging of Covent Garden in 1784 and again in 1791, metal spikes protected the musicians in the orchestra from often riotous audiences in the pit.

In the British provinces, the tradition of strolling players continued. Performances were given at fairs, and in such playhouses as those at Bath, Leicester, Bristol. Richmond and Edinburgh.

AMERICAN THEATRE

During the early part of the 18th century, what theatre there was in America consisted lately of touring companies from England, playing in temporary buildings.

In the later years of the century, the first permanent theatres appeared. New England divines managed to stop playgoing during the Revolution, except in British-held areas, but these latter-day Puritans had no long term success. The New Theatre in Philadelphia, for example, was built in 1791, with a capacity of 1,165. It had proscenium doors and was modelled on the London theatres of the early 18th century. In 1798, the Park Theatre was built in New York, using similar models. It was rebuilt in 1821, after being destroyed by fire, on much more contemporary lines. It had four tiers of seats and could accommodate an audience of more than 2,000.

THEATRE IN THE NINETEENTH CENTURY

Two movements characterised the theatre of the 19th century: on the one hand a move towards increased spectacle; on the other a bias in favour of increased naturalism. Both movements affected theatre form, and reciprocally theatre form influenced both movements. In 1812, for example, when Drury Lane was rebuilt after the fire of 1809, it had a proscenium opening of 33 feet and an audience capacity of 3,200. Similarly, when Covent Garden was rebuilt in 1809 following the fire of the previous year, it had a proscenium opening of 42 feet and an audience capacity of 3,000. The sheer size of such theatres made it difficult for detailed actions to be seen and for speech to be heard and understood. In consequence, the theatres favoured pantomime and spectacle, and in the age of Edmund Kean, did the legitimate drama no good. The introduction of gas lighting in the early 19th century (1817 at Drury Lane) enhanced the spectacular side of productions.

In Britain, the process of theatrical evolution

was hastened, as noted, by the 1843 Act for Regulating the Theatres, which allowed 'legitimate drama' to be played in any theatre. New theatres appeared, and the old 'non-patent' theatres could if they wished compete for a new audience. The stage in front of the proscenium arch was increasingly reduced to make way for more audience seating. When the Haymarket Theatre reopened after alterations in 1843, the forestage had disappeared and the space was given over to 'orchestral stalls'. By the mid-century, the proscenium doors had been abolished, the actor was confined entirely behind the proscenium arch, and the curtain was universally in use to indicate the end of acts.

Alongside the increase in spectacle was a move towards increased historical accuracy in scenery and costume all over Europe. In 1823, James Robinson Planché designed sets and costumes for Kemble's production of *King John*, which aimed at accurate reproduction of the scenes and dress of the period. The production was highly successful and set a trend which ran throughout the century.

This demand for accuracy took other forms. Not only had sets and costumes to be historically accurate, they had to be 'real'. The principal exponent of this type of 'realism' was Thomas William Robertson (see page 47), who insisted on real doorknobs and real doors in his sets. The movement produced the 'box set', which replaced the earlier side wings and eventually established the 'fourth wall' convention.

In Germany, the Saxe-Meiningen company developed the more naturalistic use of crowds. In Norway, Henrik Ibsen emerged as the leading dramatist of the new realism. The movement produced a number of 'independent' theatres such as the London Independent, the Paris Théâtre Libre and the Berlin Freie Bühne. Literary and artist merit was looked for, rather than commercial success. The movement also produced the highly influential Moscow Arts Theatre under the direction of Konstantin Stanislavsky and Vladimir Nemirovich-Danchenko (see next chapter).

Electricity was used in the theatre towards the end of the century -- the Savoy was the first London theatre to be completely electrified in 1881. The increased flexibility that electricity gave had less effect on the lighting of performances than might have been expected, but it did mean that for the first time the auditorium could be completely blacked out.

America

By the middle of the 19th century, the U.S.A. led the world in luxurious theatres, and Broadway was established as the home of extravaganza. Booth's Theatre, opened in New York in 1869, had a hydraulic lift for handling three-dimensional scenery, and a tower over the stage allowed backcloths to be lifted out of sight without being rolled.

Permanent theatres and permanent companies were established in most major cities of America by the later years of the century. Touring companies visited the smaller towns and the mining communities of the West. The saloon was transformed into a theatre, with lace curtains decorating the boxes. An orchestra was engaged and performances were a good deal more civilised than the cinema Western suggests. A British touring opera company, complete with international stars, gave Lucia di Lammermoor in Cheyenne only eight years after Custer's Last Stand in 1876.

The drive towards increased realism was an strong in America as in Europe. In 1899, realism was pushed to its limits with the production of *Ben-Hur*. The chariot race was staged with the use of treadmills, which allowed teams of racing horses to come to a gallop in front of the audience. The production was so lavish and realistic, that only eight theatres in North America had the facilities necessary for mounting it.

The revolt against this kind of production began in the university theatres. In the later eighteen-hundreds, they began a process of experimentation which they have never abandoned.

THEATRE IN THE TWENTIETH CENTURY

The early years of the century saw the final development of the 'realist' theatre, with its box sets and proscenium arch and absence of forestage. The later years have seen its decline, as actors and writers and directors have struggled to break free from its restrictions.

Experiments to find new theatrical forms characterise the whole period. The ideas of Gordon Craig and Adolph Appia, broke with the realist tradition in the fields of set design and lighting. William Poel founded the Elizabethan Stage Society in 1894, devoted to the mounting of Shakespeare plays in the Elizabethan tradition. Much of the work of Max Reinhardt broke with the orthodox proscenium theatre. In the Berlin Grosses Schauspielhaus the

actors worked well in front of the proscenium opening and theatre owes its inspiration to the classic theatre of Greece. In Vienna, Reinhardt worked in the Redoutensaal, a ballroom turned into a theatre, where the actors performed in front of a structure reminiscent of the Teatro Olimpico. In Paris, Jacques Copeau was making similar theatrical experiments in the Théâtre du vieux Colombier, where steps led from stage to auditorium.

In America, the university theatres and innumerable other small companies experimented with a wide range of theatrical forms, from pure proscenium to completely open stage. In Britain the 1939–45 war created many small companies, which toured military camps and isolated rural areas. These companies found it necessary to improvise theatres in village halls and barracks. Increased contact became the norm between actors and audiences, and these improvised theatres created a wide range of shapes and audience relationships which influenced British theatre buildings of the post-war period. The open stage of the Mermaid with no proscenium arch (1960) has been influential as well as very successful, but the most influential Anglo-American theatre has been the Festival Theatre at Stratford, Ontario, conceived by Tyrone Guthrie and Tanya Moiseiwitch, an exciting open stage in a tent in 1952, a permanent building in 1957. An arena stage with the audience on three sides, it has inspired, amongst others, the Festival Theatre at Chichester. All these theatres are dealt with in more depth in the next chapter.

Theatre-in-the-Round, with the audience surrounding the actors, was established at Scarborough and Stoke-on-Trent, its high priest in Britain being the brilliant Stephen Joseph. For all its advantages, many simply will not accept a theatre in which actors' faces and eyes cannot be seen by everyone at crucial moments. In France, André Villiers's Théâtre en Rond de Paris was established in 1954, while the movement to create 'freer acting shapes and more immediate actor-audience relationships has been particularly strong in America. However it was France which took the ultimate and most striking step when, in 1972, Ariene Mnouchkine's *1789* had the audience joining in the opening of the French Revolution, being placed in the play.

One of the first modern theatres to have adaptable stages, suitable for every style, was designed by Michael Warre for the London Academy of Music and Drama (1963), while companies with real money at their disposal can enjoy more than one auditorium and style of stage: the new National Theatre, etc. The old theatres, beautiful or not, pleasant to visit or actively uncomfortable, will be with us for generations. Even at their best they cannot easily be adapted to every sort of drama, though resourceful directors can transfer a production, even *The Royal Hunt of the Sun* (John Dexter) – from Chichester to the National (1964) without loss.

The immediate future is likely to see smaller playhouses in which actors and audiences are more closely associated with one another than they have been since the supreme period of world drama, the Elizabethan Age.

ii~Famous Theatre Buildings

(*Note: Theatre organisations – the Comédie-Fran-çaise, the Royal Shakespeare Theatre, etc. – may be found in Chapter 5.*)

ASTLEY'S AMPHITHEATRE. A famous London circus (1759–1803) built by Philip Astley near Westminster Bridge, it reopened in 1804 in Wych Street and became famous for equestrian shows, which soon developed into battle spectacles like *The Burning of Moscow*, etc. Fire was a regular hazard, with *Richard III* being given as an equestrian show between disasters. The most famous show of all was *Mazeppa* with Adah Isaacs Menken (1864). Lord George Sanger later took over, and the theatre finally closed in 1895.

BLACKFRIARS. The most famous Elizabethan private theatre, opened in part of an old Dominican monastery in 1576 and originally used by the Children of the Chapel Royal, a company of child actors. Closed in 1584, it was reopened by James Burbage, after adaptations, in 1596. In 1608 or 1609 the King's Men took it over as their private theatre along with the Globe. Shakespeare's 'Romances' are assumed to have been played there. It was demolished in 1655.

BOOTH'S. A New York theatre built for the great Edwin Booth (1869), who hoped to found a national theatre there. He failed, but gave many memorable performances. Later performers before its closure in 1883 included Charlotte Cushman, the Calverts, Modjeska and Salvini.

BOWERY. There were several Bowery theatres in New York from 1826–1929, in the first of which Edwin Forrest had some of his greatest triumphs. Charlotte Cushman made her début there in 1835, and later every conceivable type of entertainment took place there from aquatic drama to burlesque, and the New York début of Ada Rehan.

CITIZENS' THEATRE, GLASGOW. Scotland's most significant theatre since its foundation by James Bridie in 1942.

COVENT GARDEN. After Drury Lane, the most historic theatre in London, though there have been three theatres on the site. The first was opened by John Rich in 1732, the play being *The Way of the World*, though not until the late 1760s did it achieve fame under George Colman, who in 1773 put on *She Stoops to Conquer*. Before the theatre was burnt down in 1808 Mrs. Siddons and her brother, John Philip Kemble, had played there, also Master Betty, the boy prodigy. Riots greeted the opening night of the new theatre in 1809, the crowds shouting 'Old Prices', for Kemble had raised the prices to pay for the new building. He finally gave way. Edmund Kean, Macready and Mme. Vestris were among those who played in the theatre, which was burnt down in 1856. Today's building, the Royal Opera House, dates from 1858. Since the 1850s it has been mainly an opera house, ballet finally getting equal time with the opera after the Second World War (during which it was a dance hall). This was when the Sadler's Wells Ballet moved from Sadler's Wells Theatre in 1946 and the Covent Garden Opera Company was founded. Today they are the Royal Ballet and the Royal Opera.

DRURY LANE, The THEATRE ROYAL. London's most historic theatre: there have been four on the site. The first was built in 1663 by Thomas Killigrew, burnt in 1672 and rebuilt, using Wren's designs, in 1674. David Garrick first appeared there in 1742 and was a supreme actor-manager from 1746–76. Mrs. Siddons first appeared in 1775, the year of *The Rivals*, but did not triumph in London until 1782. Meanwhile, Sheridan took over the management in 1776 and produced his masterpiece, *The School for Scandal*, the next year. In 1794, the third theatre opened, holding 3,611 (compared with 2,000) and still with Sheridan as a frequently bankrupt manager. John Philip Kemble and Mrs. Siddons were among his actors, and elephants and dogs trod where once Garrick had acted. Fire destroyed it in 1809 and the final theatre, today's (though the auditorium was rebuilt in 1921), was opened in 1812. Two years later Edmund Kean made his immortal début as Shylock before a half-filled house on a bleak winter's night, and, for a managing committee which included Lord Byron and Whitbread, who had raised the money for the theatre, proceeded to give the public seasons of the most thrilling acting in the theatre's history. A later high point were the performances of Macready, and of the incomparable actress-singer, Malibran, both of whom worked for Alfred Bunn, part charlatan, part showman of genius. The rest of the century was given over to every sort of entertainment, including well-staged melodramas and pantomimes; among the managers were Augustus Harris and Arthur Collins.

Big musicals have been the main fare of the 20th century, interspersed with opera, ballet, Shakespeare, pantomime and even films; also Irving's final London season, Ellen Terry's Jubilee and Forbes-Robertson's Farewell. During the Shakespeare Tercentenary performance of *Julius Caesar* in 1916, Frank Benson was knighted in the theatre by George V. Famous events of the inter-war years included Coward's *Cavalcade* (1931) and four Ivor Novello musicals, while since 1945 several famous American musicals have been staged – along with other musicals and shows – most notably *Oklahoma* (1947) and *South Pacific* (1951). During war, the theatre had been the headquarters of ENSA, the Forces' entertainment service, run in both wars by Basil Dean. (The length of this entry, it should be stated, does not reflect the author's bias in the theatre's favour, but rather its historic importance, and its position for several centuries as Britain's unofficial National Theatre.)

FUNAMBULES, THÉÂTRE DES. This famous theatre, later immortalised in the film, *Les Enfants du Paradis*, replaced a booth for acrobats and pantomime in the Boulevard du Temple in Paris in 1816. The incomparable pantomimist Deburau became the great attraction as Pierrot, and the great Frédérick Lemaître appeared there in pantomime before he was famous. The theatre was also renowned for its scenery and trick effects. It survived the death of Deburau, but was pulled down in 1862 during Parisian rebuilding.

GAIETY. There were two theatres on this Aldwych site, the first from 1868–1902, the second from 1903–39. There was more to them than the legendary Gaiety Girls. Under John Hollingshead everything from extravaganzas to Shakespeare was given. George Edwardes took over in 1886, and six years later transferred *In Town* from the Prince of Wales's to the Gaiety, a show which ranks as the first musical comedy. The tradition continued at the New Gaiety, opened in 1903, with *The Orchid*. The cast included Gertie Millar, a supreme Gaiety star, George Grossmith Jnr., etc. Leslie Stuart and Lionel Monkton were among Gaiety composers, and later stars included Leslie Henson and Evelyn Laye. Also see **EDWARDES, George**, page 143.

GLOBE. The most famous theatre in history, its details remain a mystery. In December 1598 or the following January the Burbages and their friends dismantled The Theatre in Shoreditch (its lease had expired) and took the wood from it across the Thames to a site on Bankside where they erected The Globe, the most easterly of the four theatres on Bankside. Shakespeare's greatest plays were first given there, but in 1613 it was accidentally burnt to the ground at the première of *Henry VIII*. A new Globe was rapidly erected, but was 'pulled downe to the ground, by Sir Matthew Brand, on Munday the 15 of April, 1644, to make tenements in the room of it'. Rival theories about this most romantic and historic playhouse can be studied in, amongst others, *The Globe Theatre* by C. W. Hodges, and *Shakespeare's Wooden O* by Leslie Hotson.

HAYMARKET. This is London's second oldest theatre, originally built in 1720, when it opened with a French company. Fielding ran the theatre in the 1730s, his *Tom Thumb the Great* being given there. Walpole's Licensing Act nearly ruined the theatre, but finally Samuel Foote made it famous and it became a Theatre Royal. Today's theatre was opened in 1821, and its casts have included Phelps, Barry Sullivan, Edwin Booth, Mrs. Kendal, the Bancrofts, Tree, Maude and nearly every famous actor of modern times. It has represented the commercial theatre at its finest for many years, some would say at its safest, but it rarely drops below a high standard of performance. A modern highlight was Gielgud's 1944–5 season of Hamlet, *The Duchess of Malfi* (Ashcroft), the *Dream*, *Love for Love* and *The Circle*.

HER MAJESTY'S. Built by Beerbohm Tree, it opened in 1897 to its begetter's enormous pride. Many of its greatest successes have been musicals, notably *Chu-Chin-Chow* and *West Side Story*.

HOTEL DE BOURGOGNE. The first theatre of Paris, used from 1548, and later a component of the Comédie-Française (1673). It did not resemble a modern theatre, being a long wide hall with a deep stage lighted by candles at its front, and with two galleries on each side of the auditorium, and a pit in which the audience walked about or stood. The building later became the Comédie-Italienne, the Italian actors using it until 1783 when it was abandoned. It had seen the premières of many of Corneille's and Racine's masterpieces.

LINCOLN'S INN FIELDS. Originally a tennis court, it was converted into a theatre by Sir William Davenant in 1661; Pepys saw Betterton play Hamlet there that year. Later it was run by Rich who put on *The Beggar's Opera* in 1727. Soon after, its decline began and it was finally pulled down in 1848.

LYCEUM. The first Lyceum (1765–1830) was a mainly musical theatre; the second (1834), now a dance hall, had one period of total glory from the first night of *The Bells* with Irving in 1871 to his leaving it in 1902, having been its manager since 1878. Only the war later saved it from demolition. Happily the last performances at the Lyceum were worthy of its past: Gielgud as Hamlet (1939).

MARAIS, THÉÂTRE DU. This forerunner of the Comédie-Française opened in a converted tennis court in 1634, the company being that of the great actor Montdory. Many Corneille premières were given, most notably *Le Cid* (1636). It was abandoned in the 1670s.

PALAIS-ROYAL, THÉÂTRE DU. This was a small playhouse in Cardinal Richelieu's home, which opened in front of the King and Queen in 1641. It was given to Molière in 1660 and later enlarged. Molière played there in *Le Malade Imaginaire* on the night of his death (1673). It was twice burnt down in the 18th century. A later theatre opened in 1831.

PARK. America's 'Old Drury' and first great playhouse was opened in 1798 with *As You Like It*. Nearly every major native and foreign actor of the early 19th century played the Park, among them Edmund Kean, Macready, Forrest and Charlotte Cushman. The theatre burnt down in 1848 and a second Park was opened in 1874. Fire destroyed it on the day Lily Langtry should have made her début in 1882. Brooklyn's first professional theatre was also called the Park. It opened in 1863 and was later the last New York theatre to have a stock (repertoire) company which supported visiting stars.

PETIT-BOURBON, SALLE DU. France's first Court theatre, its professional debut was in 1577, when a *commedia dell'arte* troupe played there. Molière later shared it with Fiorillo's troupe, then, in 1658, the first of his own farces was seen there, *L'Etourdi* and *Le Depit amoureux*. It was scheduled for demolition in 1660: Molière managed to get away with the boxes and fittings.

SAVOY. This was opened by Richard D'Oyly Carte with *Patience* in 1881, and was the first London theatre to be fully lit by electricity. It is still a major commercial theatre, but historically it is important first as the home of the Gilbert and Sullivan operas and secondly as the theatre where Granville Barker staged his simple, revolutionary Shakespeare productions (1912–14), *The Winter's Tale*, *Twelfth Night* and the *Dream*.

SOUTHWARK. America's first permanent theatre, built in 1766 in Philadelphia. It opened with *The Provoked Husband*, but ceased to be a playhouse in 1821.

THEATRE, THE. This was the first permanent playhouse building in England, and opened in 1576 on land between Finsbury Fields and the road from Bishopsgate to Shoreditch Church outside the boundaries of north London. James Burbage, father of Richard, was the history-maker. Little is known about the building, but admission to it was a penny, with another penny to get into the galleries. Theatrically its history was not a great one, but by being the original, it helped trigger a golden

age. Its timber was later put to good use by the Burbages. When the lease expired in the winter of 1598–9 they and their friends pulled the Theatre down and transported as much wood as possible across the river to build the Globe (see above).

WALNUT STREET THEATRE. America's oldest theatre, opened in Philadelphia in 1809 and became a playhouse two years later.

A scene from John Osborne's A Hotel in Amsterdam, *first given by the English Stage Company at the Royal Court in 1968 and directed by Anthony Page. On the sofa are Judy Parfitt and Paul Scofield; behind are Joss Ackland (left) and Ralph Watson. (Photo: Zoe Dominic)*

CHAPTER 5

COMPANIES AND ORGANISATIONS

ABBEY THEATRE. This most famous of Irish theatres became the home of its equally famous company in 1904, five years after the founding of the Irish Dramatic Movement (first called the Irish Literary Theatre) by W. B. Yeats, Lady Gregory, Edward Martyn and George Moore. This was devoted to encouraging an Irish poetic drama, and the theatre was taken over with the help of Miss Horniman, who was to be the founding figure of British Rep. In its stormy, glorious history nearly all notable Irish dramatists have had their

work performed. Synge's *The Playboy of the Western World* caused a riot when first given there (1907), and O'Casey's three most famous plays, *The Shadow of a Gunman* (1922), *Juno and the Paycock* (1924) and *The Plough and the Stars* (1926) – the last two outright masterpieces – also had their premières there; however he fell out with the Abbey when they later rejected *The Silver Tassie*. Though the Abbey lost ground to the Gate (see below) in the mid-1920s, it has remained Ireland's National Theatre, very influential and a company where Irish acting talent has been fostered. As a reaction to large-scale productions at the turn of the century, it opted for simplicity, which was also sound economic sense. Like other Irish theatre institutions it has had to combat censorship, emigration, internal crises and financial troubles. It survives – and remains world famous.

ACTORS' COMPANY. Founded in Britain by Ian McKellen in 1972, it is a genuine and important actors' co-operative, with a repertoire of plays in which all the players (notably good ones) take it in turns to play leads and smaller rôles. So far the company has toured, playing varying lengths of time in different cities, and giving Shakespeare, Chekhov, Feydeau, Ford, Congreve etc., with casts that have included Edward Petherbridge, Robert Eddison, John Woodvine, Caroline Blakiston and McKellen himself, etc. Its importance is that while it employs good directors (David William, David Giles, Richard Cottrell), it offers the public a chance to enjoy an ensemble of leading players. In the age of Director's Theatre, and ensemble (in the great subsidised companies) as the rightly desired aim, the casualties can be the major classical parts, which are sometimes woefully undercast. A company of first-rate actors working in dedicated group freedom is not better or worse than the Royal Shakespeare Company, but different – and none the less welcome.

ACTOR'S STUDIO. See **METHOD** (Chapter 7).

AMERICAN NATIONAL THEATER AND ACADEMY (A.N.T.A.). Founded in 1935 by Act of Congress to encourage theatre, it became (from 1945 onwards) a spokesman for the American theatre at home and overseas, while helping experimental theatre schemes and stage training. Its Experimental Theater had three exciting, challenging seasons of non-profit-making theatre which worried Broadway and the Unions, but when it ended in 1950, productions had included *Galileo* with Charles Laughton, and Robinson Jeffers' *Tower Beyond Tragedy* with Judith Anderson, also a Black version of Gorky's *Lower Depths* called *A Long Way from Home*. Recent famous productions in the A.N.T.A. theatre have included *Our Town* (1969) with Henry Fonda and Mildred Natwick, produced by the Plumstead Playhouse, also James Stewart and Helen Hayes in *Harvey*, put on by the Phoenix Theater (see below).

AMERICAN SHAKESPEARE FESTIVAL. This has taken place at Stratford, Connecticut, since 1955 when it was launched thanks to Lawrence Langer, an original director of the Theater Guild. Criticisms of the theatre, of the lack of a house style, the use or absence of stars over the years cannot blunt the achievements. These include the thousands of school-children who visit the Festival, Morris Carnovsky's Lear(s) and Shylock, Bert Lahr's Bottom, Hepburn and Alfred Drake as Beatrice and Benedick, Hepburn as Portia, Earle Hyman and Drake as Othello and Iago, and plays regularly sent out on tour. Oddly, some of the most acclaimed productions have been non-Shakespearean, including *Major Barbara* (1972), directed by Edwin Sherwin and starring Jane Alexander and Lee Richardson. A major factor in the Festival's success was the engagement of John Houseman as Artistic Director (1956–9).

ARTS COUNCIL OF GREAT BRITAIN. This crucially important body began as the Council for the Encouragement of Music and the Arts in 1940, changing its name at the end of the war, and being run since 1942 entirely on such money as can be extracted from the Treasury. Without the Arts Council all opera, ballet and nearly all that is best in the British theatre would vanish overnight. As there is never more than just enough money available, criticism of the Council is constant and usually grossly unfair. Though both major political parties support subsidies for the arts, latent philistinism in Britain ensures that they will never be as heavily subsidised as they are in many European countries. Perhaps the Arts Council's most important contribution to the theatre in the 1960s was to save and revitalise Rep in Britain, which had seemed in danger of disappearing.

ARTS FOUNDATION. The U.S. Government and Congress, having at last accepted the idea of financial help for the theatre (albeit in a very modest way), a National Arts Council was set up in the mid-1960s led by Roger Stevens. With millionaire patrons now in short supply, it can only be hoped that Americans will cease to fear subsidised art on a national level and make suitably massive funds available.

BERLINER ENSEMBLE. See **BRECHT** (Chapter 2), for the great dramatist was the begetter and director of this famous company, whose influence has been so great, not least on British dramatists. He founded it in 1949 and it was directed by his widow, Helene Weigel, after his death in 1956. Until 1954 it played at the Deutches Theater in East Berlin, its repertoire being entirely devoted to Brecht or adaptations by him. The company moved to the Theater am Schiffbauerdamm in 1954. Having had to share its previous home, it was now an independent State Theatre. It has played twice in London, first the very fruitful visit in 1956, and again in 1965.

BURGTHEATER. This most famous of Austrian theatres was founded in 1741 as the Theater an der Burg and later as the Hofburgtheater. It became a National Theatre in 1776, the Emperor Joseph II modelling it on the Comédie-Française, and it has remained such ever since. In 1789, Schröder joined the company and in his four years with it reformed the current ranting and over-broad comedy technique, replacing it with subtle ensemble, a thing which became the Burgtheater's trademark. Light opera and vaudeville were banished from the repertoire in 1817 to the Leopolderstader Theater. The Burgtheater continues to flourish, sometimes playing abroad, including a visit to London (1973).

CHICHESTER FESTIVAL. This began in 1962 after a theatre had been built with an open arena-type stage, with seats on three sides of it. The theatre was the idea of Leslie Evershed-Martin, who had been inspired by the success of the theatre at Stratford, Ontario, and the first Director was Laurence Olivier. His second season saw a company that was mainly destined to be the National Theatre Company, which opened at the Old Vic in September 1963. John Clements took over the Festival in 1966, by which time a wide range of plays had been given, including works by Ford, Fletcher, Shaffer and Arden. Clements extended the season to over four months and made Chichester a Festival of Acting. His choice of plays was 'safer' than the National's (which has a big subsidy) – 1972 saw Shaw, Shakespeare, Gay and Fry – but no one complained except the more morbid Malvolios of higher drama, who managed to sneer at the audiences as well. The year 1974 sees Keith Michell take over. For the historical record, Chichester was the first to see Olivier's *Othello* (1964) and his incomparable production of *Uncle Vanya* the year before. Transfers to London in

Clements' day have included *Vivat! Vivat Regina!*; also *The Magistrate* and *Dandy Dick*, both complete with Alastair Sim at his riveting best.

CIVIC REPERTORY THEATER. This was created by Eva Le Gallienne, idealist and very fine actress, and survived from 1926–32. Salaries were inevitably low and performances were given in what Howard Taubman has called a 'huge, decrepit barn of a house on West 14th Street'. Over 1,500 performances were given of Shakespeare, Chekhov, Dumas, *Alice in Wonderland*, etc. See also **NATIONAL REPERTORY THEATER** below.

COMÉDIE-FRANÇAISE. France's National Theatre, founded in 1680 by combining three companies, including Molière's, whose name it bore at first – the Maison de Molière, or the Théâtre Français. Gradually, it became known by its present name to distinguish it from the Comédie-Italienne (see below). It has moved theatres several times and undergone a major crisis in the Revolution, when the actors were split into two factions. Napoleon later stabilised matters (1803), redrafting the company's constitution. It remains today a co-operative, actors holding a share or a part thereof, while there are two membership grades, *pensionnaire* and *sociétaire*. The first grade can be reached by an audition, the second by the death or retirement of a senior member. A retiring actor (usually not until he has served twenty years) can be granted a life pension, while the oldest actor in terms of long-service, not age, is known as the doyen. Many major actors have felt unable to endure the weight of tradition and lack of an adventureous policy at the theatre and have broken away long before the 20-year period, including Jean-Louis Barrault, and there have been various upheavals. The Comédie-Française represents all that is best in the history of French drama and is a true ensemble, but security and tradition do not always make for excitement and living art, which is why the French theatre has a love-hate relationship with its senior company. The 1970s find Molière and the classics still dominating the repertoire (rightly), but modern plays are now more welcome. Pierre Dux was appointed to modernise 'the House of Molière , modernisation which included the first performance there of Strindberg, *The Dream Play*. Terry Hands of the Royal Shakespeare Company successfully staged *Richard*

III with two of France's finest actors, Robert Hirsch and Jacques Charon, as Richard and Buckingham; and Harold Hobson, critic and Francophile, was moved to announce that the Comédie-Française had re-established itself as one of the world's great companies (*Sunday Times*, June 4, 1972). In fact, whether it reaches the heights or plumbs the depths, it cannot but help be one of the world's great companies as long as it survives.

COMÉDIE-ITALIENNE. Italian troupes of *commedia dell'arte* players were performing in Paris at least from the 1570s onwards, but Italian actors first became well-known in 1658 when a company shared the Petit Bourbon with Molière's players. In 1680, the Italians took over the Hôtel de Bourgogne. Their most famous actor of this period was Tiberio Fiorillo, the magnificent Scaramouche. Then the company was known as the Comèdie-Italienne to distinguish it from the Comédie-Française, and gradually over the next 40 years it became less Italian and more French, except in name. When opera-buffa became the rage in Paris in the 1750s, the Comédie-Italienne moved towards music and became the ancestor of the famous Opéra-Comique, amalgamating under that name with another company in 1801. *Commedia dell'arte* had vanished a century before, the repertoire having ranged from the plays of Marivaux to ballet-pantomimes and vaudevilles before comic opera finally took over. The company's history was as important as it was remarkable.

EDINBURGH FESTIVAL OF MUSIC AND DRAMA. This world-famous festival, founded in 1947, was the inspiration of Rudolph Bing of Glyndebourne and, later, New York 'Met' fame, and has always been more MUSIC than DRAMA. Theatre economics – the difficulty of assembling a top-flight cast in a major play for three weeks or less – has not helped, nor has the lack of a Scottish National Theatre (as opposed to the very fine Scottish Opera). It has been left to companies on tour, or the often significant unofficial Fringe to supply drama, though in the 1950s no less than three T. S. Eliot plays had their premières in Edinburgh, including *The Cocktail Party* (1949). A rare example of a 'local' drama has been Sir John Lindsay's *The Three Estates* (1540), directed by Guthrie in 1947 and revived a number of times.

EQUITY is the actors' trade union. American Actors' Equity, founded in 1913, had to call a strike to procure decent treatment for its members. British Actors' Equity was started in 1929.

ENGLISH STAGE COMPANY, The, was formed by George DEVINE (1901–66) and others in 1956 with its headquarters at the Royal Court. Its aim was to discover and promote new writing talent and its success has been such that it can be claimed as the most important theatre organisation in Britain. New directors, designers and actors, as well as already established dramatists have been encouraged as well, but the original concept of a 'Writers' Theatre' has been kept, along with Devine's belief in an author's right to fail.

Though the first season saw plays by established writers, including Arthur Miller and Angus Wilson, the breakthrough play was John Osborne's *Look Back in Anger* (1956). It was almost as influential a play as *Tamburlaine*, for suddenly young writers not only wished to become dramatist, but were encouraged to do so, including, Wesker, Arden, N. F. Simpson, Ann Jelicoe, and later, Storey, Charles Wood, Edward Whitehead and Bond. Many foreign plays have also been given along with some classical revivals and the re-discovery of D. H. Lawrence as a viable dramatist (thanks, in particular, to the director, Peter Gill). Directors who have played a notable part in the Company's history have included Tony Richardson, William Gaskill, Lindsay Anderson, Anthony Page, etc., and designers, the brilliant Jocelyn Herbert. Productions Without Decor have been given, and the Theatre Upstairs, started in 1969, has given new and often experimental playwrights their chance. The policy is now to produce runs of a month or so, with a number of plays transferring – though repertoire was tried at first. Great names like Olivier, Ashcroft, Richardson, Gielgud, Guinness, Scofield, Finney and Harrison have played at the Court, while the number of younger actors who first made their names their are too numerous to list in full; they include Joan Plowright, Frank Finlay, Robert Stephens, Kenneth Haigh, etc. In 1972, Oscar Lewenstein became Artistic Director.

FEDERAL THEATER PROJECT. Between 1935–9, when it was abolished by political pressure, this scheme resulted in more than 1,000 plays and shows of every kind, both amateur and professional being given. Elmer Rice started *The Living Newspaper* (productions about topical affairs) while Orson Welles and John Houseman staged productions which included an all-Black *Macbeth* and Blitzstein's anti-capitalist opera, *The Cradle will Rock*. An anti-fascist play, *It Can't Happen Here*, had its première in 21 cities at once. Mrs. Hallie Flanagan was the organiser of the great scheme, worthy of the New Deal at its best, but she and others were accused of being Communists and the scheme collapsed.

GATE THEATRE. Founded in 1928 by Hilton EDWARDS (b. 1903) and Michéal MACLIAMMOIR (see Chapter 3), it rapidly became the most exciting and adventurous Irish theatre, and remains famous.

GROUP THEATER was started by Harold CLURMAN (b. 1901), the American director, writer and manager in 1931, whose book, *The Fervent Years*, describes its thrilling decade of existence. He, Lee Strasberg and Cheryl Crawford were the directors,

The historic Moscow Art Theatre. (*Photo: Novosti Press Agency*)

Alexei Gribov as Firs in The Cherry Orchard *at the Moscow Art Theatre in 1964.* (*Photo: Novosti Press Agency*)

while the company included Stella and Luther Adler, Franchot Tone, Morris Carnovsky, Mary Morris, Elia Kazan, J. Edward Bromberg, John Garfield and Clifford Odets, whose *Waiting for Lefty* (1935) caused a tremendous stir and saw the beginning of American social conscience drama. Left wing and corporately very strong until lucrative offers tempted some of the company away, the Group was able to stage Odets, Saroyan, Irwin Shaw, Sidney Kingsley, Robert Ardrey, etc., and its influence was to be colossal.

LINCOLN CENTER FOR THE PERFORMING ARTS in New York dates from the early 1960s, and has become the home of music, ballet, opera and arts' schools as well as the Lincoln Center Repertory Theater. It was originally the idea of Robert Whitehead, who was the first co-director with Elia Kazan, beginning work in a temporary theatre. Board difficulties led to their resignation (1965), and the theatre has never truly fulfilled the hopes placed in it. Herbert Blau and Jules Irving left the San Francisco Actor's Workshop to take over the new theatre, called the Vivian Beaumont after its patroness, but Blau resigned in 1967. The building was designed by Eero Saarinen and Jo Mielziner and a new and experimental playhouse, the Forum, was added. Critics have generally been harsh at standards, but there have been many notable productions directed by John Hirsch, John Barry and others, of American and foreign plays by Schiller, Bond, Miller, Shakespeare, etc. Irving resigned in 1972, to be replaced by Joseph Papp, the many-sided and brilliant director of the New York Shakespeare Festival (see below).

MALVERN FESTIVAL. Started by Barry Jackson in 1929, it flourished until 1939 and was revived after the war for a few seasons. It was a major Shaw festival, which saw seven premières of his plays, but rare classics and also Priestley, Bridie, etc., were also given.

MALY THEATRE. Moscow's oldest theatre company dates from 1806, its name meaning small (Bolshoi means large). Productions suffered less from government interference than other Russian theatres, while a wide repertoire was given, ranging from Shakespeare to Ostrovsky, the staging being realistic. The company took the Revolution in its stride and, after playing safe with classical productions, began giving Soviet plays in the mid-1920s.

MEININGEN PLAYERS. These were formed in 1874 by the Duke of Saxe-Meiningen, a brilliant director, and were a true ensemble. The company's influence on Europe as a whole, by its tours, was very great, particularly in the handling of crowd scenes, of which the Duke was a master. He also influenced lighting, costume and scenery, being a firm believer in detail and historical accuracy. His morganatic wife, the actress, Ellen Frantz, helped him in his work which benefited, amongst others, the Moscow Art Theatre.

MERCURY THEATER was founded by Orson Welles and John Houseman (1937) after working for the Federal Theater Project (see above). This short, glorious venture included a modern dress *Julius Caesar*, also plays by Dekker, Shaw and Büchner, with Welles, Joseph Cotten and Vincent Price, etc. Then came closure – and *Citizen Kane*.

MERMAID. This most admirable theatre was the creation of Sir Bernard MILES (b. 1907), whose knighthood (1969) was one of the most deserved in stage history. His early career included work as a designer, stage manager, props, carpenter and actor, his most notable part before the Mermaid adventure being Iago for the Old Vic on tour and at the New (1941–2). His parts at the Mermaid have included Falstaff and Long John Silver. The first Mermaid was an Elizabethan-style theatre in his back garden (1951) where the great Kirsten Flagstad sang Purcell's Dido for a glass of stout per performance. There followed a season at the Royal Exchange of *Dido* and Shakespeare (1953), then he built today's Mermaid at Puddle Dock, the first theatre to be erected within the City of London in 300 years. The opening show was *Lock up your Daughters* (1960), a musical from Fielding's *Rape upon Rape*, and since then the Mermaid's range has been colossal – everything from Mystery Plays to Spike Milligan, including Greek drama, Shakespeare and *Treasure Island*. Current policy is short runs of a month or so, with great successes like *Cowardy Custard* (1972–3) given longer runs, and occasional transfers. Miles's promise to provide a 'bird's-eye view of World Theatre in ten years' has been kept, and his theatre is one of the few in London which is a pleasure to visit for itself, a true social centre with good food at different price ranges, exhibitions, concerts, etc.

MOSCOW ART THEATRE. Also see STANIS-

LAVSKY (Chapter 6). This most famous Russian theatre was started in 1898 by Stanislavsky and Nemirovich-Danchenko and became one of the most influential in the world. From the beginning its naturalistic style was a challenge to the florid acting then fashionable in Russia, and Stanislavsky's precepts remain in vogue today, having to a greater or lesser degree spread right through the theatrical world. The fifth production in 1898, a revival of the previously unsuccessful *The Seagull* by Chekhov, made the dramatist's name and that of the company, which went on to perform *Uncle Vanya*, *The Three Sisters* and *The Cherry Orchard*, also (before 1917) Gorky's *Lower Depths*, etc. Thanks to Anatoli Lunacharsky (see next chapter), the company survived the Revolution and, indeed, was allowed to make a long European and American tour before finding its place in the new scene. If few striking Soviet plays have been presented, the standards of Chekhov production and the beliefs of Stanislavsky have kept the theatre in the forefront of the theatrical world. Its ensemble remains unmatched, as visits to London and elsewhere in recent times have shown. Many of the original actors, including Chekhov's distinguished widow, Olga Knipper-Chekhova, stayed with the company until they retired. This long-term policy, which has deadened some famous companies, has only enhanced the Moscow Art Theatre – striking tribute to the actors in general and Stanislavsky in particular.

NATIONAL THEATRE. Also see **OLD VIC** below. The idea of a National Theatre was first mooted in 1848 by Effingham Wilson and optimistically planned by William Archer and Granville Barker in 1903. In the event it took until 1951 for a foundation stone to be laid on the South Bank, and until 1963 for the National Theatre to open at the Old Vic with *Hamlet*. The actual theatre, designed by Denys Lasdun, is due to open in late 1974. There could only be one first Director, Laurence Olivier, whose original Associate Directors were John Dexter and William Gaskill. At the time of writing (late 1973) there is a transitional period, with Peter Hall having just taken over from Olivier (the selection of Hall was as inevitable as the original choice of Olivier), and with Michael Blakemore and John Dexter as Associates, and Frank Dunlop in charge of the strikingly successful Young Vic (see below). With Hall will be Jonathan

Miller, Pinter, Schlesinger and John Russell Brown. Despite the attacks of certain jaundiced directors, dramatists and critics, the National has had a strikingly successful first decade, apart from a poor patch in 1971 – which was redeemed by the tremendous production of *Long Day's Journey into Night* (Michael Blakemore: Olivier, Cummings, Quilley, Pickup). The policy of Olivier and his literary manager, Kenneth Tynan was to make the theatre national and international. Those who have railed that there has not been a steady stream of new plays are unable (wilfully) to grasp the nature of the exercise, and conveniently forget that London already has the English Stage Company and the Royal Shakespeare Co. at the Aldwych. In the event, there have been several admirable new plays, including Shaffer's *The Royal Hunt of the Sun*, Stoppard's *Rosencrantz and Guildenstern are Dead* and especially his *Jumpers*, and Nichols' *The National Health*; also a brave near-success by Charles Wood, *H*, Osborne's adaptation of de Vega's *A Bond Honoured*, and from abroad, Arrabal's *The Architect and the Emperor of Assyria*, Frisch's *Andorra*, etc. Guest directors have included Zeffirelli (*Much Ado* and *Saturday, Sunday, Monday*), Jacques Charon (*A Flea in Her Ear*), Brook (Seneca's *Oedipus*), Byam Shaw (*The Dance of Death*), Guthrie and others, as well as a constellation of designers.

Exceptional productions have included Gaskill's *The Recruiting Officer*, Olivier's *Uncle Vanya*, Dexter's *The Royal Hunt of the Sun*, Charon's *A Flea in Her Ear*, Clifford Williams' all-male *As You Like It*, Miller's realistic *The School for Scandal*, Blakemore's *Long Day's Journey*: space forbids the inclusion of several more. Criticism has been levelled at the National for not holding its finest players, but what theatre can?

Peter Hall may be able to arrange some long, loose contracts of the sort he organised at the Royal Shakespeare. The irritation stems from the fact that the original company was exceptionally strong: in the early years it included Olivier, Robert Stephens, Frank Finlay, Colin Blakely, Jeremy Brett and Derek Jacobi; and Joan Plowright, Joyce Redman, Maggie Smith, Geraldine McEwen, etc., with guest appearances by Redgrave, Gielgud and others. Of this galaxy, only Olivier and Plowright are still with the company at the time of writing, though Finlay has returned. However, major talents have arrived, most notably Denis

Michael Hordern and Diana Rigg in Peter Wood's production of Jumpers *by Tom Stoppard, National Theatre, 1972. (Photo: British Tourist Authority)*

A scene from Exiles *by James Joyce, produced by the Royal Shakespeare Company at the Aldwych in 1971 and directed by Harold Pinter. From left to right are John Wood, Vivien Merchant and Estelle Kohler. (Photo: Peggy Leder)*

Quilley, Ronald Pickup, Alan MacNaughtan, Paul Curran and Constance Cummings – some already established, some 'made' at the National. In any short selective account several memories stand out: Olivier's Othello, Shylock, James Tyrone and performances in Restoration comedy; Plowright and Redgrave in Chekhov; Stephens and Blakely in *The Royal Hunt of the Sun*, Maggie Smith as Desdemona, Michael Hordern in *Jumpers*, Olivier, Cummings, Quilley and Pickup in *Long Day's Journey* . . . but, happily, the list could be extended beyond the permits of space.

NATIONAL YOUTH THEATRE. This was founded by Michael Croft, a schoolmaster who directed notable Shakespeare productions at Alleyn's School. Old boys asked him to continue and his theatre followed, playing in London since 1959 and also touring in Europe. Though not a forcing house of professional talent, some of his actors have succeeded significantly, including Derek Jacobi, John Stride, Simon Ward, Hywell Bennett, Martin Jarvis and Helen Mirren. Apart from Shakespeare, the N.Y.T.'s most regular dramatist has been Peter Terson. It now has a centre of its own, the Shaw Theatre in London.

NEW YORK SHAKESPEARE FESTIVAL. This free annual festival was founded by Joseph Papp (see Chapter 6) in 1954 and has run ever since – since 1956 in Central Park where its own theatre, the Delacorte, was opened in 1962. Papp (a man of fierce determination, according to Howard Taubman) has extended his festival to include winter performances throughout New York State, rock musicals in its indoor Public Theater, and also the hit musical version of *The Two Gentleman of Verona*, given free in Central Park in 1971 and less cheaply later on Broadway and in the West End. Many productions are directed by Papp himself.

OLD VIC. From 1963 until the opening of its new home, the National Theatre's playhouse, but for many years before the most famous theatre company in the English-speaking world. The building dates back to 1818, when it was the Coburg, later the Victoria Theatre. In 1880 it was turned into a temperance hall by Emma Cons; in 1914, her now-legendary niece, Lilian Baylis (see Chapter 6) took over to present opera in English, and Shakespeare, both at popular prices. Her directors included Matheson Lang, Ben Greet, Russell Thorndike,

Robert Atkins, Andrew Leigh, Harcourt Williams, Tyrone Guthrie and Henry Cass; by the time of her death (and with the theatre still unsubsidised) in 1937, the Old Vic was already world-famous. Atkins, Williams and Guthrie were the most influential of her directors. In 1931 she re-opened Sadler's Wells which soon became the home of her opera and new ballet company. In the mainly frivolous London theatre of the 1920s and early '30s, the Old Vic kept great drama and the idea of great acting alive. Nearly all the great classical actors of the 1940s and '50s worked for her between the wars.

The Old Vic used the New as a wartime base when the theatre was bombed in 1940, and it was there that its supreme seasons (1944–8) took place, under the triumvirate of Olivier, Richardson and John Burrell. Later directors (the return to the Vic was in 1950) included Hugh Hunt, Guthrie, Michael Benthall, Douglas Seale and, after a period with no overall chief, Michael Elliott. Except in Benthall's day, when Shakespeare alone was given, often with distinction over several seasons, the policy was mainly Shakespeare, other classics and some European dramas. A list of actors being out of the question, some books may be recommended, notably *Four Years at the Old Vic* and *Old Vic Saga* by Harcourt Williams; *Old Vic Drama*, Parts 1 and 2 by Audrey Williamson; *Lilian Baylis* by Sybil and Russell Thorndike, autobiographies by Gielgud, Guthrie, etc., and *Shakespeare on the English Stage* 1900–64 by J. C. Trewin. With the exception perhaps of the English Stage Company, the Old Vic ranks as the most important British theatre company of the century.

PHOENIX THEATER. This was started off-Broadway in 1953 by T. Edward Hambleton and Norris Houghton and included in its first season *Coriolanus*, directed by John Houseman, and *The Seagull* directed by Houghton, with Montgomery Clift, Kevin McCarthy, Maureen Stapleton and Judith Evelyn in the cast. It survived financial crises and mixed standards with its ideals intact, then became the Phoenix-A.P.A. in 1964, merging with the fine touring company of Ellis Rabb, and taking over the Lyceum on Broadway. The Phoenix split from the A.P.A. (Association of Producing Artists) in 1969, both having had major successes since. In 1973, the new Phoenix Repertory Co. had particular successes with Durrenmatt's *The Visit* and

Feydeau's *Chemin de Fer.*

PICCOLO TEATRO DI MILANO. See **Giorgio STREHLER** (Chapter 6).

ROYAL SHAKESPEARE COMPANY. Now possibly the most famous British theatre company, it was previously the Shakespeare Memorial Theatre Company. The theatre grew out of Shakespeare's 300th birthday celebrations in 1864. Charles Flower, a rich brewer whose family has been associated with the theatre ever since, proposed a permanent playhouse, which was opened in 1879. Though its stage was too shallow, and few admired its Gothic architecture except Oscar Wilde, actors and audiences liked the theatre. But not until 1886 was there any theatrical continuity; from then until 1919 Sir Frank Benson performed there almost every Spring, adding a summer season in 1910. W. Bridges-Adams was in charge from 1919 to 1934, during which time the old theatre was burnt down and today's building opened (thanks to very generous Americans) in 1932. A chasm divided audience and actors, which was not finally rectified completely until the 1960s and, with low salaries keeping famous actors away, and with critical attacks, the period between the wars is often damned as provincial. However audiences grew and distinguished performances were given by Wolfit, Baliol Holloway and, most notably, Randle Ayrton as Lear. Directors after Bridges-Adams were Ben Iden Payne (1935–42), Milton Rosmer (1943), and Robert Atkins (1944–5); then came a turning point with Sir Barry Jackson taking charge (1946–8). He brought in the young Peter Brook and Paul Scofield and other talents who removed the never really fair provincial tag, but on grounds of age he was replaced by Anthony Quayle (1949–52), Quayle and Glen Byam Shaw (1952–6), and Byam Shaw (1957–9).

This last decade before the Hall regime is often berated by the ignorant because companies dispersed annually and no true ensemble was possible. The marvel is what was achieved in the circumstances, though considering the casts which have never been equalled, perhaps it is not so marvellous: Edith Evans, Ashcroft, Gielgud, Tearle, Richardson, Olivier, Scofield, Helpmann, Harry Andrews, Wynyard, Redgrave, Tutin, etc. The Shakespeare Memorial Theatre was now world-famous and had toured Russia and Australia. The supreme performances of the decade were perhaps the Brook-Olivier *Titus Andronicus* (1955), the finest *Antony and Cleopatra* of modern times (Byam Shaw: Redgrave, Ashcroft, 1953), Guthrie's *All's Well that Ends Well* (1959), and Olivier's *Macbeth* (1955) and *Coriolanus.*

The latter was directed in 1959 by Peter Hall, who took over the next year (aged 29). He transformed the company into a permanent one with long-term contracts flexible enough to allow actors to make money between work at Stratford; he took over the Aldwych for a London home; he broadened the repertoire to include important modern plays there; and he created a true ensemble, and – after a breaking-in period – a company style. Brook and Michel Saint-Denis were fellow Directors, and younger directors who soon made their mark included John Barton, Clifford Williams, and later, Terry Hands, David Jones and Trevor Nunn, who took over from Hall in 1968. The design team, who have also created a style for all their individuality, consists of Christopher Morley, John Bury, Farrah and Timothy O'Brien. Robin Phillips and Ronald Eyre have been among the guest directors.

The turning point of the Royal Shakespeare Company's fortunes – its name changed in 1960 – was *The Wars of the Roses* (1963–4) which consisted of the three *Henry VI* plays plus *Richard III*, turned into three plays by John Barton and directed by Hall. It later built up into a sequence of seven Histories. Meanwhile at the Aldwych plays were given by Pinter, Albee, Mercer, etc., plus productions from Stratford. The R.S.C. pretends to eschew stars, but has plenty on its books: Ashcroft, Sinden, Dench, Paul Rogers, Richard Pasco, etc., and a number developed within the company, including Elizabeth Spriggs, Helen Mirren, Susan Fleetwood and Ian Richardson. Sometimes a part which must have a star (in the best sense) is woefully undercast but 'names' are brought in, including Michael Hordern, Dorothy Tutin, and Richard Johnson – an R.S.C. player before going into films who returned to play both Antonys in 1972–3 with marked success. The most famous production of the decade has been Brook's *A Midsummer Night's Dream* (1970), an international as well as a national success, but more significant perhaps is the way that the R.S.C. can (under Nunn) mount Shakespeare's four Roman plays (1972; London, 1973), not as natural a sequence as the Histories, but compelling and often thrilling, and almost entirely cast from within the company. Apart from a perverse

King Lear *at the Stratford Festival, Stratford, Ontario, in 1972—the Festival's 20th year. The director was David William. Left to right, Kenneth Welsh as Edgar, Mervyn Blake as Kent, William Hutt as Lear and Edward Atienza as the Fool. (Photo: Stratford Festival Theatre)*

Romeo, and a shocking "improvement" of *King John* by Barton, the Company at the time of writing is in excellent theatrical health, while its brilliant *Richard II*, directed by Barton, and with Richardson and Pasco alternating in the leads, has been seen in America.

Meanwhile, the Company's Theatregoround group plays all over Britain and important experimental seasons are given at the Place in London. The most acclaimed production there, however, was a classic: *Miss Julie* (1971), directed by Robin Phillips, with Helen Mirren, Donal McCann and Heather Channing.

The stage and auditorium of the parent theatre at Stratford were altered yet again in 1972 and mechanically the stage is more versatile than ever, while it is hard to imagine that there was ever a chasm. The action is thrown behind the proscenium arch out-of-season when touring shows visit the theatre: out-of-season is now a few short weeks. Those with any feeling for theatrical history should not fail to visit the theatre's Picture Gallery with its many theatrical treasures. Meanwhile the R.S.C. is in the safe hands of people who care deeply about Shakespeare and who firmly believe that because he is truly 'for all time', he can and should be interpreted freshly for each generation. They are worthy possessors of the world's supreme house dramatist'.

STRATFORD, ONTARIO, SHAKESPEAREAN FESTIVAL. Conceived by a journalist named Tom Patterson who had seen Shakespeare and the classics in Britain and opera in Italy in the war, the first festival took place in 1953. The events of the previous year during which the worthies of Stratford sent Patterson to Britain to consult Tyrone Guthrie, are described in *Renown in Stratford* by Guthrie and others. The first season took place in a large tent with an open stage, *Richard III* (with Guinness) and *All's Well* being given with Anglo-Canadian casts directed by Guthrie in designs by Tanya Moiseiwitsch. Since then a permanent theatre has been opened (1957), casts have become mainly Canadian, and the playhouse itself has influenced others, including Chichester's. Canadian actors who have made their names at Stratford have included Christopher Plummer, John Colicos, Douglas Rain and William Hutt, while guest players have included Scofield, Irene Worth, Julie Harris, Jason Robards, Jnr. British directors

since the glory man have been Michael Langham, Douglas Seale and Peter Hall, while Douglas Campbell not only played and directed regularly for many years, but also founded the touring Canadian Players (1955).

Currently Jean Gascon is Artistic Director, having been directing at the theatre for a number of years, including operas since 1965. A typically interesting Stratford idea was to give *Henry V* with French-Canadians playing the French, with Plummer as Henry V. The company is the most important Shakespearean company in North America and its standards are totally international.

THEATER GUILD was started in 1918–19 to present good, but not necessarily commercial plays and has been 'the most enlightened and influential theater organisation' that New York has ever enjoyed (Brooks Atkinson). Lawrence Langner was the chief organiser of the original directors of the group which began by giving foreign plays because of shortage of native talent. These included the world premières of three Shaw plays, *Heartbreak House*, *Back to Methusalah*, and *St. Joan*. Foreign plays and classics continued, as did plays by O'Neill, Elmer Rice, Sidney Howard, etc., and by the 1927–8 season the Guild had 30,000 subscribers who could enjoy O'Neill's *Marco's Millions* and *Strange Interlude*. Unfortunately these golden years saw the Board becoming steadily less united and, with a number of dramatists setting up their own group, including Sherwood, Anderson, Behrman and Howard, and Lee Strasberg and Harold Clurman leaving to start Group Theater (see above), though it was assisted by Theatre Guild, the situation was less rosy. Yet it was the Guild which premièred *Mourning Becomes Electra*, *Porgy and Bess* and other famous plays and shows. Its standards remained high, though it became conservative, then a commercial management, but its place in American theatre history is assured.

THÉÂTRE NATIONAL POPULAIRE. This was founded in 1951 by Jean VILAR (b. 1912), who had previously started the Compagnie des Sept (1943) and the Festival of Dramatic Art at Avignon (1947). His most famous productions have been classical, but interpreted in a modern manner. Vilar is renowned for demanding clarity of diction and economy of movement and his company has divided its time between Paris and Avignon.

Joan Littlewood, who for many years made the Theatre Workshop at the Theatre Royal, Stratford East, the most exciting playhouse in London. (Photo: Camera Press)

Shakespeare, Racine, Molière have been among the company's classical authors, Brecht and Pirandello among the moderns. Though the company is permanent, guest artists appear: Gérard Phillipe played in *Le Cid* (1951).

THEATRE WORKSHOP was founded in Manchester by Joan LITTLEWOOD who, after touring in the north of England with semi-topical plays by Ewan MacColl and classical plays, took over the Theatre Royal, Stratford East in 1953. A scintillatingly brilliant director, she made her theatre the most dynamic in Britain until the early 1960s, not perhaps as important a showcase for new drama-

tists as the English Stage Co., but in terms of sheer theatrical excitement, second to none. Social commitment, Brecht, song, dance and music hall were used by her to create her own brand of popular theatre, with the text by no means sacred. However she often contributed to her authors' successes very fully, notably to Shelagh Delaney's *A Taste of Honey* (1958). Her classical forays were less happy.

Among her outstanding productions were Behan's *The Quare Fellow* (1956) and *The Hostage* (1958), Frank Norman's *Fings Aint Wot They Used T'Be* (1959) and finest of all, an impassioned, tragic, sometimes hilarious evocation of the First World War, loosely linked by the songs the soldiers sang, *Oh What a Lovely War!* This was her masterpiece, an unclassifiable show, great and simple, which was leagues ahead of every single example of the Theatre of Fact, and actorish, smugly well-meaning pieces like Brook's *US*. Miss Littlewood's casts, which were true co-operatives, included James Booth, Avis Bunnage, Barbara Windsor, Victor Spinetti, etc., but transfers to the West End inevitably weakened and then destroyed her marvellous ensemble, in which every actor was expected to contribute to the whole. She has ranged the world since those epic days dreaming of Fun Palaces and children's entertainments when not directing plays, but London has only occasionally had glimpses of the fire and the glory.

YOUNG VIC. *1.* A touring company run by George Devine, playing to children and students (1946–51), with casts that included Derek Godfrey and Keith Michell. It toured Europe as well as Britain, but collapsed from lack of funds. *2.* The offspring of the National Theatre, opening in 1970, with Frank Dunlop as its Director. Its theatre, near the Old Vic, holds 456 people who are mainly young, and the repertoire is both classical and modern: revivals have ranged from Shakespeare to *Look Back in Anger* and *French Without Tears*, and some of the National's actors play there. With the limited and expensive seating at the Old Vic, the existence of this intimate, friendly theatre where the prices are cheap, has been entirely beneficial.

Peter Hall, seen at an Aldwych Press Conference. Having triumphed at Stratford and in London in charge of the Royal Shakespeare Company, taking in operatic and administrative successes along the way, he now faces his greatest challenge as Director of the National Theatre. (Photo: Camera Press)

CHAPTER 6

BACKSTAGE

A Who's Who of Directors, Producers and Designers

ABBOTT, George (b. 1887). American dramatist, director, actor and play-doctor, best-known for his musicals (writer and director), including *On Your Toes* (1936) with Rogers and Hart, *The Boys from Syracuse* (1938), *The Pyjama Game* (1954), etc. He helped shape the fast-moving side of the Broadway scene between the wars.

AKIMOV, Nikolai (b. 1901). Russian designer and director, famous for his experimental, often eccentric settings between the wars at the Vakhtangov Theatre and later (and less wildly), at Leningrad's Theatre of Comedy. His *Hamlet* (1930) at the former theatre was more a rewriting of the text than a new interpretation and caused a scandal. Not surprisingly: Hamlet faked the Ghost, Ophelia was drunk when she drowned, etc.

ALBERY, Sir Bronson (1881–1971). British theatre manager who owned the Wyndham's, the New and the Criterion for many years and helped raise public taste in a poor period. Gielgud, Olivier, Ashcroft, Edith Evans and Guthrie were among those whose careers he helped, and he put on Sybil Thorndike in *St. Joan* (1924). Best of all, he housed the Old Vic at the New (1944–8) in its greatest period. An administrator of genius, the New is now named after him. His son, Donald Albery, succeeded him in 1962.

ANTOINE, André (1859–1943). French manager and director, who founded the Théâtre Libre in 1887 which introduced Ibsen, Strindberg, Verga, etc., to France. It failed in 1894, but he remained a key figure until he retired in 1916, and helped inspire Copeau (see below).

APPIA, Adolph (1862–1928). Swiss designer and theorist, with Gordon Craig (see below), the leader of the anti-realistic, symbolic revolution though he rarely worked in the theatre itself. Opera (especially Wagner) and Shakespeare were the spheres he hoped to influence, not realistic drama, but his reduction of the actor to a mere part of the stage picture, albeit a mobile part, has not had the effect that his theories on lighting have had. He wanted atmospheric effects built up by light playing on and shifting over non-realistic settings of masses of grey or white, and most important modern theatre productions owe something to him. His two major works are *La Mis-en-scène du drame Wagnerien* and *Die Musik und die Inszenierung*. Not until post-war Bayreuth under Wagner's grandsons were his operatic ideas put into practice.

ARONSON, Boris (b. 1900). American designer who worked with the Group Theater and later on major productions including *The Rose Tattoo* (1951), *Fiddler on the Roof* (1964), etc.

ARTAUD, Antonin. See **CRUELTY, THEATRE OF** (Chapter 7).

ATKINS, Robert (1886–1972). English director, actor and Rabelaisian wit, a major influence on the Old Vic as a director in its infancy (including the first *Peer Gynt* in Britain in 1922), and whose parts included Lear. He ran the Open Air Theatre, Regent's Park from 1933–60, apart from two years at Stratford (1944–5), and played Bottom, Sir Toby, etc. Most of the stories told about him are true, and he urgently needs a biographer.

BANCROFT, Sir Squire (1841–1926) and **Marie** (née **Wilton) BANCROFT** (1839–1921). English actor-managers, who helped start the vogue for drawing-room comedy and drama at a time when both were much needed. They patronised Tom Robertson of *Caste* fame (1867) and helped bring a much-needed realism to a theatre in dire need of reform. They provided 'real' doors and a ceiling to three wall rooms, following ideas of Mme. Vestris (see below), and were also popular actors, especially in comedy.

BARKER, Harley Granville (1877–1946). English director, playwright and writer, whose influence has been immense. He gave Shakespeare simply and swiftly, following the precepts of Poel (see below) including a built-on apron stage. His historic productions included *The Winter's Tale* and the *Dream* (1914), and earlier he had been the first Marchbanks in *Candida* and, with John Vedrenne, had run the Court where he directed Shaw, Ibsen, Euripides, Galsworthy, etc. (1904–7). In 1921 he virtually retired, but wrote his very influential *Prefaces to Shakespeare*.

BARNUM, Phinea T. (1810–1891). American showman extraordinary, who presented Tom Thumb, Jenny Lind, etc., and from 1871 ran 'The Greatest Show on Earth', the circus to end all circuses.

BARRAULT, Jean-Louis. See page 99.

BAYLIS, Lilian (1874–1937). English theatre manager who created three national theatres, the Old Vic, Sadler's Wells Opera, and Sadler's Wells (now the Royal) Ballet. This semi-educated, courageous, God-intoxicated, earthy, glorious woman took over the Vic from her aunt, Emma Cons, and began in 1914 to give Shakespeare and opera at popular prices. In 1932 she re-opened Sadler's Wells, having already managed to secure up-and-coming actors (Gielgud, Richardson, etc.) at minimal salaries. Also see **OLD VIC**, Chapter 5. Without subsidies, with plenty of faults, she achieved miracles not least as a picker of talents. She is an immortal.

BEATON, Cecil (b. 1904). English designer and photographer, whose best work has been in Pinero, Wilde, etc., and for *My Fair Lady* (1956).

BEAUMONT, Hugh (1908–1973). English manager who made the firm of H. M. Tennent Ltd. (founded in 1936) the most powerful British commercial management of modern times, especially in the 1940s and '50s. He put on classical revivals (before subsidised theatre) as well as fine commercial plays and his influence was mainly good.

BELASCO, David (1889–1931). American producer, dramatist, actor and showman, who staged a wide range of plays from classics to corn, and who was famous for his realistic staging. His adaptation of *Madam Butterfly* inspired Puccini, as did his original *The Girl of the Golden West* (1905). When directing *The Easiest Way* (1909), set in a theatrical boarding house, he bought one and used it on stage.

BEL GEDDES, Norman (1893–1958). American designer and director, a very talented disciple of Appia and Craig. His abstract settings included *Hamlet* (1931), while a famous naturalistic departure was for his own production of Kingsley's slum drama, *Dead End* (1934). His daughter is the distinguished actress **Barbara BEL GEDDES** (b. 1922), the first Margaret in *Cat on a Hot Tin Roof* (1954).

BENTHALL, Michael (b. 1919). English director in charge of the Old Vic (1953–9). During his notable regime all the First Folio plays of Shakespeare were staged, many being directed by himself.

BÉRARD, Christain (1903–1949). French designer and fashion artist who, after distinguished work in ballet in the 1930s, designed for Jouvet, Barrault and Cocteau, etc., on stage and screen, including *La Machine infernale* (1934) of the last-named. A

superb sense of period was added to his romantic gifts which were seen in fine revivals of Molière, Marivaux, etc.

BERGMAN, Ingmar (b. 1918). Swedish director and dramatist best known abroad for his internationally famous films, but a noted stage director, including a spell at Malmö (1947–52), where his productions included *Le Misanthrope*, *Peer Gynt* and Strindberg's *Dream Play*.

BIBIENAS. Italian family who helped develop the Baroque theatre in the late 17th century and the 18th century. Bologna-based, they travelled throughout Europe working on pageants and spectacles as well as designing theatres and introducing diagonal perspectives. **Giuseppe Bibienas** (1696–1757), son of one of the family's founders, was the first to use transparent scenery lit from behind, while his brother **Antonio** (1700–1774) designed the famous Teatro Communale at Bologna.

BLIN, Roger (b. 1907). French director and designer, particularly associated with Artaud's Theatre of Cruelty, Jean-Louis Barrault, and the Theatre of the Absurd. Plays he has directed include *Waiting for Godot* (1953), playing Pozzo, Genet's *Les Nègres* (1959) and *The Screens* (1966).

BROOK, Peter (b. 1925). English director, the most remarkable of our day. Only the late Tyrone Guthrie equalled him in inventiveness in the British theatre, though Brook is less capricious. He first made his name at Birmingham Rep and Stratford (1945–7), Barry Jackson calling him 'the youngest earthquake I have known'. His *Love's Labour's Lost* (1946) remains a theatre legend. Since then he has become an international, as well as a national director, ranging from Shakespeare and opera to musicals and commercial plays. Twin peaks of achievement have been *Titus Andronicus* at Stratford (1955) with Olivier, and *A Midsummer Night's Dream* (1970) at Stratford and later London, Europe and America – the most acclaimed staging of a Shakespearean comedy in memory: a radical interpretation which sounds gimmicky, but which used circus techniques in a bare white setting to concentrate on both verse and story as is rarely possible, it was truly historic, a much over-used word but not in this case.

Among many other highlights have been a powerful *Measure for Measure* (1950); a famous Becket-

Peter Brook, master director of total theatre, dramatic excitement and unease. (Photo: Zoe Dominic)

tian *Lear* (1962) with Scofield; the ultimate Director's Theatre piece, *Marat-Sade* (1964), the last two being for the Royal Shakespeare Company, of which he has been a Director since 1962. This 'greatest explorer among our directors' (Ronald Hayman) formed a Parisian International Centre for Theatre Research which performed *Orghast* in Persia in 1972, using an international language invented for the occasion by Ted Hughes. Brook is often controversial, often maddening, but always important, even in *US* (1965), his sincere comment on Vietnam conceived by him, but too actorish and self-indulgent to be truly effective. He finds time to direct films, write books, design sets and com-

pose: he did both for *Titus*. Even remotely conventional theatre seems to be appealing to him less, which is our loss. Two things are certain: his work is never less than brilliantly conceived and never trivial. The Director's Theatre is justified by him for, at his best, he is that rare theatrical being, a genius. See *Peter Brook* by J. C. Trewin and his own *The Empty Space*.

BUNN, Alfred (1798–1860). English theatre manager famous for his quarrels with Macready and many others, his stormy rule of Drury Lane and Covent Garden, his attempts to establish English opera – he wrote the libretto of the once-popular *The Bohemian Girl* – and his general buccaneering methods. However his *The Stage; Before and Behind the Curtain* is a marvellous glimpse of the age of Edmund Kean, Macready and Maria Malibran, the most thrilling of all actress-singers, whom he engaged for Drury Lane.

BURY, John (b. 1925). English designer who made his name at Theatre Workshop (1946–61), then at the Royal Shakespeare Co., especially working with Peter Hall: *The Wars of the Roses* (1963), plays by Pinter, etc. They have also collaborated very successfully on operas. He is a great believer in authentic materials. The *Roses* plays had a steel look, and iron props and furniture, and he has said that his job is to give a 'sounding board for the actor's imagination to supply him with the basic imagery that he needs'.

CHARLOT, André (1882–1956). French-born English impresario, famous for his London revues. *London Calling* (1924) was Coward's début as a revue writer, while *Revue of 1924* saw a triple-début on Broadway that can never have been surpassed: Gertrude Lawrence, Beatrice Lillie and Jack Buchanan. He also presented comedies and farces.

CLEMENTS, Sir John (b. 1910). English actor-manager and director, and the Director of the Chichester Festival from 1966–73 (see previous chapter). His classical parts have included Coriolanus at the Old Vic (1948), and Macbeth, Shotover, Prospero, Antony and Sir Antony Absolute at Chichester. As an actor-manager his triumphs have included a record-breaking run of *The Beaux' Strategem* starring himself and his wife, **Kay HAMMOND** (b. 1909), a delectable Mrs. Sullen, famous for her seductive sugar-plum drawl of a voice. They also played together in his production of the complete *Man and Superman* (1951). At the Saville (1955) he presented Ibsen, Sheridan, Shaw and Congreve with superb casts, while he made Chichester into a 'festival of acting' to the huge enjoyment of all except the more tight-lipped, trend-conscious critics. Miss Hammond is the daughter of the actor, Sir Guy Standing, and the mother of that fine actor, John Standing, at the time of writing (1973) starring in *Private Lives*.

CLURMAN, Harold (b. 1901). American director, producer and manager, who founded the very influential Group Theater (discussed in the previous chapter) in 1931. When it broke up in 1940 he became an independent director. Recommended strongly in his *The Fervent Years – The Story of the Group Theater*.

COCHRAN, Sir Charles (1873–1951). English impresario, the greatest of his day, who presented boxing, rodeos, Houdini, Reinhardt's *The Miracle* (1911), Coward's *This Year of Grace, Bitter Sweet* and *Cavalcade*. The first was staged at the London Pavilion, where he presented revues from 1918–31. A charming man, he found time to write three books of memoirs.

COHAN, George M. (1879–1942). American actor, song-writer, song-and-dance man, and superb showman, regarded by many as the founding father of American musical comedy with shows like *The Little Millionaire* (1911), etc. When his style became out of date he successfully turned to straight acting. He wrote the First World War hit song, *Over There*.

COPEAU, Jacques (1878–1949). French director and manager. Though an anti-realist, like Appia and Craig, he was not their disciple, rather preaching the sanctity of the text of a play, given as straightforwardly as possible without distractions. He made his name with his own company at the Vieux Colombier (from 1913), specialising in Shakespeare and Molière, with as little scenery as possible, clear, light speech and economic movements. In 1931 he left his company to his nephew, Michel Saint-Denis (see below), after several years of performing in Burgundy, renewing 'contact with the soil' and playing to countryfolk. From 1936–41 he was a director of the Comédie-Française.

CRAIG, Edward Gordon (1872–1966). English designer, director and theorist, the son of Ellen Terry and the architect, Edward Godwin. Apart from two busy years (1902–3), when he directed a number of plays, including Ibsen's *The Vikings at Helgeland* and *Much Ado* with his mother in both, he only had a hand in four productions, including *Hamlet* at the Moscow Art Theatre (1911) with Stanislavsky, a more practical man. From then on he became a theorist, his most famous testament being *On The Art of the Theatre* (1911). His views were not unlike Appia's (see above) but although he was anti-realist and stressed the importance of the director, lighting and colour, he became less interested in words, demanding that the theatre should be an extension of mime and dance. This naturally means a demotion of the actor, and his influence has been greatest in parts of the French theatre, especially on Jean-Louis Barrault. But his overall influence on unrealistic design and lighting and the building of atmosphere has influenced the theatre as a whole.

DALY, Augustin (1839–1899). American manager and dramatist, famous in New York and London for his theatres and generally high standards of productions to be seen in them. The first actually named Daly's opened in New York in 1879 and saw many major classical revivals; London's Daly's opened in 1893, having been built for Daly by George Edwardes. Though Duse and Bernhardt played there it is best remembered for its musicals, especially *The Maid of the Mountains* which ran for 1,352 performances.

DAUBENY, Sir Peter (b. 1921). English impresario and manager, whose World Theatre and other seasons (1951–73) have not only brought many great companies to Britain, but have influenced the English stage, as when the Berliner Ensemble played in London in 1956. For several years his assistant was **Michael WHITE** (b. 1936), now a leading producer himself.

DEVINE, George. See **ENGLISH STAGE COMPANY** (Chapter 5).

DEXTER, John (b. 1925). English director particularly associated first with the English Stage Co., then with the National Theatre, and famous for his skill in organising stage business on a large scale, since Wesker's *The Kitchen* (1961); this was at the Royal Court, where other productions included Wesker's *Trilogy* (1958–60). His most acclaimed productions at the National have included the Olivier *Othello* (1964), his stunning *The Royal Hunt of the Sun* (1964) and *The Misanthrope* (1973). Also a notable director of opera.

DUKES, Ashley (1885–1959). English dramatist (*The Man with a Load of Mischief*, 1924) and manager who founded the Mercury Theatre in 1933. It became especially famous for its productions of foreign plays, many of them adapted by him, and as the home of the Ballet Rambert, founded by his wife, Dame Marie Rambert. It was also something of a haven for English verse drama before and after the war, including plays by Eliot, Fry and Ronald Duncan.

DULLIN, Charles (1885–1949). French director, manager and actor and a very notable teacher of acting. After working with Copeau he founded a troupe in 1918 which later played at the Théâtre de l'Atelier. His most famous productions were of plays by Shakespeare, Jonson and Aristophanes, and, of the moderns, Pirandello.

EDWARDES, George (1852–1915). English manager famous for his reign at the Gaiety from 1885. He later ran Daly's, which he had built for Augustin Daly in 1893. His enormously popular productions of musicals included *The Geisha* and *The Merry Widow* (1907), the latter being turned from operetta into musical comedy to suit current British taste.

FAGAN, J. B. (1873–1933). English director and dramatist (including *And So To Bed*, 1926) whose most remarkable achievement was a two-year spell at Oxford Playhouse where his casts included Robson, Robert Morley, Gielgud, Guthrie, etc., and where, in one amazing eight-week season, he gave Wilde, Shaw (twice), Congreve, Goldini, St. John Hankin, Yeats, Maeterlinck and Sophocles. This was an earlier Playhouse than that of today, run so successfully for many years by **Frank HAUSER** (b. 1922), an exceptionally wide-ranging director of plays and opera.

FROHMAN, Charles (1860–1915). American manager, the best-known of three brothers in the business, who was a greatly respected figure and an Anglophile and who at one time ran five West End theatres, most notably the Duke of York's; he presented the first *Peter Pan* there in 1905. He went down in the *Titanic*.

GLENVILLE, Peter (b. 1913). English director, son of the comedian Shaun Glenville and *the* pantomime principal boy, Dorothy Ward. Beginning as an actor, his productions have included *Separate Tables* in London and New York (1954–6), *A Patriot for Me* (New York, 1969) and *Bequest to the Nation* (London, 1970).

GRÜNDGENS, Gustav (1899–1963). German actor and director, and a famous Hamlet who also appeared in films. Director of the Preussisches Staatstheater, Berlin (1937–54), the Deutches Theater, Berlin (1946–7) and, later, leading theatres in

Tyrone Guthrie, director of plays, founder of theatres, author, talker, and enfant terrible until he died. (Photo: Walter Bird)

Düsseldorf and Hamburg. His parts in his own productions included Richard II, Mephisto in *Faust* and Wallenstein. A very gifted administrator as well as a director, his career was as remarkable as it was influential.

GUTHRIE, Sir Tyrone (1900–1971). Anglo-Irish director, theatre founder, writer and talker, prodigiously energetic and incapable of dullness. This first English world-famous star director could be capricious in the extreme in Shakespearean plays he was directing for the second or third time. He could be a stern taskmaster, but most actors adored working for him. He was an enfant terrible until his death and no respecter of stars, and he was practising ensemble long before it was fashionable.

He advocated the open stage, theatre-in-the-round, the arena stage – but not the proscenium theatre, where many of his greatest triumphs occurred. He was the Old Vic's youngest Director (1933), in charge of the Vic and the Wells (1939–45), the first Director of the Stratford, Ontario Festival (1953) and Director of the theatre at Minneapolis which bears his name (1962–5). He also directed plays in Israel, New Zealand, Australia, etc., and was a notable, if erratic, director of opera. He first made his name in the early 1930s in Priestley and Bridie, while still acting occasionally, handicapped by his 6 feet 5 inches. Among his finest productions were his *Dream* at the Old Vic, *The School for Scandal* for Gielgud (1937), *Peer Gynt* with Richardson at the New – which inaugurated the greatest

Jesus Christ Superstar on Broadway. (*Photo: Camera Press, London*)

stretch of Old Vic seasons – and *Tamburlaine* at the Vic (1951), with Wolfit, a tempestuous success in which this master of spectacle and movement excelled even himself. Later triumphs included *Troilus and Cressida* at the Vic (1956), and his *All's Well that Ends Well* (1953) was one of his biggest Canadian successes. He wrote the play, *Top of the Ladder* (1950), also two splendid books, *A Life in the Theatre* and *Tyrone Guthrie on Acting*.

HALL, Peter (b. 1930). English director, the Director of the National Theatre from 1973 after a remarkably successful career embracing plays, opera and films, and a famous spell in charge of the Royal Shakespeare Co. (1960–9). Director of the Arts (1955–6), where his productions included the historic British première of *Waiting for Godot* (1953). His achievements at Stratford included producing all seven Histories, including the epic 3-part *Wars of the Roses* (with John Barton) which comprised the three *Henry VI* plays and *Richard III* (1963–4). He created a permanent company on long term contracts, which made a genuine ensemble possible, and gave the R.S.C. its famous London home at the Aldwych (1960). Shakespeare apart, he has been particularly noted for his Pinter productions, also directing Livings, Albee, etc. He has often and very successfully worked in the theatre and opera with the designer, John Bury (see above), and it was inevitable that this born administrator and complete man-of-the-theatre should be asked to succeed Olivier at the National. Also see **ROYAL SHAKESPEARE COMPANY** in Chapter 5.

HARRIS, Sir Augustus (1851–1896). English manager known as 'Druriolanus' because of his long connection with Drury Lane, which he made famous for its melodramas and pantomimes. He was the first to bring music hall stars into pantomime. The son of another Augustus Harris, who was best known as a manager of opera and ballet, his knighthood was not a theatrical one, but because he happened to be the City's Sheriff when the German Emperor visited it.

HENSLOWE, Philip (d. 1616). English manager and theatre owner who built the first Bankside theatre, the Rose, in 1587. Five years later his step-daughter married the great actor, Edward Alleyn, and the two men began a very successful partnership – at the Rose, the Fortune, and the Hope,

this last being the old Bear Garden, rebuilt in 1613 for baiting and plays. He was a sharp businessman and his *Diary*, much of it an account book, is an invaluable source of information about Elizabethan theatre management and the stage in general. It spans 1592–1603.

HORNIMAN, Miss A. E. F. (1860–1937). English heiress who was one of the founders of the Repertory Movement. After re-opening the Abbey Theatre in Dublin as the Repertory Theatre of Ireland (1903), she founded Britain's first Rep at the Gaiety, Manchester, in 1908. Before being forced to close in 1921 she had produced 200 plays, half of them new, an extraordinary achievement. They included Harold Brighouse's *Hobson's Choice* (1916). A key factor in her success was the director **Ben Iden PAYNE** (b. 1888), a disciple of William Poel who since 1945 has been very influential in the American theatre as a Shakespearean director and teacher, but the final credit must go to Miss Horniman, whose example fired many others to spread Rep throughout Britain.

HOUSEMAN, John (b. 1902). American director, whose notable career has included work for Theater Guild, co-founding Mercury Theater with Orson Welles (1937) and rescuing the Shakespeare Festival at Stratford, Conn., from 'chronic provincialism' in the 1950s (Brooks Atkinson). In the 1960s he became Producing Director of A.P.A. Phoenix; in the 1970s the founder of the Acting Company in New York.

HUNT, Hugh (b. 1911). English director who directed more than 30 Irish plays at the Abbey, Dublin (1935–8). After a notable period at the Bristol Old Vic (1945–8), and at the Old Vic (including the last season at the New) (1949–53), he worked in Australia as Director of the Elizabethan Theatre Trust, then became the first Professor of Drama at Manchester University. Memorable productions have included an enchanting *Love's Labour's Lost* (1949) and an even more famous *Romeo* (1952), with Alan Badel, Claire Bloom and Peter Finch. He became Artistic Director of the Abbey, Dublin in 1969.

HURRY, Leslie (b. 1909). English designer of plays, operas and ballets, especially associated with the Old Vic (including *Tamburlaine*, 1951) and Stratford, Ontario.

JACKSON, Sir Barry (1878–1961). English manager, the founder and director of Birmingham Rep, spending his own fortune in the process. He made it the leading British Rep, and premières there included *Back to Methusalah* (1923). The Rep gave seasons in London and, at first, operas, while his rising stars included Edith Evans, Ashcroft, Olivier, Richardson, Hardwicke, Scofield, Leighton, Finney, etc., and Peter Brook. He ran the Malvern Festival (1928–37) and the Shakespeare Memorial Theatre (1945–8), banishing a certain provincialism that had reigned there. He was one of the most influential figures in modern British theatre history.

JESSNER, Leopold (1878–1945). German director of the Berlin State Theatre (1919–25) who replaced realistic scenery with different acting levels connected by steps. An expressionist and a disciple of Rheinhardt, he was considered very radical and was certainly most influential.

JONES, Inigo (1573–1652). English architect and designer who designed and staged court masques from 1605–13, often working with Ben Jonson. Using knowledge gained in Italy and his own instinct for the theatre, his sets, costumes and stage machinery were as elaborate as they were to be influential. He was probably the first English designer to use painted scenery forming a stage perspective picture within a proscenium arch and indicate scene changes by use of revolving screens.

JONES, Robert Edmund (1887–1954). American designer of exceptional talent who, wrote Brooks Atkinson, 'turned scene design to an art by his use of colour, form and lighting'. He put Broadway stage design far ahead of the West End's and inspired many young artists. Notable designs included those for Barrymore's *Richard III* and *Hamlet*, and for O'Neill's *The Great God Brown* in the 1920s, also fantastic sets for *The Green Pastures* in 1930. A revolutionary, endlessly fascinating, always relevant designer.

JOUVET, Louis (1887–1951). French actor and director, one of the key figures in the French theatre of his day. After working with Copeau from 1913 he formed his own company in 1922 at the Théâtre des Champs-Élysées where, after personal triumphs in plays by Jules Romains, he began a famous association with Giraudoux, directing his first play, *Siegfried*, in 1927. He worked with the dramatist on all but one of his plays in very close collaboration. Renowned (from his association with Copeau) for great devotion to the text, he gradually added inventiveness, combining the two in a memorable production of *L'École des femmes* (1936). He was appointed resident director of the Comédie-Française (1936), where his methods were very influential. His own finest performances were in comedy, including the title-rôle in Romains' *Knock*, and Molière's Tartuffe.

KAZAN, Elia (b. 1909). American director, born in Turkey, who acted with Group Theater (1932–9), then became one of the most brilliant and creative directors of the modern American stage, who has done more than anyone else in the U.S.A. to bring about the Director's Theatre. Some of his greatest successes have been *The Skin of our Teeth* (1942), *A Streetcar named Desire* (1947), *Death of a Salesman* (1949), *Cat on a Hot Tin Roof* (1955) and *Sweet Bird of Youth* (1959). Co-directed at the Lincoln Center from 1962–4.

KENNY, Sean (1932–73). Irish designer who trained as an architect under Frank Lloyd Wright. This influential master of stage mechanics, automation included, worked non-stop in the theatre from the late 1950s to the mid-'60s, his designs including *The Hostage* (1958), *Oliver* (1960), *The Devils* (1961), *King Priam* at Covent Garden (1962), *Pickwick* (1965), etc. *Oliver*, one of several collaborations with Lionel Bart, had sets automatically controlled by a stage crew of one. It seemed that he was about to return more regularly to the theatre when his death occurred.

KOMISARJEVSKY, Theodore (1882–1954). Russian director and designer, born in Venice, who became a naturalised Briton. After early successes in opera in Europe and America, he made his name in Britain staging Russian plays in a converted cinema in Barnes with Gielgud, Jean Forbes Robertson, Martita Hunt, Laughton, etc. Notable for his insistence on depth in acting and intensity, he observed some of Stanislavsky's methods and provided non-realistic settings which stressed mood. His Shakespearean productions were less successful because of indifference to the texts, which culminated in a horribly miscast Cleopatra; the Russian light comedian, Eugenie Leontovich,

*Limbert Spencer and The Tribe in the London produc-
tion of* Hair. (*Photo: Camera Press, London*)

who began the speech, 'O wither'd is the garland of the war,' according to Charles Morgan, by emitting: 'O weederdee degarlano devar' and continued in like manner, 'boys and girls' becoming 'boisenguls', etc. However, a *Lear* at Stratford with Randle Ayrton fared better, especially as Komisarjevsky was a master of lighting and grouping.

LE GALLIENNE, Eva (b. 1899). American actress and producer and director, born in London, who founded the Civic Repertory Theater (1926–33), presenting and acting in major American and foreign plays. Later, with Cheryl Crawford and Margaret Webster, she founded the American Repertory Company (1946). An actress of remarkable range, she excelled in Ibsen, Chekhov and as Amanda in *Private Lives*, while being dedicated to good plays and true ensemble. In the 1960s she toured, directed and acted for the National Repertory Theater. An idealist who became one of the supreme figures of the American theatre.

LITTLEWOOD, Joan. See **THEATRE WORKSHOP** (Chapter 5).

LUGNÉ-POË, Aurélien-Marie (1869–1940). French actor-manager who, between 1892–1929 at the Théâtre de l'Oeuvre, introduced plays by Strindberg, Ibsen, Haptmann, etc., to the public, helped make Maeterlinck famous and presented Claudel's first success, *L'Announce faite à Marie* (1912).

LUNACHARSKY, Anatoli (1875–1933). Russian friend of Lenin, who saved the theatre from being swept away after the Revolution by protecting the famous old institutions, notably the Moscow Art Theatre, and organising new ones. As first Commissar for Education he protected the old plays of Russia and the rest of Europe, while propounding the doctrine of Socialist Realism. Though later abused by politicians to force dramatists to toe an official line, this 'realism' had a notable effect on the classics, for – vague as the term is – it led to their reappraisal in terms of today, but not their distortion. If the classics in Russia have now become museum art in a way Western radical directors would not tolerate, that does not lessen Lunacharsky's achievements.

MARSHALL, Norman (b. 1901). English director who ran the Cambridge Festival Theatre in the 1930s and later the influential Gate Theatre, presenting many classical and modern plays. His *The Other Theatre* (1947) is essential reading for an account of the non-West End theatre between the wars, the 'Fringe' of a generation ago.

MERRICK, David. American producer and manager who, since *Fanny* (1954), has presented every type of show on Broadway from Weiss and Osborne to the very lightest pieces, and shown himself to be a master publicist.

MESSEL, Oliver (b. 1905). English director who has worked in nearly every theatre genre and is especially famous for elegant, amusing and romantically decaying designs and the power to create mysterious enchantment. Famous sets have included *The Little Hut* (1950) and, in the classics, his *Dream* (1938) and *The Tempest* (1940), both for the Old Vic. He has also designed theatre interiors in Britain and America.

MEYERHOLD, Vsevolod (1874–*c.* 1940). Russian actor and director who joined the Moscow Art Theatre in 1898 and later worked with Stanislavsky, after touring the provinces, in the Art Theatre's experimental studio. He turned to Vera Komisarjevskaya's company where his advocacy of Gordon Craig's ideals, with actors reduced to mere puppets of the director if carried to the extreme, led into trouble. After the Revolution, he directed Mayakovsky's *Mystery-Bouffe* (1918), the first Soviet play, and developed his system of 'Bio-mechanics', acrobatic training which made actors the servants of directors to an extreme degree, but which produced finely-tuned bodies. But after directing *The Bed Bug* and *The Bath House*, he fell from favour with the Regime in the 1930s and his theatre was closed. He vanished in 1939 and is assumed to have died or been killed in prison.

MILES, Sir Bernard. See **MERMAID** (Chapter 5).

MIELZINER, Jo (b. 1901). American designer whose work has enhanced over a hundred plays since 1924, ranging from the classics to Tennessee Williams and Arthur Miller, also musicals, including *Annie Get Your Gun*, *South Pacific*, *Gypsy*, etc. With Eero Saarinen he designed the repertory theatre at the Lincoln Center.

MOISEIWITSCH, Tanya (b. 1914). English designer who has worked at the Old Vic (including the legendary *Uncle Vanya*, 1945) and Stratford; with Guthrie, he designed the original Festival Tent at Stratford, Ontario, and later the Tyrone Guthrie Theater, Minneapolis.

MORLEY, Christopher. English designer, Head of Design for the Royal Shakespeare Co. Some of his best work has been with Trevor Nunn: *The Revenger's Tragedy* (1966), and the four Roman plays (1972; London, 1973). A brilliant user of colour, also of simple box-like sets.

MOTLEY. A group of English designers, Sophia and Margaret Harris and Elizabeth Montgomery, the last working solely now in New York. Their first designs were for *Romeo* at the O.U.D.S. (1932), since when they have designed very many plays, musicals and operas in Britain and America, including the whole of Gielgud's great season at the Queen's (1937) and *The Dance of Death* at the National (1967). Too 'safe' for some tastes, their record speaks for itself. Sophia died in 1966.

NEMIROVICH-DANCHENKO, Vladimir (1859–1943). Russian impresario, manager and director, who founded the Moscow Art Theatre with Stanislavsky (1898). Earlier he had already tried to make Russian acting more naturalistic, as had Stanislavsky, whom he met in 1897. At the Art Theatre his duties were mainly as literary editor, though he directed plays, more frequently after Stanislavsky's death. He also founded the Moscow Musical Theatre to improve standards in musicals and operetta.

NEUBER, Fredericka Carolina (1697–1760). German actress-manager, née Weisenborn, who married Johann Neuber. Apart from her fame as an actress, especially in breeches parts, she is best remembered for her reforms of the German stage along the lines of the French classical theatre, as suggested by the critic, Johann Gottsched, though he was too rigid in his ideas for her. Although they fell out, their association is regarded as a turning point in the history of the German stage, not least for improved standards of acting. She also brought about a relationship between the theatre and literary men, which had been a mere dream before her

An historic glimpse of Stanislavsky and Bernard Shaw in 1921. The less well-known figure of the left is Anatoli Lunacharsky, who did more than anyone to save the traditions of the Russian theatre, even the theatre itself, at the time of the Revolution. (Photo: Novosti Press Agency)

time.

NUNN, Trevor (b. 1940). English director. Artistic Director of the Royal Shakespeare Co. since 1968, where he had made his name two years earlier with his fine production of *The Revenger's Tragedy* (1966). His most striking achievement has been directing Shakespeare's four Roman plays at Stratford (1972) and in London. He is married to **Janet SUZMAN** (b. 1939), who has played Ophelia, Rosalind, Beatrice, etc., for the Company, and a fine Cleopatra, which was highly praised.

OKHLOPKOV, Nikolai (b. 1900). Russian actor and director who, after working with Meyerhold, became Director of the Realistic Theatre in Moscow where he produced plays which flowed without interruption in the manner of the Elizabethans and the Greeks, using a stage or stages and involving the spectators in the action in a way which was then revolutionary. He became Director of the Theatre of the Revolution in 1943. Some of his ideas stemmed from the Japanese *kabuki* theatre.

PAPP, Joseph (b. 1921). American director and producer of the New York Shakespeare Festival (see Chapter 5) and of the Public Theater, founded by him as a winter headquarters in 1967. Shows there have ranged from *Hair* to *Hamlet*. This extraordinary man has now (1973) been appointed Director of the Vivian Beaumont and the Forum Theater at the Lincoln Center, while still ruling his fine old empire.

PISCATOR, Erwin (1893–1966). German director who was a disciple of Reinhardt and later influenced Brecht, with whom he dramatised *The Good Soldier Schweik* (1927). He shared with Brecht the idea of Epic Theatre but his later career, apart from a spell in Moscow as Director of the International Theatre (1931–3), lay in New York and West Germany. He directed his own famous version of *War and Peace* during the 1950s, though it was written in 1936, and opened the Free People's Theatre in West Berlin in 1963.

PITOËFF, Georges (1887–1939) and his wife **Ludmilla** (1896–1951). Russo-French actors and directors of their own company. Having acted with Copeau after settling in France in 1918, Pitoeff founded his own company in 1924, introducing Shaw and Pirandello to French audiences, as well

as new French dramatists, including Claudel, Cocteau and Anouilh. Ludmilla took over when her husband died, having been his leading actress; after her death, their son **Sacha** took over.

PLANCHON, Roger (b. 1931). French director and disciple of Brecht, also influenced by Artaud and Vilar but with his own style of theatre – lively, inventive, often funny, and essentially popular – which has made his name. Appointed Director of the Théâtre Populaire de Provence in 1959, his productions have included the two parts of Shakespeare's *Henry IV* in one, an improvised burlesque of *The Three Musketeers*, Marlowe's *Edward II* and a number of plays by Adamov.

PLAYFAIR, Sir Nigel (1874–1934). English manager and director who ran the Lyric, Hammersmith, in a famous spell from 1918–34. His productions included Drinkwater's *Abraham Lincoln* (1918), his classic revival of *The Beggar's Opera* (1920) which ran for 1,463 performances, *The Way of the World* (1924) with Edith Evans' incomparable Millimant, and *The Importance of Being Earnest* (1930) with Gielgud as Jack Worthing. Earlier he had been an actor with Benson and Tree. He played Bottom in Granville Barker's famous *Dream* (1912).

POEL, William (1852–1934). English actor and director whose Shakespearean productions were as nearly as possible in the style of the Elizabethan originals. Founding the Elizabethan Stage Society in 1894, he presented *Twelfth Night* in 1895 on a reconstruction of an Elizabethan stage, and by the time the Society was abandoned in 1905, had directed most major Elizabethan and Jacobean plays. A very influential figure, not least on Harley Granville Barker.

PRINCE, Harold (b. 1928). American director and producer who since *The Pyjama Game* (1954) had been associated with many major musicals, including *West Side Story, Fiddler on the Roof, Company*, etc., also with plays, including Durrenmatt's *The Visit* for the Phoenix Repertory Company (1973).

QUINTERO, José (b. 1924). American director who founded the Circle-in-the-Square theatre, and whose 1950–1 season was a turning point in the fortunes of Off-Broadway when Tennessee Williams'

Summer and Smoke was produced. His two famous productions of O'Neill, *The Iceman Cometh* (1956) and the first performance of *Long Day's Journey into Night* (1956), finally established the playwright's supreme position in American drama, since when he has produced Genet, more O'Neill, etc., also films and opera.

REINHARDT, Max (1873–1943). Austrian director, manager and actor whose real name was Goldmann, and who had to leave Germany in 1933 when Hitler came to power. After acting from 1893, he switched entirely to direction ten years later. Though he first made his reputation in small theatres, the Deutches Theater and the intimate Kammerspiele, he is best remembered for his spectacular productions and control of huge stage crowds, and as the most successful exponent of Gordon Craig's theories on lighting, design and the stage picture. An inspiring leader, he attracted notable collaborators. He used stylised settings, sometimes dwarfing his actors with vertical lines, sometimes having them tower over the sets by horizontal lines, and he brought actors and audiences into closer contact whenever possible, being an early modern exponent of arena theatre. His famous productions included *Oedipus Rex* in Vienna (1910), *The Miracle* in London (1911), and *Oedipus* in London the same year, with Martin-Harvey. He founded and ran the Salzburg Festival (1920), where he regularly staged *Everyman*, and during the 1920s directed not only in the two smaller theatres mentioned above, but at the huge Grosses Schauspielhaus, also in Berlin. In a famous tour of America (1927–8), his company gave the *Dream* (which he later filmed oddly but sometimes gloriously in Hollywood), *Danton's Death* and *Everyman*, while one of his British productions was *Helen* (from Offenbach's *La Belle Hélène*) for Cochran (1932). The next year he directed the *Dream* for the O.U.D.S. Despite his masterly intimate productions, critics sometimes accused his large productions of vulgarising the theatre; popularising would be a better word. He found time to start the first school for directors, at Schönbrunn in Vienna, and obtained the collaboration of famous painters and musicians. He made Berlin Europe's theatre capital. He has had no modern successor: one would have to imagine a combination of Peter Hall and Zeffirelli to conceive his influence.

RICH, John (*c.* 1682–1761). English manager of the Lincoln's Inn Fields theatre after the death of his father, Christopher Rich. He put on *The Beggar's Opera* (1728), having earlier established the popularity of pantomime in Britain (from 1717), with himself as a famous Harlequin.

RIX, Brian (b. 1924). English actor-manager, famous for his farces, first at the Whitehall, then elsewhere. His authors have included Colin Morris, John Chapman, Anthony Marriott, Ray Cooney, Michael Pertwee, etc., and the style has been broader than that of the Aldwych farces, but suitably hilarious. His Whitehall career began with Morris's *Reluctant Heroes* (1950), with himself as the gormless Godfrey, and his casts have included Leo Franklyn, Alfred Marks, Dennis Ramsden, Derek Farr, Muriel Pavlow, Moray Watson and Rix's wife, Elspet Gray.

ROBBINS, Jerome (b. 1918). American choreographer and director who, apart from his distinguished work in ballet, devised and choreographed *On The Town* (1944) and also *West Side Story* (1957) which he also directed and which revolutionised the musical, though, alas, without leading to adequate successors. His many other successes includes the staging and choreography of *Fiddler on the Roof* (1964).

SAINT-DENIS, Michel (1897–1971). French director who founded the Compagnie des Quinze (1931) as a successor to his uncle, Jacques Copeau's, Vieux-Colombier company. Andre Obéy was resident dramatist and the company was notable for a collapsible rostrum as the basic setting, plus occasional very stylised pieces of scenery, also for its skill in mime. After its close Saint-Denis settled in London (1936) where he became a great influence on the serious British theatre. He directed *Macbeth* at the Vic (1937) and more significantly *The Three Sisters* for Gielgud (1938), an early and rarely equalled example of ensemble playing, and the most famous production of Chekhov ever seen in Britain, which finally established his popularity. The cast was amazing: Gielgud, Ashcroft, Redgrave, ffrangcon-Davies, Angela Baddeley, Devine, Byam Shaw, Guinness, Harry Andrews, Quartermaine, etc. He founded the London Theatre Studio and was head of the very influential Old Vic Theatre School (1946–52). He directed Olivier in

Oedipus Rex (1945) and Stravinsky's *Oedipus Rex* at the Wells (1960). A Director of the Royal Shakespeare Co., he staged *The Cherry Orchard* for them (1962). He was also a consultant for the Lincoln Center Repertory and Dramatic School in New York.

SHAW, Glen Byam (b. 1904). English director and actor, now Director of Productions for Sadler's Wells Opera. After the 1930s, in which his parts included Laertes, Horatio, etc., and war service, he became a leading figure in the classical theatre (plus West End productions) as a director of the Old Vic School and Centre (1946–52), co-director of the Shakespeare Memorial Theatre with Anthony Quayle (1953–6) and sole director (1956–9). His most famous productions include *Antony and Cleopatra* with Ashcroft and Redgrave (1953) and, for the National, *The Dance of Death* (1967), also *The Ring* with John Blatchley for the Wells. A respecter of the text and a fine teacher of actors and singers, he is married to the excellent actress, Angela Baddeley.

SHUBERT, Lee, Sam and **Jacob**. American producers and theatre managers who wielded colossal power on Broadway from early in the century until the 1950s, after destroying the monopoly of a syndicate dominated by Abe Erlanger. They were not interested in Art, but they kept many theatres open instead of making fortunes selling them off, and they produced over 500 shows. (Sam Shubert died in 1905.)

STANISLAVSKY, Konstantin Sergeyevich (1865–1938). Russian director, teacher and actor and very influential theorist who founded the Society of Literature and Art in 1888 and became well-known in the early '90s with productions of Tolstoy and a version of Dostoyevsky's *Selo Stepanchikhov*. Already he was insisting on relaxed realistic acting (against current fashion) in naturalistic sets, and his career soared when, in 1898, he founded the Moscow Art Theatre with Nemirovich-Danchenko (see above and, for the theatre, Chapter 5). His productions of Chekhov are theatre history, from *The Seagull* (1898) onwards; perhaps less humorous than Chekhov wanted, but realistic, poetic and atmospheric, rather than literal, factual recreations, and always psychologically suggestive. Later, Stanislavsky became more concerned with the development of character and less with naturalism,

and wrote several key books, *An Actor Prepares* (1926), *Building a Character, Stanislavsky Rehearses Othello* and his autobiography, *My Life in Art*. The first, because it was more concerned with the psychology of acting than technique (in which Stanislavsky was a great believer), flawed the otherwise admirable American Method school of acting (see **METHOD** in Chapter 7), for which the great man is sometimes blamed. Those who criticise him for earnestness and over-many rehearsals forget the revolution he created when it was needed, and the fact that no one has done more to make actors and directors realise the importance of *thinking* about their art and taking it seriously.

STRASBERG, Lee (b. 1901). American director and teacher who was co-founder with Harold Clurman (see above) of the Group Theater in 1931 (see Chapter 5). He founded the Actor's Studio in 1948 where he has been the leading exponent of the Method (see Chapter 7). He has lectured widely about his beliefs.

STREHLER, Giorgio. Italian director and manager who, with Paolo Grassi, founded the Piccolo Teatro di Milano in 1947, which played – and plays – a major part in advancing the cause of Italian theatre after many years of isolation under the Fascists. Also a brilliant director of opera.

STIGWOOD, Robert (b. 1930). Australian impresario and, at the time of writing (1973), the fastest rising producer on the British theatre scene, via *Jesus Christ Superstar*, etc.

TAIROV, Alexander Yakovlevich (1885–1950). Russian director who founded the Kamerny Theatre in 1914 along lines directly opposed to Stanislavky's. A believer in 'theatricalism' (i.e. that theatre is theatre, not life), he stressed the importance of settings and lighting and downgraded the actor, as Appia and Craig had suggested in their different ways, making them near-puppets of the director. His productions of Shakespeare, Racine, Claudel in the early 1920s seemed neo-realistic to some, despite Cubist designs and balletic acting; later, he directed O'Neill and other moderns along the lines of Craig and Meyerhold, and finally ran into trouble with the authorities at a time when socialist realism demanded realism of a sort that would not obscure a play's message, whether it was a modern or a classical work. Not surprisingly, brilliance was reduced to competence.

Luchino Visconti, aristocrat, Marxist and director of plays, films and operas. (Photo: Camera Press)

TORELLI, Giacomo (1608–1678). Italian designer, a supreme figure in the Baroque theatre, who was the pupil of Aleotti, designer of the Teatro Farnese at Parma. The complete set of wings there, the first known, may have been his work. He later designed Venice's Teatro Novissimo (1641–5), then moved to Paris, where he rebuilt the backstage area of Molière's Petit-Bourbon theatre to allow spectacular effects to be achieved. His influence was felt throughout Europe.

VAKHTANGOV, Yevgeny (1883–1922). Russian director and actor, and a disciple of Stanislavsky. He became head of the Moscow Art Theatre's acting studio in 1914, which later embraced other groups to become the Third Workshop (1920). His work became non-realistic and Expressionist, but not at the expense of the actors (unlike Meyerhold at the same period). His early death was a tragedy for the Russian theatre, for his productions were showing a happy blend of Stanislavsky and Meyerhold. He died during the final rehearsal of one of his most famous, Gozzi's *Princess Turandot*.

VILAR, Jean (see **THÉÂTRE NATIONAL POPULAIRE**, Chapter 5).

VISCONTI, Luchino (b. 1906). Italian director and designer of plays, films and opera (it was he who discovered the fact that Callas was potentially a great actress, and helped her achieve greatness). His range of plays produced has been vast, many being given by the Paolo Stoppa-Rina Morelli company from the mid-1940s onwards, including *Death of a Salesman* (1951) and *A View from the Bridge* (1958). His most famous drama production abroad has been *'Tis Pity She's a Whore* in Paris (1961), with Alain Delon and Romy Schneider. A rare lapse has been Pinter's *Old Times* in Rome (1973), or rather, not Pinter's. His work reflects his Marxism and his aristocratic background, a potent mixture, while his Covent Garden *Don Carlos* (1958) in its first season was possibly the finest production of a 19th-century Italian opera ever seen in Britain.

WANAMAKER, Sam (b. 1919). American actor, director and producer currently engaged in re-

claiming Bankside for Shakespeare. A temporary Globe arose in 1972 and the omens are favourable. His varied career has included directing and playing Bernie in *Winter Journey* in London (1952), directing *The Threepenny Opera* in London (1956) and Tippett's *King Priam* at Covent Garden (1962), also playing Macbeth in Chicago (1964). He has also directed films, and the first opera, *War and Peace*, in Sydney's new opera house (1973). But it is his Globe project which will, if all goes well, make him the most valuable export to Britain, artistically speaking, ever to come from America.

WEBSTER, Margaret (1905–1972). Anglo-American director and actress, whose classical productions

Sam Wanamaker is hoping to reclaim Bankside for Shakespeare, and give a new Globe Theatre to Shakespeare's heirs. (Photo: Tom Blau)

Franco Zeffirelli, a true Renaissance Man who has been giving audiences superb productions of plays and operas since the 1950s, often designing his own sets. He has been a major figure in films for almost as long. (Photo: Camera Press)

included Robeson's *Othello* (1943). A founder of the American Repertory Theater with Eva Le Gallienne (see above).

ZEFFIRELLI, Franco (b. 1924). Italian director and designer of plays, films and opera who, after working with Visconti as a designer, became internationally known as an opera director. His searingly realistic *Romeo and Juliet* (John Stride and Judi Dench) at the Old Vic in 1959 followed closely on his *Lucia* (with a transformed Joan Sutherland) and *Cavalleria Rusticana* and *I Pagliacci* at Covent Garden. At the time of writing (1973) he has delighted London audiences yet again with his production for the National of di Filippo's *Saturday, Sunday, Monday*. His Shakespeare films, *Romeo and Juliet* and *The Taming of the Shrew*, *The Lady of the Camelias* in New York, *Hamlet* in Rome, and operas in Dallas, Vienna, Milan, London, New

York, etc. (given adequate rehearsal he can make the most recalcitrant singer act), make him a modern Renaissance man.

ZIEGFELD, Florenz (1867–1932). American impresario who set about 'Glorifying the American Girl' with remarkable success in Follies that ran from 1907 through no less than twenty-four editions. He rightly claimed them as 'An American Institution'. He also staged straight plays and musicals, including *Show Boat* (1927), helped talents like W. C. Fields and Eddie Cantor, and possessed superb flair and legendary judgement. The creative personalities and list of players who worked with him is huge, while his Girls included Marion Davies, Irene Dunne and Paulette Goddard. Renowned for lavishness in and out of the theatre, he was an American Institution himself.

America's greatest actor, Edwin Booth, assists at a benefit performance for his sister-in-law. Benefits could mean the difference between penury and affluence a century ago. (Central Office of Information)

CHAPTER 7

THEATRE TERMS

ABSURD, THEATRE OF THE. A convenient grouping of a number of playwrights. The absurdity and purposelessness of Man's existence has been explored for centuries, but only in the 1950s – following Camus's *The Myth of Sisyphus*, 1942 – did a number of dramatists produce a body of work which could be usefully grouped into a school of the Absurd. These include Ionesco, Beckett, Genet, Pinter, N. F. Simpson, Frisch, Albee, etc., though not necessarily in all their plays. Methods have varied, which means that the term is useful rather than completely accurate, but basically the style is anti-realistic. Absurd objects and images are often used because of a distrust of language and, as John Russell Taylor has put it, 'The ideas are allowed to shape the form as well as the content.' The movement has gradually faded possibly because of the difficulty of keeping Absurd plays going any length of time. Beckett's *Waiting for Godot* is the supreme example of the genre, but his

157

later plays have become more and more concise. But the influence of the Absurd has been very widespread. It has even spread to Shakespearean production via Peter Brook's Beckettian *King Lear* (1962) inspired by Jan Kott's *Shakespeare Our Contemporary*.

ACTING AREA. The space on stage enclosed by scenery (if any) where play is performed. It contains nine acting areas: centre stage; down-stage centre; down-stage right and left; right; left; and up-stage centre, right and left.

ACTOR MANAGER. The best summing-up of the old-time Actor Manager was Ronald Jeans: 'One to whom the part is greater than the whole.' They faded gloriously with Donald Wolfit in the 1940s and 1950s and, except at their most abysmal, were no bigger a menace than brilliant directors gone berserk. From the 1930s a new style of actor manager appeared in Britain: Gielgud at the Queen's (1937–8), Olivier at the St. James's in the 1950s, also John Clements at the Saville in the 1950s, etc.

ALIENATION. See **BRECHT**, page 63 .

AGENTS try to place plays and players for a percentage. It is harder to place the latter unless they are already known, and an agent without contacts and advanced knowledge of events is of little use. Consequently, a good agent is worth every penny of his ten per cent, a bad one is a disaster. Yet such is the complexity of show business today that few actors can manage without one.

AMATEURS are vital to the well-being of the theatre. Companies range from talented and dedicated ensembles to ego-boosting groups with no interest in the theatre outside their own little world. A few companies are famous, notably (in Britain) Unity, the Questors, Ealing, the O.U.D.S. (Oxford University Dramatic Society), etc., but what ultimately matters is that many thousands of other companies exist in all parts of the world.

ANGEL. A play's backer who, if it is a hit, will make steady money; if a flop, will lose his outlay. The gamble is biggest with musicals, which cost many thousands to stage and – nowadays – flop with remarkable regularity, partly because they need a long run to begin to recover their costs. Also a verb – to angel, i.e. to back a play or actor.

APRON. That part of the stage which extends from the (imaginary) setting line behind which scenery is set beyond the proscenium (if any) towards the audience. An extension of this is the open or thrust stage pushing out into the audience, the most famous example being the Elizabethan platform stage thrusting into the courtyard where the groundlings stood. A modern example is the arena stage with the audience on three sides, the first famous post-war one being at Stratford, Ontario (1953).

ARISTOTELIAN PLAY. Aristotle (384–322 B.C.), the Greek philosopher analysed tragedy in his *Poetics* (also comedy in a book that has been lost). For him tragedy must imitate action, not an actual but a possible one, poetic licence colouring the dramatist's work. The action has to be complete, with a coherent beginning, middle, and end and be of enough magnitude to stir audiences to pity and fear, and therefore be purged of their emotions, 'catharsis'. He stressed the importance of the action through which characters are revealed. His ideal hero was a famous man whose lack of judgement brings him down: he need not have flaws of character nor be particularly noble. Aristotle's ideal dramatist was Sophocles, whose *Oedipus Rex* obeys his dictums; he did not demand the three Unities – of time, place and action – as was claimed by Renaissance writers; he only insisted on Unity of Action, though he mentioned in passing the advisability of the tragedy taking place over some 24 hours. Though many moderns have challenged Aristotle, notably Brecht, much great drama, including many Elizabethan tragedies and Ibsen's *Ghosts* can be seen as direct descendants of his ideas turned into theatre.

ASSISTANT STAGE MANAGER (A.S.M.). See **STAGE MANAGER.**

AUDIENCE. As important to the theatre as the playwright and the actor, its influence can be everything from disastrous to crucial. Debased Roman tastes helped destroy the Roman theatre; the Elizabethan audience, characterised by the ignorant as little better than a chattering mob eating nuts and apples, seems, whatever its Puritanical enemies and disappointed playwrights claimed, to have been as appreciative and inspiring (to an author and his cast) as it was lively. Even the less bright groundlings would 'clap their brawny hands T'applaud what their charmed soul scarce understands' (Dekker). What written evidence there is suggests an audience which was the perfect sounding board for great drama. And all classes went to the theatre, a very rare happening in history. The nearest modern equivalent – a whole people enraptured by a form of theatre – occurred in Italy in the 19th century, the form being opera. The reverse occurred in the 1840s–'50s in Britain where Macready, a great or near great actor, was exposed to audiences who were as bad as the current state of the drama in his time, i.e. fourth-rate. A breakdown of today's audience trends would take thousands of words. Suffice to say that in western Europe and America it is the middle classes who make up the vast bulk of theatre audiences, while the longed-for worker element stays away.

AUDITION. A form of torture endured by applicants for parts, sometimes in the form of a reading, sometimes by reciting a speech, often in a theatre peopled only by a few of the Management sitting unseen in the darkened auditorium. As some of the best actors are not good sight-readers, or are very nervous at such contests, the system is fraught with hazards and flaws. Happy the star or well-known player who is spared such anguish. 'We'll let you know!' is the classic last line from the darkness out front.

AUDITORIUM. Where the audience sits, often called 'out front' by actors.

AUNT EDNA. Terence Rattigan's typical theatre-goer, now more than 2,000 years old, the eternal average audience, without whose patronage no author, dead or alive, subsidised up to the hilt or commercial, will succeed in the long run. She is not Puritanical and will never reject the first-rate, according to Rattigan, but one cannot help feeling that she is sometimes a little late in spotting it.

BACK-STAGE STAFF vary in number depending on the size of the theatre, but basically consist of the Stage Carpenter, Electricians, Property Men, Flymen, Stagehands, Dressers, Firemen and the Stage Door Keeper.

BARNSTORMERS. A 19th-century word to describe touring actors who played in barns and

stormed (ranted and raved) to country folk. Also see **HAM**.

BENEFIT. Though this now usually refers to a performance for a charity or an organisation, it used to refer to a performance from which all the proceeds went to one or, possibly, two members of a cast. In Britain it lasted from the 18th to the mid-19th century, and could mean the difference between penury and affluence to an actor, who was allowed to act in the play of his choice, and would sometimes present one of his own. However, it could lead to abuses and humiliation. It was still a custom outside London in the early 19th century, a famous fictional example being in *Nicholas Nickleby*.

BLACK COMEDY. Much comedy is based on disaster and suffering from the basic gag of man slipping on banana skin, but Black Comedy, particularly in the plays of Joe Orton, goes even further, shocking the audience with violent language and incident, using murder, madness, death and perversion to create laughter. This is done either by using farce techniques, or by 'refined' language and sentiments and deadpan jokes. It is impossible to convert people to even the best Black Comedy: either it is enjoyed or it is not.

BOOM. A tubular bar on which spotlights or floods can be suspended one above another. It is placed at the side of a scene.

BOX SET(TING). A scene in which flats represent three walls of a room, as opposed to an open scene.

BRECHTIAN. See **BRECHT**, page 63 .

BROADWAY. A New York street on or near which most of the city's leading commercial theatres are situated. The word's British equivalents are West End or Shaftesbury Avenue. Also see **OFF-BROADWAY**.

BURLESQUE. A parody or travesty of a play, or caricature of a famous person. A take-off of someone or something, as part of a revue. In America it can also mean an entertainment which is part leg show, part low comedy.

BUSKIN. The thick-soled boot worn by Greek actors in tragedy to give them extra height. It can also refer to acting in, or writing, tragedy.

CATHARSIS. The emotional relief gained after watching tragedy. See **ARISTOTELIAN PLAY**.

CENSORSHIP of plays ended in Britain in 1968 (the law of the land apart), having reigned via the Lord Chamberlain's Office since the 18th century. Few playwrights, even the seemingly most innocuous, escaped his dead hand. Nevertheless it survives in many countries.

CHRONICLE PLAY. A historical play, usually one which features a famous figure: Shaw's *St. Joan*, Drinkwater's *Abraham Lincoln*, etc.

CHILDREN'S THEATRE. Not until the 20th century were plays written in any great number for children, and even now there are few really popular ones. Far and away the most successful in Anglo-American countries has been *Peter Pan* (1904) by James Barrie, but most nations have tried to find suitable and worthwhile plays, and there are a number of companies specialising in them. Caryl Jenner was the leading pioneer in Britain, while Russia leads the world with over 30 theatres specially for children, including a famous one in Moscow developed by Natalia Satz. Today more and more children are being encouraged to sample suitable adult theatre.

CLAQUE. Hired applauders, known as claquers. Opera houses are their usual stamping ground where they are often highly organised. They have their standards. At the notorious Teatro Regio, Parma, the claque once gave a tenor back his money and proceeded to boo all his later performances.

CLARENCE DERWENT. An award named after an Anglo-American actor and producer, which is given annually to the best supporting actor and actress in New York and London.

CLUB THEATRES were particularly important in Britain when there was theatre censorship. Between and after the Wars, banned plays were safely given at the Arts, Everyman, Mercury and Gate, and by the English Stage Company at the Royal Court theatre. Also see **FRINGE**.

COMEDY OF MANNERS. A comedy, usually witty and often satirical, which portrays the customs,

manners and outlook of a society. English Restoration drama saw the genre at its finest.

COMMEDIA DELL'ARTE. Italian improvised comedies given by special troupes of actors, which were at their most popular in the 16th and 17th centuries. The basic plots were pre-arranged and the stock characters included such favourites as Pierrot, Columbine, Pantaloon and the quick-witted Arlecchino, who was later to reappear in Britain as Harlequin. Pulcinella gradually became Punch. Later in the 17th century and into the 18th writers like Molière and Marivaux – and in different ways, Goldini and Gozzi – were all influenced by the old traditions which linger on today, especially in French mime, most notably Marcel Marceau's.

COMPLIMENTARY. A free ticket for a show. Local shopkeepers expect complimentaries for displaying bills, and members of a cast can sometimes or always (if they are stars) provide 'comps'. Also see **OAKLEY**.

CONSOLE. A mobile remote control unit, looking like an organ console, used for stage lighting. The most modern have a memory device attached that can store instructions; this enables the operator to make difficult changes at high speed.

CORPSE. This used to mean to kill another actor's speech or business or laugh by cutting in too soon, or to forget one's lines. Now it normally mean to get the giggles on stage, either by seeing or hearing something which should not happen, or because some fellow actor has deliberately done or said something reprehensible, but funny, i.e. he has 'corpsed' one. Trying not to let the audience know that one has been corpsed can be a nightmare, whether it has happened accidentally or deliberately.

CRITICS endure rude comparisons with eunuchs, basically that 'they know how it is done but can't do it themselves' – not strictly true because a number have written successful plays, including a supreme critic, Bernard Shaw. The critic must love the theatre, add knowledge (not necessarily technical) to that love, he must write well and he must have a sense of history. He is expected by some actors to give constructive criticism, though one

Mary Martin, star of musicals on both sides of the Atlantic. Her greatest rôle has been English Nellie Forbush in South Pacific *in which she was 'as corny as Kansas in August' and washed 'that man right out of her hair' on the stage. (Photo: Karsh of Ottawa)*

famous actress once said: 'I don't want criticism. Fulsome flattery is good enough for me.'

The wit of some critics can be savage, however entertaining, and is unforgiveable unless based firmly on truth. Was Dorothy Parker really right when she claimed: 'Katherine Hepburn ran the whole gamut of emotion from A to B?' And was Percy Hammond being quite fair when he memorably wrote: 'Of the acting of Miss Bergere's company one may not speak candidly unless one is in a trench.' George Jean Nathan, who once summed up Barrie's work as 'the triumph of sugar over diabetes', was probably the most brilliant American critic of the century, but his waspish wit savaged many harmless plays while he was championing the new major dramatists admirably. It is the less savage, but very influential and admirable Brooks Atkinson who had had a theatre named for him. The greatest British critic of the last half century, James Agate, was far sounder on acting than on new plays. His most notable successor has been Kenneth Tynan, a better judge of plays, a splendid judge of acting, but the possessor of a scimitar wit which has been known to promote effect to the top of the league of writing virtues.

The critic is the actor's best hope of immortality. Happy the country which allows its critics to think before committing their thoughts on a play to paper. Yet those who advocate their being given a play in advance to read forget the primary purpose of surprise and stimulation *in the theatre*. The influence of critics varies from place to place. Very few in Britain have been able to sway public opinion in modern times to the extent of swaying in favour of new, but unusual, talent. Tynan's famous review of *Look Back in Anger*, a superbly understanding tribute, did not cause a box-office stampede, nor did Harold Hobson's early championing of Pinter. A rare example of a critic creating a hit on the strength of a single review was Agate's notice of Wolfit's Lear in 1944, which sold out not only *Lear* but a whole season which had previously been doing poor business.

Few countries suffer a worse critical situation than America. In New York, the public pays too much attention to critics, not so serious a matter when there were 'Seven Butchers of Broadway', but now, with fewer papers, and costs spiralling so fast that a show is an instant success or an instant total flop, the public decides what it will see by reading the *New York Times*. This puts the British-born critic, Clive Barnes, in a position of power which a Roman Emperor might envy. Those who resent his (i.e. *The Times*'s) power can console themselves with the fact that he loves the theatre. His successor may not.

One gibe against the critics by actors is unfair: that actors automatically know the truth about performances because they are actors. They know far more about technique but, like everyone else, are influenced by personality, and disagree amongst themselves as much as critics. Meanwhile these pariahs of the profession, abused, occasionally banned, rarely liked, even more rarely loved, perform a useful, sometimes vital task. P. G. Wodehouse must have the last word on them, for he speaks for all show business, and who can blame it? 'Has anyone seen a dramatic critic in the daytime? Of course not. They come out after dark, up to no good.'

CRUELTY, THEATRE OF. The French director and dramatist, Antonin Artaud (1986–1948), believed that an audience's violent, sexual and disorderly instincts – its repressions – could be banished by a style of theatre where words were merely emotional, incantatory and part of a total theatre of music, mime, ritual, dance, frenzy and cruelty. A superb example of his theories put into practice was Peter Brook's production of Weiss's *Marat-Sade* (1964), but it must be said that just as savage tribes are not purged of their latent cruelty by dancing, there is no proof that 'civilised' audiences will be purged of their cruelty, repressions, etc., by the Theatre of Cruelty. It makes for exciting viewing and listening however.

CURTAINS in the modern theatre came in with the proscenium arch in the 17th century, the late Roman theatre having used ones that were lifted up. The famous Curtain Theatre in Elizabethan London was not the forerunner: it was named for the land on which it stood. At first the curtain was raised after the prologue, then lowered at the end of a play. Around 1750 it was dropped between acts and soon replaced by a painted cloth, the Act-drop. In the 1880 revival of *The Corsican Brothers*, Irving brought back the curtain and also had it dropped for scene changes. At the time of writing (1973) it would seem that the curtain's days are numbered, in the straight theatre at least, though its innumerable fans will find that it survives, in the commercial theatre at any rate, for years. Yet they will probably admit how easy it is to get used to a view of the stage as they enter an auditorium, and scene changes in full view of the audience.

DARK. The word used to describe a theatre which is closed before the opening of a play. It comes from the absence of illuminations and signs on the building.

DEPUTY STAGE MANAGER (D.S.M.). See **STAGE MANAGER**.

DEUS EX MACHINA. The god from a machine who comes down to sort things out at a play's end. The Greeks lowered him on a crane, which made it look as if he was flying. In the theatres and opera houses of the 17th century and later it was applied to the chariots that came down, and it is sometimes used today about a late arrival who sets things right.

DIRECTOR. He is responsible for staging and rehearsing plays and, sometimes, altering them in rehearsals with or without the dramatist's blessing. Until recently he was called the Producer in Britain, but not in America. He is now the most powerful figure in the theatre, having only existed in Britain for some 70 or 80 years: before that direction was usually in the hands of a stage manager, star or author. The first British director may have been Lewis Winfield, Lily Langtry's director for *As You Like It* (1890). One of the first European directors was the Duke of Saxe-Meiningen, who formed his ensemble company in 1874. In the 1890s

Adolph Appia and Gordon Craig were publicising the need for a director's theatre, and early major directors were Stanislavsky, Harley Granville Barker, Reinhardt and André Antoine. Perhaps the most influential American director has been Elia Kazan; the most influential modern British, Tyrone Guthrie, Peter Brook and Peter Hall. These and other Europeans and Americans are discussed more fully in Chapter 6.

The finest directors are the inspired servants of the playwright; the worst – often the same man can be in both categories – are insensitive and totally arrogant. Not all directors understand actors, although those who have been and are actors normally do. This does not necessarily matter in performance terms. Today's ensemble theatre has the director as king. He often deserves to be.

DOCK. A space adjoining the stage, or part of the stage, where scenery is stored.

DRAG. The word was first used in the 1800s in its present sense of a man playing a woman's part, or dressed as a woman. It refers to the man dragging his skirt across a stage.

DRAMA SCHOOLS cannot teach anyone to act, though they can improve basic equipment: voice, movement, relaxation. In many countries such schools can be started by anyone, and frequently are. It is safest to go to a really reputable school – RADA, the Central, LAMDA and a few others – and best to avoid infant drama schools, so beloved by stage-struck-at-second-hand mamas. Ballet schools are a different matter: dance training *has* to be started young.

DRAMATURG. A German word best translated into English as Literary Editor (as Kenneth Tynan, first Literary Editor of the National Theatre). The *dramaturg* has to advise about suitable plays, read new ones, sometimes work with authors on alterations, write programme notes and be prepared to act as an extra Public Relations man.

EPIC THEATRE. See **BRECHT**, page 63

ENSEMBLE. Originally the picture or general effect of the cast in the setting; also the cast acknowledging their applause; also (in America) the singers and dancers of the chorus. Today it is a consummation devoutly to be wished in permanent companies, and signifies teamwork. It is the justification of the Director's Theatre as opposed to the star system, though directors who forget that certain parts demand stars (albeit ones who can fit into an ensemble) can spoil a play as much as lack of ensemble.

EXPRESSIONISM. A reaction against realism stemming, it can be argued, from the later plays of Strindberg. Realism portrays the psychology of the individual and represents actual life, while Expressionism, which flourished mainly in the Germany of the 1920s, explores the typical. Leading Expressionists were Toller, Kaiser, Capek and Elmer Rice, while O'Neill (*The Hairy Ape, The Great God Brown*) and O'Casey (*The Silver Tassie*) sometimes experimented with it. The Expressionists were concerned with man versus machine and the class struggle, and their characters tend to be types, their designs stylised and their scenes short. Their techniques have proved more lasting than their aims.

FACT, THEATRE OF. Normally fiction based mainly on fact, the writers feeling themselves more 'significant' than mere purveyors of historical dramas, despite their inevitable selective bias. See **HOCHHUTH**, page 75

FALSE PROSCENIUM. Two wings and a framed border set up-stage of the true proscenium, the 'false' one being semi-permanent.

FARCE. Though originally farces were broad, often knockabout, comedy – from Greek times to the mid-19th century – and often interludes in dramas, for British and French audiences at least, it is an austerely classical form at best: Feydeau, Ben Travers. Americans often label plays farces which the British would call farcical comedies, i.e. the delightful *You Can't Take It With You* by Moss Hart and George Kaufman. Two definitions of this hard-to-define genre are 'possible people in impossible situations' and 'tragedy turned upside down'. A freer attitude to sex and marriage has weakened the famous form – bedroom farce.

FIT-UP. A temporary proscenium, not necessarily used over a stage, 'fitted up' in a hall or outside. Carried round by a company, it forms the basis of a portable theatre. Hence 'fit-up tours', 'fit-up' and 'one-night stands'.

STRODE'S COLLEGE

FLAT. The basic piece of theatrical scenery, painted canvas on a wooden frame.

FLIES. The area above the stage, which includes one or two galleries from which scenery can be lowered or raised. Americans call the area the 'wings'.

FLOATS. Footlights. Originally wicks that floated in a trough of tallow. 'Foots' in America.

FLOODS. Lanterns with no focusing adjustments. They can give a wide-angle light beam for lighting backcloths.

FRINGE. Originally this referred to the unofficial companies playing at the Edinburgh Theatre, now it more often refers to London's small companies, who are sometimes referred to as the other Theatre and the Underground. Performances take place in London basements and pubs at lunchtime and in the evening (the thriving theatre restaurant at the King's Head, Islington, performs at both times), while the Roundhouse and Charles Marowitz's Open Space are 'grander' institutions; the latter, founded by Marowitz in 1968, is London's leading experimental theatre, its repertoire being reinforced from time to time by its founder's Shakespearean 'collages', the best of which has been *An Othello* (1972). The Fringe is already significant and may become more so. One of the earliest companies to make its mark was the playwright, David Halliwell's Quipu, now operating at the Little Theatre Club. The Fringe has attracted actors as well-known as David Warner and Kenneth Haigh, and the outlook is bright.

GHOST WALKS ON FRIDAY, THE. Treasury day in the theatre is on Friday and for more than a century 'the Ghost walks' that night. 'Has the Ghost walked yet?' can be a plaintive query. Allegedly an actor was playing the ghost of Hamlet's father and, when the Hamlet said: 'I will watch tonight. Perchance t'will walk again,' the off-stage Ghost shouted back at him: 'I'll be damned if he will unless our salaries are paid!'

GREEN ROOM. A club or waiting room, for actors in some theatres. As a term it dates back to the 17th century and is thought to derive from the presumed fact that one of them was decorated in green.

GROUND CLOTH or **STAGE CLOTH.** A canvas sheet covering the entire acting area. The setting is built up on it and it may be painted with 'paving stones', boards', 'carpets', etc.

GROUND ROW. A low piece of scenery which represents a hedge, a grassy bank, a wall, etc., and enhances the effect of distance in relation to the backcloth. It can also refer to a row of lights to illuminate a backcloth.

HAM. A derogatory term for an actor who is bad because he overdoes things, or because his technique is crude. It was much used between the wars, even about good actors who dared to *act* at a time when restraint was in vogue. Its origin is obscure, but the most probable explanation is American. It may be short for 'ham-fatter', a raw country actor who made up with ham fat as a base, or removed his make-up with ham fat. It may also be linked with acting in hamlets.

HARLEQUINADE. A feature of British pantomimes until the 20th century, starring Harlequin, Columbine and Pantaloon in a madcap mixture of magic, mime and music. Just occasionally one is given today, by a traditionalist like Cyril Fletcher.

HEROIC TRAGEDY. A large-scale, grand form in heroic couplets, and concerned with Love and Honour, which flourished in England in the second half of the 17th century. Inspired especially by Corneille, its best practitioner was Dryden whose heroic tragedies, though extinct, are at least of literary value.

I KNEW IT IN THE BATH. A (probably accurate) statement after 'drying' at rehearsal, to 'dry' being to forget one's words.

IMPRESARIO. A presenter of spectacles, shows, opera, ballet, concerts, etc., really a glorified producer. By thinking and living big the latter can hope to become one.

INTERLUDE. The short, often broad entertainment which linked medieval church dramas with Elizabethan comedy, the link being John Heywood (see page 113). In Italy the interlude was known as the intermezzo; in Spain, the entremes; in France, the entremets. Later, interludes developed into masques.

INTIMATE REVUE. See **REVUE.**

LEGITIMATE or **LEGIT.** The straight drama, rather than musicals, music hall, vaudeville, burlesque, etc. The term is not arrogant for it dates back to the 18th century in London, when the officially licensed theatres, Drury Lane and Covent Garden (which presented dramas), were fighting the rivalry of unlicensed theatres which could slip in dramatic pieces along with singing, dancing and spectacle. Later, there was an element of snobbery in the term; now it is another word for 'straight'.

LIGHTING became important with the coming of indoor theatres, c. 1600, but even then it was a matter of lighting the stage and whole auditorium with chandeliers and lamps, rather than illuminating the stage alone. Footlights (shielded candles) were being widely used later in the century, while chandeliers over the stage were a menace to playgoers seated high up in some theatres because the naked candles produced enough glare to be trying, and also the line of sight was impeded. By the mid-18th century lighting had improved, but was still basically a matter of chandeliers, with footlights and lights on wing ladders. David Garrick and other 18th-century reformers added refinements like controlled and directed side-lighting and concealed footlights, and many spectacular effects were achieved. However the great turning point was the introduction of gas-lighting in the early 1800s. The first British theatre to be lit entirely by gas was Drury Lane in 1817. Gradually, it was learnt how to make the maximum use of it by control.

Darkening the auditorium became general after Irving and others practised it in the early 1880s – it had been advocated in the 1590s – and at the same time electricity was introduced to the theatre. It had first been tried out for certain effects at the Paris Opéra in the 1840s. The first London theatre completely lit by electricity was the Savoy in 1881, though some, like Irving, had become so skilled with gas that they took some time to make the change-over.

A modern development, though anticipated in the 19th century, has been the gradual discarding of footlights, and now they are often not used even in proscenium theatres. They are of course impractical on open stages, theatre-in-the-round, etc. This trend away from 'floats' became noticeable in the 1920s. Since the 1940s and, especially, in the 1960s, the job of lighting a show has been given more and more frequently to a lighting expert or 'consultant'; until then, it was the director's job (as it still is in the sense that he is in overall charge); earlier still, the stage manager's or, if he wished to do it, the actor manager's. Technical improvement have now revolutionised this branch of theatre art. Also see **CONSOLE** and **LIMELIGHT**.

LIGHTING PLOT. The recorded details of a play's lighting, and the cues for lighting changes.

LIMELIGHT. A brilliant white light developed in the early 1800s, much admired for moonlight and fairyland effects. The lime or calcium light was also used for following actors about and spot-lighting. It outlived the gas age and lives on as a phrase, 'in the limelight'.

MARIE TEMPEST. As a door can sometimes swing of its own accord because of the rake of the stage, a metal hinge with a screw lever adjustment can be attached to the door and the reveal (a board attached at a right angle indicating a window's or a door's thickness), and this allows an opened door to stay in one position. It is named after the actress Dame Marie Tempest (1864–1962) who demanded that the hinges should be used in one of her plays.

MATINÉE IDOL. An inter-war term to describe a limited number of handsome 'romantic' actors whose presence in a play in the West End ensured full houses at matinées, houses of devoted female admirers. Famous examples were Owen Nares, Ivor Novello (the word could apply to musical comedy as much as straight plays) and Sir Gerald du Maurier; Laurence Olivier was something of a matinée idol in the early 1930s. The matinée idol, handsome in appearance and dress, might or might not be a good actor. Nares, without the rugged virility of some of the breed, tended to be underrated as a performer despite a very fine technique. The movies also had matinée idols in profusion at the time, but now they too are an extinct breed, along with most of the plays and films in which they appeared.

MELODRAMA originated in mid-18th century France and Germany; in the former with a character miming and music expressing his emotion and, later, speaking to music; in the latter, as a spoken

Ivor Novello, the ultimate matinée idol of the British Theatre. He became steadily more handsome, especially in profile, while unlike some matinée idols, he had real talent. (Photo: Author's Collection)

passage in opera with a musical accompaniment. By the turn of the century melodrama had become the simple, direct and popular entertainment it was to remain for a century: strong drama comedy and sentiment, plus music, spectacular scenery and lighting to increase the effect. Gradually music was dropped or relegated to a minor place, but the drama remained the same. Its headquarters at first was the 'Boulevard du Crime' with its second-class theatres in Paris (1797–1835), and it soon crossed the Channel, where famous early examples were *Maria Marten, or the Murder in the Red Barn* (based on an actual case) and *Sweeney Todd, or the Demon Barber of Fleet Street*.

The influence of melodrama spread into more serious works of the Romantic era, notably the melodramatic plays of Hugo and Dumas Père. It helped the French Romantics to an appreciation of Shakespeare and other allegedly barbaric play-

wrights. Gradually, some melodramas became more subtle, and it was in one, *The Bells* (1871), from the French, that Henry Irving became famous. The genre reached its height in Britain with *The Silver King* (1882) by Henry Arthur Jones, at a time when the word was becoming suspect. Melodrama can still hold the stage today, though the temptation of both artists and cast to guy the plays is sometimes irresistible. Melodramas in the original sense occur in the operas *Fidelio* and *Der Freischutz*.

METHOD. A 'method' of acting, and also directing, developed and taught at the Actors' Studio in New York by Lee Strasberg and others (since 1948). It is an adaptation of Stanislavsky's ideas, being based on the building of character as outlined in his *An Actor Prepares*, not on his teaching about the all-important performance. Though this very influential system has been endorsed by some very famous players (who would have succeeded anyhow), it suffers – for many – a fatal flaw, a lack of interest in technique, diction, etc., which would have amazed Stanislavsky. The losing of the actor in his part to discover the truth about a character may indeed find the truth – for an audience of one, himself. Every actor has his own method, some starting with an external – a trick of walking or voice. However, the Method has had notable successes in some naturalistic plays and films. Far more influential however is its insistence on improvisation and exercises to explore character. This, too, stems from Stanislavsky.

MIME. Though it now means acting without speech, in ancient times mime usually meant a short, broad, improvised and often indecent comedy or farce, though there were also more literary mimes, meant to be read rather than staged. Women could take part, and by Imperial times anything went on stage, including copulation and the execution of criminals. Modern mime stems from the *commedia dell'arte* plays (see above), but did not become purely silent until the last century. It is called pantomime in many countries, but not in Britain and some parts of the Commonwealth, where the word refers to the Christmas entertainment (see below). Famous mime artists have included Deburau (1796–1846), immortalised by another famous mime, Jean Louis Barrault, in the film, *Les Enfants du Paradise*, and Marcel Marceau.

MUSICAL. Now, thanks to America, a blanket term which serves to describe musical comedies, operettas (outside the opera house), folk operas, etc. Musical comedy has always been a particularly unsatisfactory term, for the difference between it and operetta can be impossible to define. The incomparable *The Merry Widow* (1905) by Lehar is an operetta but became musical comedy in London because more lightly sung and played broader by the comics, and is again operetta via Sadler's Wells. *My Fair Lady* (1956) could be termed either; whereas to label the serious, masterly, *West Side Story* (1957) a musical comedy or operetta would be an abuse of language. This classic integration of song, dance and speech, master-minded by the choreographer Jerome Robbins and aided by many others, including Leonard Bernstein (music), is a . . . musical.

The musical's roots are many, but are basically to be found in the operettas and light operas of the late 19th century to which was later added native American genius for the form in every department. This book is not primarily concerned with it, but its assets and limitations should be pointed out. Musicals cannot get over ideas and thoughts as well as the best plays but, especially if composer, lyricist and choreographer are masters, they can give the Theatre of Entertainment an emotional and most vivid experience, or maximum enjoyment, or both. With a few exceptions – Coward's *Bitter Sweet*, Bart's *Oliver* – the finest exponents have been Americans or naturalised Americans, though many of the stars have been from Britain or elsewhere, including Gertrude Lawrence, Julie Andrews, Jack Buchanan, Jessie Matthews, the actor-composer Ivor Novello, and the Master, Noël Coward.

American masters have included two of the old European traditional school, whose tunefulness covers a mass of improbabilities: Rudolf Friml (1881 –1972) of *Rose Marie* and *Vagabond King* fame, and Sigmund Romberg (1887–1951): *The Desert Song*, *The Student Prince*, etc. Jerome Kern's *Show Boat* (1927), with Book and Lyrics by Oscar Hammerstein II, advanced the form, not so much because of its incomparable score, but because the story was quite serious and it fused music with drama, and presented believable characters on stage. George Gershwin, with his brother Ira, wrote a series of Broadway hits: a near operatic masterpiece, *Porgy and Bess* (1935), and a political

musical, *Of Thee I Sing* (1931), which helped the form grow up. The famous partnership of Rodgers and Hart produced brilliant shows: *On Your Toes* (1926), *The Boys from Syracuse* (1938) and, their masterpiece, *Pal Joey* (1940), the composer later noting that the show – the mood is cynical, the atmosphere sleazy – 'wore long pants'. Later Rodgers, whose incomparably skilful and witty lyricist died in 1943, teamed up with Hammerstein to become the most popular double since Gilbert and Sullivan. Their *Oklahoma* (1943) was a milestone that blended music, a strong story and dancing (choreographer, Agnes de Mille) into a marvellous whole. Their successes continued with *Carousel*, *South Pacific* (their best work), *The King and I* and other shows, finishing with their biggest moneymaker, *The Sound of Music*.

Even the shortest account cannot leave out two other shows: Irving Berlin's finest achievement, *Annie Get Your Gun* (1946) and Cole Porter's *Kiss Me, Kate* (1948), perhaps the most witty and stylish of all American musicals. Frederick Loewe and Alan Jay Lerner immortalised themselves with *My Fair Lady* (1956), aided by Moss Hart's staging, Cecil Beaton's designs, and Rex Harrison, Julie Andrews and Stanley Holloway, etc. – and Bernard Shaw, who could hardly have objected at the brilliant use of his *Pygmalion*. Since that classic and *West Side Story* the musical has proliferated, but not improved, partly because the major composers have either died or given up. Fortunately experiments abound. Quasi-religious shows have been found to have real worth – *Godspell*, *Jesus Christ Superstar*; rock-operas and rock-musicals vie with serious thoughts on marriage, as in *Company*, a splendid show, but a reminder that a musical cannot comment as deeply as a play. If the great years are over, the future is not discouraging.

The careers of the great American musical stars do not belong in this book, or European ones like Richard Tauber. However several names cannot be omitted – in alphabetical order for safety: George Abbott, writer and director; Fred Astaire, Ray Bolger; Jack Buchanan; Gower Champion, Carol Channing; Alfred Drake, also a noted straight actor; the English-born singer turned actor, and a Broadway star as both, Dennis King; Bert Lahr; Beatrice Lillie; Mary Martin; Jessie Matthews; the trumpet-toned Ethel Merman; Marilyn Miller; Sandy Wilson of *Boy Friend* fame; and Vincent

Youmans, whose *No, No Nanette* (1925) has been revived triumphantly in the 1970s. Also see **REVUE**.

NATURALISM. An extension of Realism, and one which tries to record the actualities of life, with form and the dramatist's ideas taking a lesser place. This places it on the borderline of art, and only master dramatists stay on the right side and great ones triumph. Examples are Strindberg's *Miss Julie* (1888), Gorky's *The Lower Depths* (1902) and, some claim, Stanislavsky's productions of Chekhov, though for many Chekhov in any form is too great to be contained by such a suspect label. However, it should be stressed that Naturalism was 'invented' to combat the artificiality of the theatre in the late 19th century. See **REALISM**.

OAKLEY, AN ANNIE. A complimentary ticket (in the U.S.), named for 'Little Sure Shot' Annie Oakley, an even better shot than the musical, *Annie Get Your Gun*, claimed. Her shooting at card targets gave rise to the term, because a 'comp' in America is often punched so that it can be checked when counting receipts.

OFF-BROADWAY. For years production and running costs have ensured that Broadway has either hits or flops (unlike the West End, where a short run is still a possibility). To counteract this, small theatre groups began appearing in halls, cellars, theatres, etc., in Greenwich Village and elsewhere from the 1940s onwards, the actors and technicians – the latter get far more than their London equivalents – being paid less than the Unions would allow on Broadway. The turning point in the fortunes of Off-Broadway, which had always been significant, was in 1950–1, the season at the Circle in the Square, directed by José Quintero, which included a hit, Tennessee Williams's *Summer and Smoke*, starring Geraldine Page. In the '60s, Genet's *The Balcony* and the première of *Long Day's Journey into Night* also took place there. Jason Robards, George C. Scott, Dustin Hoffman and Coleen Dewhurst are among other talents to emerge, along with most new American dramatists of worth; but even Off-Broadway is now being affected by the troubles of New York's theatres as a whole. It should be noted that some claim that the very first Off-Broadway season was given by the Provincetown Players in 1916, the company that first staged O'Neill and brought Strindberg's plays to America. Among many theatres Off-Broadway, the

Living Theater and the American Place Theater have very fine records. There is also an 'Off-Off-Broadway', highly experimental and of varying standards.

ONE-NIGHT STAND. See **FIT-UP**.

OPEN COLD. A play that opens in London without a pre-London tour.

OPEN STAGE. Strictly speaking this means an acting area free from obstructive settings, the extreme need being by ballet dancers, but much desired also by opera and plays with large crowds. Now, however, it tends to mean a stage without a proscenium arch, as at the Mermaid, or an apron stage, thrusting out into the audience, as at the original Globe.

PANTOMIME. Apart from its similar meaning to mime (see above), it refers to the splendidly irrational British Christmas entertainment which can embrace everything from a fairy tale complete with magic, to pop songs and a bicycle act. Beginning in the 18th century, it stemmed from the *commedia dell'arte* and harlequinade, both described above, and reached its present weird and wonderful form in the late 19th century. 'Musts' include audience participation, topical gags and, until recently, a principal boy played by a girl and the dame played by a man. A responsible pantomime remembers the children and has real humour and slapstick, and not just a string of blue jokes, also it has at least one transformation scene. The most popular story remains Cinderella, complete with the lovable Buttons and two principal boys, the second, Dandini, being borrowed from Rossini's *La Cenorentola*.

PAPER THE HOUSE. Filling empty seats with complimentary ticket holders, making it easier for the cast and, hopefully, spreading a good report of the play from the 'comp' holders and boosting bookings. Nurses are popular candidates for house-papering.

PIT. Now the orchestra pit or the back few rows of the stalls, but once the entire ground floor of the theatre between the stage and the lower boxes. Seats were cheap and playgoers sat on benches. They were often the most knowing – 'The Pit rose at me!' a great actor could say with pride. Stalls first appeared in the 1830s and '40s. Comfort increased and so did prices.

PRODUCER. A word complicated by the fact that, until recently, it was the British name for a play's

Audition time for the Drury Lane pantomime in 1858. Mrs. Worthingtons abound. (From the Author's Collection)

director. Now 'Director' is used on both sides of the Atlantic. But in Britain both 'Production' and 'produced by' can still be used to mean 'directed by', and those directors from the theatre who also work in opera suddenly return to being producers. An American producer is the manager of a company, arranging finance, putting on a show, arranging contracts, etc., but in Britain he has been known – until recently – as the Manager. Now he too is often called the Producer, but 'The Management' is still used. See also **IMPRESARIO**. The French term is régisseur; a word widely used on the Continent.

PROMPT CORNER. Where the stage manager sits, or his deputies, to prompt the cast, and where the cue board for running a show is placed. It is behind the proscenium arch if there is one. Most theatres' prompt sides are on the left of the stage facing the audience, so that side is sometimes referred to as 'prompt side' (PS) and the other as 'opposite prompt side' (OPS). As anyone who has ever stage-managed at the St. Martin's, or other theatres with a prompt side on the right, will agree, this is confusing. Fortunately, more usual is 'stage right' and 'stage left', L and R for short.

PROSCENIUM. Strictly speaking, the wall before the curtain which divides stage from autitorium. The **PROSCENIUM OPENING** is the proscenium arch through which the audience watches the play. It is called the **PORTAL** in the U.S.A. Though this 'picture-frame' effect is disliked in most advanced theatre thinking, so many of the old theatres have a 'pros arch' that the proscenium will last at least for several generations and in the opera house, for as long as opera lasts. See also Chapter 4.

RAKE. The slope of the stage down to the front,

which can be increased by scenery. The slopes are becoming so severe in some Wagnerian productions that muscular strains are becoming as challenging as vocal lines. A rake in the auditorium is vital as well.

REALISM. A less radical form that naturalism (see above). It was introduced in the late 19th century to combat over-acting and the over-mechanical aspects of the 'well-made play' (see below). Though artificiality was banished, construction remained important. The supreme master of the movement was Ibsen whose influence on others, including Shaw and Stanislavsky, was colossal. 'Theatrical truth' could be said to describe Realism but, like so many theatrical terms, it is useful rather than conclusive.

REPERTOIRE. The group of plays that a company is giving over a season or part of a season. It can also apply to an actor's rôles. The National Theatre, the Royal Shakespeare Co., the Comédie-Française, etc., perform in repertoire, as do opera and ballet companies, as opposed to the long and short runs of the commercial theatre. Now some Reps also perform in Repertoire.

REPERTORY. Strictly, as above, but British Rep, begun by Miss Horniman (in Dublin and Manchester before the First World War) and others set the Repertory Movement on a different course, i.e. runs of a week, a fortnight, three weeks or a month. It has become fashionable (among theatrical infants, or the merely ignorant) to sneer at old-time Rep, excepting of course the leading companies – notably Sir Barry Jackson's Birmingham Rep, on which he spent his fortune and from which came Olivier, Ralph Richardson, Evans, Ashcroft, Scofield, Leighton, Hardwicke, Finney, etc., etc.

In fact much good (and bad) work was done even in weekly Reps. For instance John Hale at Lincoln in the 1950s, when major and minor Reps were suffering from the advent of mass television and spiralling costs, was doing far better work than some of today's subsidised companies, few of whose members know the 'best of times and worst of times' that was weekly Rep for young actors. Rep was transformed in the 1960s by adequate Arts Council grants; weeklies could suddenly become fortnightlies or even aspire to 3-week runs and, at last, new theatres were built. Actors are actually paid living wages. Few Reps could afford to pay enough in the old days – except the generous

Derek Salberg of the Birmingham Alexandra, and John Counsell, now the doyen of the Rep movement after years of admirable work at the Theatre Royal, Windsor.

Even a short account of the Rep movement, which has kept theatre alive so admirably, and gave so many fine actors to the West End and the national companies, cannot omit certain names, apart from those already mentioned. With deepest apologies for deliberate omissions for space reasons, one can briefly note William Armstrong (Liverpool); Val May (Nottingham, Bristol Old Vic, etc.); Hazel Vincent Wallace (Leatherhead); John Neville (Nottingham); J. B. Fagan and Frank Hauser (Oxford); Ronald Russell and Peggy Ann Wood (Bristol Little); those kings of the twice-nightly Reps, Harry Hanson and Frank Fortescue; David Scase (Manchester Library Theatre); Stuart Burge (Nottingham); Warren Jenkins (Belgrade, Coventry) which was the first new British post-War theatre, 1958); Hugh Hunt, Denis Carey and Val May (Bristol Old Vic); A. R. Whatmore (Dundee); Donovan Maule (Nairobi), etc. Other outposts have included and include Barry O'Brien's seaside companies, also Wilson Barrett's Scottish companies, the Glasgow Citizens' – founded (1942) by Bridie – Edinburgh's Traverse (now Scotland's chief experimental theatre), York, Perth, Northampton, Folkestone, Derby (where once was John Osborne), Richmond, Ipswich, Colchester (Robert Digby), etc.

Rep even reaches London occasionally, including Douglas Seale's famous *Henry VI* from Birmingham (1953), and the (Manchester) 69 Theatre Company's *Journey's End* (1972), directed by Eric Thompson; the company's Artistic Director is Michael Elliott.

RESTING. The actor's euphemism for being out of work, and unhappy state that the majority are in most of the time in Britain – whose actors are the admiration of the world. **AT LIBERTY** is the American equivalent.

RESTORATION COMEDY refers to the comedies produced between the restoration of Charles II to his throne in 1660 and the death of George Farquhar (1707). In the history of English drama it is a period only excelled by the Elizabethans and Jacobeans and can be regarded as a whole. Its characters are 'wicked, witty creatures without morals or scruples – and they were a reflection of the people who paid to see them' (Stephen Joseph in *The Playhouse of England*). Inevitably, with brilliant writers to hand, the 'comedy of manners' flourished mightily; the greatest of them, Wycherley, Dryden, Farquhar and especially Congreve, are all featured in Chapter 2.

It must be admitted that a reaction against the genre was inevitable.

The first major blast was Jeremy Collier's *A Short View of the Immorality and Profaneness of the English Stage* (1698). Under William III and Anne, Court patronage declined. And managers decided to attract a wider cross-section of the public, which meant that lewdness gave way to sentiment. The result was artistic disaster but good financial returns. Not until Goldsmith and Sheridan appeared in the 1770s did major talent reappear, and then only for a few short years.

REVUE. A nearly extinct entertainment combining song, dance and satirical and comic sketches. It flourished especially from the 1920s to 1950s, the 40s and 50s seeing Intimate Revue, the same on a smaller scale, attracting huge numbers of devotees. A particular peak was *Sweet and Low* (1943) and its two successors, with Hermoine Gingold helping win both the war and peace with a personality and voice like a glamorous serpent. Ian Carmichael, Dora Bryan and Kenneth Williams are among the stars made from Intimate Revue, while supreme stars of the genre included Gertrude Lawrence, Beatrice Lillie, Jack Buchanan and Noel Coward; and major impresarios – legends like Ziegfeld and André Charlot. One-woman revues have been enormously successful: Ruth Draper and Joyce Grenfell; and one of the last, *Beyond the Fringe* (1960), made stars of Peter Cook, Alan Bennett, Dudley Moore and Jonathan Miller. The death of Revue is puzzling. Probably a form, which attracted talents ranging from Alan Melville to Harold Pinter, was almost annihilated by TV. The huge success of *Cowardy Custard* at the Mermaid (1972–3) showed the public what they had lost.

SATIRICAL PLAY. Few writers have the ironic wit and detachment to succeed in this genre, which demands indignation and some emotion, but great control to prevent audience hostility. Shaw was the supreme master. Elizabeth Locke, author of the masterly drama section in *Pears Cyclopaedia*, suggests that satirical plays flourish in a stable society (Swift and Voltaire in the 18th century) and notes that modern exponents, Frisch and Dürrenmatt, are both Swiss.

SATYR PLAY. Broad, farcical burlesque dramas given in ancient Greece along with the trilogy of tragedies, and written by the same author. Euripides' *The Cyclops* survives complete; it formed part of the drama competition. A legendary character would find himself in a ludicrous situation and be surrounded by satyrs, bawdy half-men, half-beasts. Little is known about the origin and importance of the plays which have nothing to do with satire.

STAGE. See Chapter 4 Part I and various entries in this chapter.

STAGE MANAGER. A superman (if available) in charge backstage during performances; in rehearsal, the director's right-hand man; director of understudy rehearsals; possibly an understudy himself; often the Company Manager, too, meaning he pays the cast and is the representative of the Management. On tour his duties include arranging the lighting in every theatre visited and being in charge of 'get-ins' on Mondays or, occasionally, Sundays, also the 'get-outs' on Saturday nights. Fortunately, most companies will have a touring Stage Carpenter who directly supervises these. Another key task, difficult in some companies, is to ensure that a production is kept up to standard after its director has left, sometimes never to return (though he will pocket his percentage happily if on one). Also the Stage Manager must be a diplomat and get on with permanent theatre staffs. This little-known backstage maestro was known in Britain as Stage Director until the 1950s, but the reversion to his earlier title, never abandoned in America, is now complete. He has as assistants a Deputy Stage Manager and one or more Assistant Stage Managers. Good S.M.s, D.S.M.s and A.S.M.s, who do not lust after acting, are not only treasures beyond price, but have a higher expectation of employment than their acting colleagues. Don't put your daughter on the stage, Mrs. Worthington: make her become an A.S.M. instead.

STAR. A star cannot be hidden, be he Edmund Kean or a lesser talent. Only fools object to stars who are also dedicated, gifted actors, if the parts in question call for star performances. Some Shakespearean and other rôles must have a star, a fact of life sometimes challenged by star directors and by companies who rightly praise ensemble but try hard to breed their own stars or borrow them from elsewhere. The word though has emotional overtones which results in theatrical purists raging against stars when they are actually attacking a star system that has vanished.

STRIKE. To dismantle and remove a setting after use, or a property or piece of furniture, or lighting equipment.

STURM UND DRANG (Storm and stress). This late-18th century literary movement emphasised the battling individual opposed to rational enlightenment. Shakespeare was one of its heroes, and the chief dramatic followers of the movement were Goethe and Schiller.

TABS. The curtain or act drop, also tableau curtains which are divided in the middle and can be opened outwards.

THESPIAN. An adjective for both actors and their art, from the semi-legendary Greek, Thespis, who can be claimed as the founder of drama.

THRILLERS can be chillers, melodramas, detective plays and psychological dramas. They are generally not liked by actors, who resent playing one-dimensional parts in plays in which everything is subsurvient to the plot and which require considerable discipline to sustain tension night after night. A very popular form, perhaps the finest in recent years, is Emlyn Williams' *Night Must Fall* (1935), followed closely by Anthony Shaffer's conjuring trick of a play, *Sleuth* (1970).

UNDERSTUDY. One who is ready (given enough understudy rehearsals) to go on at a moment's notice if necessary in place of a member of a cast who is absent or ill. A 'walking understudy' is employed simply for this task; others may have small parts, or be part of the stage management. Mean managements, willing to risk disasters (which sometimes happen) have one person understudying several parts. The author of this book knows of a tour of a Priestley play in which the Stage Manager understudied *all* the seven men. Good directors and helpful and likeable casts make an understudy's unsatisfactory life bearable, even pleasant. Note for hopefuls: very few understudies have ever found fame overnight, but to go on in a suitable part may lead to management recognition. It is a very professional job. The phrase 'stand-by' is now often used.

UP-STAGE. Any place on the stage away from the footlights, including especially the part furthest away. Older theatres with steep rakes caused actors literally to walk up-stage. 'Up-stage' is theatre slang for conceit or aloofness, while 'up-staging' occurs – in the wrong sense – when an actor deliberately plants himself in a dominating position up-stage. This 'old pro' trick can be combated by down-staging the up-stager, i.e. looking out front in an intense manner. Of course, in these days of ensemble and no star nonsense, such tricks are never resorted to (?).

VERSE DRAMA. There have been many attempts in our century to revive verse plays, spurred on by the incomparable success of Renaissance dramatists, and undeterred by the fact that modern poetry has become the least popular of the arts. Each attempt has raised hopes: Stephen Phillips' *Paolo and Francesca* (1902), the plays of Yeats, Eliot and Fry after the Second World War; but despite successes the re-birth of a new verse tradition has not occurred. Poetic prose and the poetic flavour of both story and imagery, as in *Under Milk Wood* by Dylan Thomas, have been more effective, and many find poetry in the language of Beckett, Pinter and others. The most highly regarded verse play of the last two decades in London has been Robert Lowell's *Benito Cereno* (1967). The struggle continues.

WALTER PLINGE. The name once regularly given to an actor playing more than one part. It was first used by Frank Benson's Shakespearean company, *c.* 1900, when they were playing at the Lyceum. Opposite the stage door was a publican named Plinge and on one occasion a young actor objected to his doubling being revealed on the programme. The Acting Manager, Henry Jalland, played along with him and substituted the name Walter Plinge. The Bensonians were to be regularly joined by Plinge, as were other companies. In America **GEORGE SPELVIN** is the man, origin unknown.

WARDROBE. The actors' clothes in a show, also the dressing room, ruled by the **WARDROBE MISTRESS**, where they are cleaned, mended, ironed, etc. All sensible actors keep in with the Wardrobe Mistress. The late, legendary 'Wattie' of Peter Pan backstage fame judged the characters of Pirates and Lost Boys alike by how they kept their costumes.

WELL-MADE PLAY. The phrase can mean just that, but is basically hostile. Scribe (1791–1861) 'invented' this type of thin, mechanically-effective drama, and Bernard Shaw was the most notable opponent of it, calling it 'Sardoodledum' after Sardou, the second most famous name in the trade. However it is frequently aimed at really well-made plays, i.e. Rattigan's *The Browning Version* and *The Deep Blue Sea.*

WEST END. A blanket name for the whole of London's commercial theatre, not just that part of it in the West End. **SHAFTESBURY AVENUE** is an even more localised version of it. Also see **BROADWAY**.

WINGS. The stage space on the left and right of a play's acting area.

WORKING LIGHT. A single, bulb hanging above a stage, giving just enough light for a rehearsal.

ADDENDUM 1974

All authors of reference books have been affected by the 1974 publishing crisis and resulting delays, triggered by the national economic crisis. Fortunately, thanks to a sympathetic publisher, I am able to bring certain aspects of this compilation up to date, September 1974. Inevitably, these are British, not international, the latter not being possible to check at a moment's notice.

*   *   *

First, as always, Shakespeare. . . . 1974 has not been a good year for him, in Britain at least. At Stratford his admirers have been forced to endure an unnecessary 'adaptation', complete with new lines by the usually admirable John Barton, who presumably thinks his *King John* to be better than the Bard's. Worse has followed; a rising director named Keith Hack, having taken his cue from Edward Bond, the main opponent of all Authority on earth, presenting us with a version of *Measure for Measure* which straitjackets Shakespeare into Bond-Shakespeare with disastrous effect on the characters. That the critics were unanimously hostile can be no consolation. Reluctantly, and remembering the sick *Romeo* of 1973, one can only urge Trevor Nunn to purge his extremists by making them go back to the plays – humbly. My own optimistic remarks about the R.S.C.'s current attitude to Shakespeare on page 136 seem sadly out of date.

*   *   *

Elsewhere too, Shakespeare has suffered, appearing in a biographical play at the Royal Court (after an earlier reincarnation at the Northcott, Exeter) not as Shakespeare, but as Bond-Shakespeare in *Bingo*. Anyone can create Shakespeare the man in his own image, but such a creation cannot be divorced from his period and given 20th century values. Shakespeare was not against Order, as is Bond, indeed no thinking person was in Elizabethan and Jacobean England. Too much was known about anarchy. So Bond's admittedly fascinating play tells us about – Bond, not least in his weird idea that Shakespeare killed himself.

*   *   *

Like scores of others, Alan Ayckbourn (b. 1939) was left out of the dramatists' section, despite notable successes including *Absurd Person Singular*, still running at the time of writing. Now that his superb trilogy, *The Norman Conquests*, starring Tom Courtenay, has reached London from Greenwich, the omission must be rectified. Greenwich, founded by Ewan Hooper in 1969, has within the last few months become one of the most significant theatres in the British Isles.

*   *   *

Finally, some notes: Michael Benthall, whose Old Vic regime is now so under-rated, has died, as has Ernest Milton for whose acting the word unique might have been coined. Jim Dale has become 'the toast of Broadway' in the Young Vic's *Scapino*. Nichol Williamson has yet again created a stir, this time as Malvolio. In *Doctor Faustus*, a happier reworking than *King John* by John Barton, Ian McKellan and Emrys James (as Mephistopheles) have had notable successes, the latter, who has given a fine line of villains at the R.S.C. including Shylock, being all the more effective for his restraint. Meanwhile, David Jones has directed yet another Gorky play for the R.S.C., this time *Summerfolk*, Claire Bloom is giving a major performance in *Streetcar Named Desire*, Ethel Merman of the trumpet tones is in town, and *The Mousetrap* just goes rolling along.

INDEX

A

K

M

Q